THE STORY
OF LUDGROVE

THE STORY OF LUDGROVE

Richard Barber

For Richard and Mary

In friendship and with affectionate good wishes

Richard Barber

— September 2006 —

Published for the Ludgrove School Trust
by
Guidon Publishing

Design: Adrian Hodgkins
Typesetting: Keith Rigley
Project editor: Angus McGeoch
Printed by Information Press, Eynsham, Oxon
Bound by Green Street Bindery, Oxford

CONTENTS

ACKNOWLEDGEMENTS

In writing this book I have drawn on the memories of over fifty Old Ludgrovians, former staff, governors, parents and friends of Ludgrove, whom I have visited all over Britain and who have given freely of their time to talk to me about their associations with the School. Most of them are quoted by name in the book, and to all of them I am deeply grateful. I would particularly like to thank Hugh Bevan and Brian Warren, who provided valuable information on the early history of Ludgrove House and Trent Park; Roland Pym, who specially drew the delightful and witty school scenes from the 1920s to illustrate his memories of Ludgrove; and Captain North Dalrymple-Hamilton RN, for his intriguing insights into the atmosphere and the causes of decline of Wixenford School, whose premises in Wokingham were taken over by Ludgrove in 1937.

It is a matter of especial regret to me that two Old Ludgrovians who spoke to me most enthusiastically about their time at the School – Andrew, Duke of Devonshire and Paul Foot – did not live to see the publication of this book.

In connection with one of the earliest Ludgrovians, the late Robert McCormick, I received invaluable transatlantic support from Eric Gillespie, Carrie Hoye and Walter Wojtowicz of the *Chicago Tribune*.

At Ludgrove itself I spent countless hours talking to my beloved aunt Dorothy Barber, now aged 98, whose memories of people and events still seem as clear and as colourful as ever. Sue Neame and Peter Shaw, the children of Tim Shaw, helped me greatly with memories of their father.

I have had constant encouragement and guidance from Ned Boldero, grandson of Arthur Dunn, the founder of Ludgrove, who is a former Chairman of the Ludgrove School Trust; and also, of course, from Gerald and Janet Barber and Nichol Marston.

Finally, my most sincere thanks go to Sally Whittaker at Ludgrove, whose energy and instant communication galvanised the whole Ludgrove team involved in the book; to Wendy Spackman, Alan Barber's former secretary, who tracked down and conjured up from far and wide the majority of photos in this book; and to Angus McGeoch, my tireless and skilful editor. With cheerful efficiency and unremitting dedication, they have provided the indispensable support without which *The Story of Ludgrove* could never have seen the light of day.

Richard Barber

And a woman who held a babe said:
"Speak to us of Children"

And he said:
"Your children are not your children
They are the sons and daughters of Life's longing for itself.
They come through you but not from you.
And though they are with you, yet they belong not to you.

You may give them your love but not your thoughts,
For they have their own thoughts.
You may house their bodies, but not their souls,
For their souls dwell in the house of tomorrow, which you cannot visit, not
even in your dreams.
You may strive to be like them, but seek not to make them like you,
For Life goes not backwards, nor tarries with Yesterday.

You are the bows from which your children as living arrows are sent forth.
The Archer sees the mark upon the path of the Infinite, and He bends you
with his might that his arrows may go swift and far.
Let your bending in the Archer's hand be for gladness;
For even as he loves the arrow that flies, so He loves the bow that is stable."

From "The Prophet" by Khalil Gibran

INTRODUCTION

If a man were called upon to name one achievement for which he would wish to be honoured by posterity, he could scarcely do better than to have founded an institution that would be flourishing over a century onward as a leader of its kind, yet still based on the principles that he himself had originally laid down. That is a measure of the achievement of Ludgrove's founder and first headmaster, Arthur Dunn.

The site, the size and the curriculum of today's Ludgrove are all very different from its modest beginnings in 1892; but the name, the reputation and the principles of the school remain unchanged. This book describes the events along the road Ludgrove has travelled since those early days, the masters, staff and pupils who have been the custodians of Arthur Dunn's legacy, and the many interactions of change and continuity that have left their mark throughout more than a century.

What were the principles which Arthur Dunn and his new institution stood for? They are epitomised in his favourite quotation – one he kept before him daily, framed on the wall of his study: the simple and magnificent words from Chapter IX of Ecclesiastes

> *Whatsoever thy hand findeth to do, do it with thy might.*

It is a tremendous statement. It is also a guide to the personality of the man, a precept that lay behind his achievements, and a fitting motto for the School which, under his inspired leadership, was to become famous throughout the land, and which remains so to this day and beyond.

Today, the present Headmaster of Ludgrove, Gerald Barber, uses a prayer in Chapel, which evokes a spirit identical to that of the Founder:

> *O Almighty God, who hath appointed unto every man his work, give us grace to try*
> *and improve whatever talents Thou hast committed to our trust. And grant that,*
> *whatever we do, we do it with all our might, to Thy honour and glory.*

The Story of Ludgrove tells how this philosophy has been deployed at the school for over a hundred years. Its full impact will become apparent in the pages that follow.

Chapter I

THE VICTORIAN
PREPARATORY SCHOOL

"If he'll only turn out a brave, helpful, truth-telling
English gentleman, that's all I want."

Squire Brown in *Tom Brown's Schooldays*, by Thomas Hughes

In the last quarter of the 19th century there was an "explosion" in the number of new preparatory schools for boys founded throughout England. This occurred several decades after the surge in the number of new boys' public schools that had started in the 1840s and 1850s. What is the reason for this lapse of time? It is a question that goes to the heart of the change in private education in England in the 19th century, and provides the key to understanding the context in which Arthur Dunn founded Ludgrove in 1892.[1]

At the start of the 19th century only a handful of great public schools enjoyed a national reputation. These schools were described by the cleric and man of letters, Sydney Smith[2], in an article in the Edinburgh Review in 1810 as

> endowed places of education of old standing, to which the sons of gentlemen
> resort in considerable numbers, and where they continue to reside from eight or
> nine until eighteen years of age.

Such schools included Charterhouse, Christ's Hospital, Eton, Harrow, Merchant Taylors', Rugby, Shrewsbury, St. Paul's, Westminster and Winchester. All these schools were Anglican, and their shared objective was to educate boys to become gentlemen and rulers of the Empire by providing a largely classical education, based on the three foundation stones of Grammar, Religion and Games – all helped along with frequent and strenuous bouts of chastisement.

The middle decades of Victoria's reign saw these old schools grow considerably in size. At the same time their ranks were swelled by a burgeoning number of new public schools founded to meet the demands of a rapidly expanding middle class, fuelled by a new-found prosperity - the fruit of England's Industrial Revolution in the first half of the century. Such schools included Mill Hill (1807); Cheltenham (1841); Marlborough and Rossall (1843); Bradfield (1850); Wellington (1853); Bloxham (1860); Malvern (1862); and the legacies of the Woodard Foundation of 1848, which gave birth to such schools as Ardingly, Hurstpierpoint and Lancing.

As the century moved on, the wide age-range for which these schools catered was to be questioned. Sydney Smith's reference to "eight to nine year old boys" shows that, when he was writing in 1810, the education of very young boys was firmly within the purview of these schools. This continued to be the case into the middle of the century. But the forces of change were gathering. Thomas Arnold, the famous Head Master of Rugby from 1828 to 1841, had promoted the prefect system, which gave older boys wider responsibilities for keeping discipline among the younger ones - a model that rapidly spread throughout the whole public school system. But it was open to abuse: the tribulations suffered by Tom Brown at Rugby are eloquent and still frightening testimony to this. Arnold was among the first to see that the education of younger boys was not helped by bringing them up in the same institutions as senior boys, and in 1837 he took the radical decision to abolish his youngest form at Rugby, Form 1. In 1838 he removed Form 2 as well. This in effect meant that, from that date, Rugby no longer took boys younger than twelve.

Thomas Arnold

This initiative was further reinforced in 1864 with the publication of the famous Clarendon Report, which promulgated the progressive view that

> the care and instruction of little boys is as important, and in some cases as difficult, as the care and instruction of older boys.

The Report went on to discuss the proper age of transfer from preparatory to public school, and formally recommended the separate education of young boys. Specifically it proposed the separation of Lower School from Upper School boys at Eton.

It was many years before public schools in general ceased to take boys at an early age. In 1861 Eton still admitted as many as 25 boys under 12, of whom four were aged 8. But the trend gradually became the norm. It was Arnold's decision, reinforced by Clarendon, which had acted as the springboard from which preparatory schools for boys up to 12 years old, as distinct institutions from the senior schools, took their great leap forward.

For the first half of the nineteenth century, the pace of preparatory school expansion was slow. Of some 202 English preparatory schools thought to have been founded prior to 1900, only 24 dated from before 1800 (these were mainly cathedral choir schools), and only 15 between 1801 and 1850. But thereafter the pace began to quicken: 47 new

19th century school scene, Rugby.

prep schools were founded between 1850 and 1875; and in the last quarter of the 19th century the movement took off, with no less than 120 being founded between 1875 and 1900. The English preparatory school had become firmly established in the educational landscape of the country. The movement was decisively reinforced in 1893, the year after Ludgrove's foundation, by the formation of the Association of Headmasters of Preparatory Schools (the AHPS – forerunner of the IAPS) which gave a collective voice for the first time to this new and expanding part of the English educational system.

This rapid growth of preparatory schools was driven by a number of wider social, economic and global influences, which were clearly discernible by the last quarter of the 19th century.

Economically, the country was experiencing ever greater prosperity flowing from the expansion of large-scale industry and of Britain's imperial trade. With this growth in wealth came growth in population: that of England and Wales expanded by over 40 per cent from 22.7 million in 1871 to 32.5 million in 1901. The standard of living of most social groups improved correspondingly: an intriguing measure of this increasing affluence is the number of domestic servants in England and Wales, which grew from 750,000 in 1850 to 1.2 million in 1870. Domestic service, broadly defined, was now the second largest employment sector after agriculture.

The cost of private education was thus within reach of a far larger number of people than ever before, who increasingly aspired to educate their sons as "gentlemen" at these schools. As Squire Brown, Tom Brown's father, said: "I don't care a straw for Greek particles…If he'll only turn out a brave, helpful, truth-telling English man, and a Gentleman, and a Christian, that's all I want". At the same time, the railway, that great product of the Industrial Revolution, was spreading its network to most parts of the country and was widely available to convey boys to and from their boarding schools.

In the wider world, the British Empire was at its zenith in the last quarter of the 19th century. The mood of the time was never better caught than by John Ruskin in 1870 who, as the newly-appointed Slade Professor of Fine Art at Oxford, delivered a famous invocation to Empire:

> There is a Destiny now possible to us, the highest ever set before a nation to be accepted or refused. Will you youths of England make your country again a royal throne of Kings, a sceptred isle, for all the world a source of delight, mistress of learning and the arts, faithful guardians of the honoured principles? This is what England must do or perish. She must found colonies as fast as she is able, formed of her worthiest and most energetic men, seizing every piece of useful ground she can set foot on, and there teaching the colonists that their first aim is to advance the power of England by land and sea.

"Discomforts of African travel", from The Graphic, 1872

The same theme was captured by a lecturer at Ludgrove in 1904 who ended with the words:

> There has never been a time in the history of this country when it was more necessary for all Englishmen, from their earliest years, to train themselves to help in the great work of building the Empire, and to maintain the reputation of the

Anglo-Saxon race for producing leaders who can…make the subject races contented and happy by carrying out what is right and just for all."

How strange these words now sound in today's world! But the British Empire then consisted of some 400 million people, covering a quarter of the world's surface. Another lecturer at Ludgrove in 1906 suggested that it would take all the subjects of the King at least 13 years to pass a given point at the rate of one a second. These vast lands and peoples were all ruled by a tiny handful of well-trained British soldiers and administrators, who went forth to accomplish the nation's mission, as captured in the famous words of Rudyard Kipling:

Take up the white man's burden
Send forth the best ye breed…

and their officer corps was indeed recruited from upper-middle class and aristocratic families, through competitive examination, into the armed forces or the Indian Civil Service. This generated a need for schools which would both fulfil the need to prepare pupils in the subjects and techniques of those exams, and would also provide places of boarding education for the children of colonial personnel who went abroad in the service of the Crown. The preparatory schools had indeed become 'cradles of Empire'.

India, "Travelling up country", from The Graphic, 1875

Of the greatest importance in the training required to rule that Empire was the playing of games – especially cricket. As Niall Ferguson[3], has said:

What made public school boys capable of heroics on the Empire's behalf was not what they learned in the classroom but what they learned on the games field…above all cricket, with its subtle, protracted rhythms, its emphasis on team spirit in the field and on solo heroics at the crease.

To excel at sport was considered to make a man not only physically but morally healthy. Sporting prowess was seen not just as the ability to make runs or take wickets: it also imparted 'character', the ability to lead and inspire a team, to "treat Triumph and Disaster just the same", to be generous to opponents in defeat, and to see the playing fields as the arena in which lifetime friendships were forged and like-minded men got on with the job of winning together – in life as much as in matches. 'Playing a straight bat' was as much a metaphor for life as for the crease, a sentiment echoed in one of the public school magazines of the period:

> *So hit hard, my lads, and through life as at school*
> *"Play fair and play square" is an excellent rule,*
> *And when things go badly, don't get in the dumps,*
> *But play all the harder and keep up your stumps.*

It was in this spirit that the cult of athleticism, based on compulsory games, came to be at the very heart of the late 19th century 'Public School ethos'. It was to prove a durable foundation for most private schools in England for the 20th century as well.

And now, the senior and junior institutions of private education, which by the 1870s had split into the separate and official categories of public schools and preparatory schools, had begun to grow together again through the gradual introduction of a common entrance exam, the proliferation of competitive scholarships on offer from the

Elstree School, Hertfordshire, about 1835

senior schools, and the status of many prep schools as recognised feeder schools for specific public schools. This trend was reinforced by the growing number of public school assistant masters who left – often with the encouragement of their headmasters – to start their own preparatory schools. One prime example of this was the Rev. John Hawtrey, who in 1869 left Eton, where he had been an assistant master for seven years, to found his new school, Aldin House in Slough (or 'Hawtreys' as it became known) which rapidly established itself as the prime feeder school for Eton.

Rev. Lancelot Sanderson, headmaster of Elstree 1869-1901, seen here with his son in 1870

Another such school was Elstree, near Borehamwood in Hertfordshire. The school is one of the country's oldest prep schools, having been founded in the late 18th century; but it had gone into rapid decline after the headmastership of the terrifying Rev. Dr. Bernays, one of the most feared of all 19th century prep school headmasters. It was revived by the Rev. Lancelot Sanderson, who went there in 1869 from being an assistant master at Harrow. He reigned at Elstree from 1869 to 1901 and during that time established the school as a principal feeder for Harrow and one of the leading prep schools in the country.

Sanderson was said to have been one of the few preparatory school headmasters at that time in England to recruit first class men to his staff, and then to treat them as friends and colleagues, rather than as second-class citizens working at arm's length from the almighty 'Head'. It is a remarkable testimony to Sanderson's skill in choosing people, and one of his enduring legacies to the preparatory school movement, that no fewer than six of his assistant masters at Elstree went on to found successful preparatory schools: A.J. Richardson of St. Peter's Court, Broadstairs; W. Hornby and C.P. Wilson of Sandroyd School, now in Salisbury; E. Smith of The Grange, Eastbourne; the Rev. V. Royle of Stanmore Park, Middlesex; and A.T.B. Dunn, who founded Ludgrove School in Barnet in 1892.

Such was the social and educational environment in which Arthur Dunn began his career as a schoolmaster, and the stable from which he went forth to found his new establishment. It is to this energetic, talented and inspiring man that we shall now turn.

What else was happening in 1892?

- In the July General Election, the Liberals defeated the Conservatives by a narrow margin, and W.E. Gladstone, now aged 83, formed a government, with H.H. Asquith at the Home Office and Lord Rosebery as Foreign Secretary.

- Keir Hardie, the founder of the Labour Party, was elected to Parliament. He entered wearing a cloth cap to the blare of a brass band.

- The first council houses had just been built, and the minimum age for children working in factories had been raised to 11!

- Oscar Wilde's first play, *Lady Windermere's Fan*, was premiered but got a sniffy review from *Punch*

- The Assisted Education Act provided for a grant of 10 shillings per pupil to all local schools, enabling them to cease charging fees.

- The first meeting of the Association of Preparatory School Headmasters took place to consider the size of cricket ball best suited to small boys.

- London's streets were still lit by gas.

- Kipling wrote *Barrack-Room Ballads*.

- A room at the Savoy cost 7s 6d (37$\frac{1}{2}$p) per night.

- In 1892 the telephone was still something of a novelty.

Chapter II

ARTHUR DUNN AND THE FOUNDING OF LUDGROVE 1892–1902

"How much we owe to his knowledge, enthusiasm
and kindly encouragement."
Cecil Sharp

Arthur Tempest Blakiston Dunn was born at Whitby on 12th August 1860, the son of John Dunn and Helen Bowen. His names indicate links on his father's side through the Tempest family to the House of Londonderry, and through the Blakistons to landed coal-mine owners from the north country. His mother was the daughter of the Rev. Bowen, Rector of West Lynn in Norfolk and descended from the Percys of Northumberland. But lineage was of no great importance to Arthur. In later life his wife Helen was to write: "My own mother went back to 1500, and Arthur's family are very old too – but what does it really matter where character and ideals are so far more important?"

Arthur's father was a distinguished mathematician, having been Second Wrangler at St. John's College, Cambridge. He became a well-known coach in mathematics, and the author of a then-famous guide to mathematical examinations called "Dunn's Previous". The family was far from rich, but Dunn Senior aspired to give his young and talented son the very best education that England could provide. By the greatest effort he was able to send Arthur to Mr. Tarver's house at Eton in 1874.

Eton, like all public schools in those days, was a harsh and forbidding environment for the very young. But Arthur Dunn had two particular talents which marked him out for success. He was a football player of brilliance who was to become a legend in his own lifetime and beyond; and he had a singing voice the like of which Eton had seldom heard before.

His singing clearly made a mark upon everyone who heard him. This was inherited from his mother, who herself had a very fine voice. She had even been compared with some of the greatest sopranos of her day such as the legendary Jenny Lind ("the Swedish

Nightingale"). She used to sing to the accompaniment of Charles Stanford and the great Austrian violinist Joseph Joachim. It seemed that she had passed on a measure of her talent to her son. The Eton College Chronicle records a school concert in 1878 (attended by his mother), at the end of which it was reported that some of the audience were in tears at the beauty of the rendition:

> The principal feature of the Finale in the Lorelei was the singing of Dunn, whose voice seems as strong and as sweet as ever through the pathos and dramatic power with which he rendered the solos…His singing was the feature of the evening. He has never been heard to greater advantage, the perfect clearness of his high notes and the rich quality of his voice could not fail to take the audience by storm.

But singing appears to have become a talent which Dunn preferred to keep largely hidden, deployed only in quartets at end-of-term concerts at his school. He could only with difficulty be prevailed upon to give his friends a sample of this wonderful gift. Later in life, after a school concert he had attended, he was asked by someone to sing

Arthur Dunn as boy at Eton

Tom Bowling, and at the end it is recorded that there was only a stupefied silence – for the audience was in tears. His voice remained a magnificent instrument to the end of his life.

The other talent, and the one that was to bring him immortality, was football. Although he was very small, weighing only about six stone at Eton, he won his House Colours when he was still too short to wear tails. His diminutive size, fleetness of foot and eye for an opening enabled him to excel at this sport at a very early age.

To this day Eton has a quite specific style of playing football – known as the Field Game – which marks its play out from that of other schools. This puts the whole emphasis of the game on fast dribbling, where the player propels the ball forward in a straight line with quick bursts of speed and without passing (or "sneaking" as it is called). One of Dunn's comments in Ludgrove's School Notes on their Football season in 1894 gives clear evidence of this:

> Skill in dribbling can only come with practice…but we hope that Ludgrove boys will make it a golden rule to *go straight*. (Dunn's italics).

His size and speed made him ideally cut out for this form of the game. He was said at the time to be:

...desperately quick, strong and certain on his feet, and a wonderful dribbler. He was at his very best on treacherous ground, and the worse the soup the more easily he slipped over the top of it.

Eton was followed by Cambridge, where Dunn went up to Trinity College in 1880. He won his Half Blue for Football in 1883 and 1884. (The sport did not merit a Full Blue until 1885, and only then in the face of furious protests by the oarsmen who apparently wished official inter-Varsity sport to be confined to rowing and cricket.)

Dunn (right) demonstrating a tackle for "Football", from the Badminton Library of Sports. The other player is G.O. Smith.

The English Football Cup

A year after leaving Eton, Arthur Dunn was selected to play for the Old Etonians in the final of the English Football Cup against Clapham Rovers, which the O.E.s won 1 – 0. An early triumph came in 1882 when he played for the O.E.s in the Cup Final against Blackburn Rovers. Under the captaincy of Lord Kinnaird, the Etonians won by a single goal, scored after a wonderful run by Dunn from the half-way line right to the Blackburn goal box, before passing across the goal to a colleague who scored on the volley. It was an electrifying moment, the more so because Blackburn Rovers had four Internationals in their side. Indeed, so confident were they of victory that they had their Victory Song printed before the match. This including such magnificent verses as

> *"All hail, ye gallant Rover lads!*
> *Etonians thought ye were but cads,*
> *They've found at Football games their dads*
> *By meeting Blackburn Rovers!"*

To cap it all, the Member of Parliament for Blackburn had arranged, "with a prescience fully worthy of British legislators", to give a banquet that evening at St. James's Restaurant to celebrate Blackburn's victory. As an Old Ludgrovian, Sir Shane Leslie (1895-1900), wrote in his memoir of Arthur Dunn[1]:

> Seldom did Nemesis wait at such an expectant table. It would have been hard to have extemporised a satisfactory toast that evening to the words "All hail, ye gallant Rover lads". An Old Etonian who had been invited to the dinner to represent the Opposition and the Football Association, wrote afterwards: "It was rather a dismal affair".

The Old Etonians played in six finals of the English Football Cup between 1875 and 1883. They won it twice, and three of their defeats were only after extra time.

Dunn had inherited a natural talent for mathematics from his father, and indeed did so well in the first part of the Cambridge Tripos that it was predicted that he would achieve a high Wranglership. But he believed that university life should be about enjoying the spirit of the place more than the learning, and for Arthur Dunn that spirit was imparted more by friendships, games and entertainment than by the mysteries of higher mathematics. Consequently he "sailed with undeserving ease into the Third Class of the

Arthur Dunn in England "strip"

honours list". He left Cambridge to seek his way in the world, secure in the knowledge that his father's keen disappointment with his academic performance was balanced by the wide circle of friends who were to be his most precious asset throughout his life.

On coming down, he was without a profession. He wondered for a time whether to pursue an opening offered to him in a lawyer's office in Newcastle. But the sequestered life of a solicitor was not for him. In 1883 he applied for a post of assistant master at the Rev. Lancelot Sanderson's preparatory school at Elstree, and was appointed there the same year.

From this stable he was able to continue the pursuit of the game in which he was in due course to lead his country. For 11 years throughout the 1880s and early '90s he regularly played two or three matches a week – over 500 games in all – for the Old Etonians, for the Corinthians, for the South v. the North, for London v. Sheffield and of course for England. He played five times for his country – three times against Ireland (as one of the two centre-forwards, the normal team formation in those days) in 1883, 1884 and 1887; and once each – both as captain - against Wales and Scotland in 1892. In the Scottish match he led ten professionals on to the field of play; and England's 4 – 0 victory that day "left England's amateur captain with as bright a memory of his international days as his contemporaries had of him".

As proof of his unique versatility and skill, he had started his international career as centre-forward, and finished it playing at full-back, an achievement never since matched. His last major game was played for the Old Internationals against Charterhouse at the Queen's Club when he scored the only two goals of the match. His football career was summed up in a book at the time[2]:

> Arthur Dunn's name will be handed down to posterity as one of the players who raised Association Football to the height of England's national game.

As a natural games player, Arthur was also an excellent all-round cricketer. It is said that only lack of time and practice kept him from playing at first-class level. He was a fluent middle-order left-handed bat, and a fast round-arm bowler – almost equally good with his left hand as with his right! He once took 5 wickets with 5 balls on tour in Ireland, at a time when there were only 5 balls in an over. His speed and eye also enabled him on occasion to keep wicket for Hertfordshire.

Arthur Dunn with G.O. Smith and W.P. Blore (far left)

As with football, his first and last loyalty in cricket was to Eton. At the same time as he was building up his new school, he became Treasurer and then Secretary of the Eton Ramblers C.C. between 1892 and 1902, and in that time rescued the club almost single-handedly from near oblivion. In 1890 the Club had had 45 members; by 1894 there were 270; and from a mere five fixtures in 1889 (three of which were cancelled) he expanded the fixture list to 45 by 1896, managing a large number of the matches himself, organising tours with legendary precision and restoring order, pride and a financial surplus to the struggling club. In the course of the 1890s he scored over 1,900 runs, and took 96 wickets for an average of 11, the best bowling average of any Rambler in the club's history. A contemporary summed him up as a cricketer:

> He was able to bat, bowl and – with his proximity to the ground and wonderful
> agility – was a first-class fielder in almost any position. An ideal captain, he always
> and without any effort extracted 18 ounces of work to the pound from everyone
> on the side, and never gave up trying until the last ball was bowled. He was a
> perfect leader of men, never playing a lone hand for himself. Good teamwork and
> unflagging keenness he insisted on and invariably obtained.[3]

It was that same style and inspiration that he brought to the much bigger task of founding and developing the school which he was shortly to start in Barnet, Hertfordshire, in 1892.

LUDGROVE HALL

The estate in Barnet on which Ludgrove Hall stands could be well over a thousand years old, since it straddles the 10th century Hertfordshire/Middlesex county boundary, suggesting that the original estate predates that.[4] The actual origin of the name 'Ludgrove' is obscure, but was possibly derived from one William Lyghtgrave who, in 1423, conveyed to William Somercotes, Thomas Frowyke and others a "messuage" in

Hadley, Hertfordshire, of '120 acres of land, 80 of meadowe and 80 of wood.' One hundred and twenty years later, in 1543, a certain John Marsh gave 'Ludgrave Farme' to the King in exchange for other lands; and in 1551 Edward VI granted it to the Earl of Pembroke. Around that time it was described as 'a very faire house, scytuate in a valley neere Enfeyld Chase'. In 1611 a Cornelius Fyshe 'alienated Ludgraves Farme' to Sir Roger Wilbraham, a distinguished courtier of both Queen Elizabeth and King James I and benefactor of Hadley church and of the almshouses on Hadley Green, who died in 1616. In the middle of the 17th century it was 'in the occupation' of Francis Atkinson, and records of the time reveal that he then called it 'the Blue House'. In a remarkable foretaste of Ludgrove's future destiny, it is recorded that his son-in-law, a Mr. J.Poole

> had charge and management of a school for the education of a select number of Gentlemen's sons of good quality, in the house of a worthy Gentleman, Mr Francis Atkinson, who kept it out of a design truly generous and publick in endeavouring to prevent the inconveniences of irregulated youth.[5]

1760 map showing Ludgrove (top) and what is now north London

The house then descended through a number of owners – Thomas and John Pelham, Ambrose Brunskill, Thomas and John Walton, Ephraim Beauchamp and the Temple Wests. In 1811 it was held by a prominent local farmer called Archibald Paris whose main residence was the magnificent Palladian house, Beech Hill Park, just to the north – now the elegant clubhouse of the Hadley Wood Golf Club.

Paris decided to increase his acreage of farmland, and extended his property southward to the road running between the hamlets of Cockfosters and Monken Hadley. This included the adjoining Blue House, which he decided to demolish and build afresh.

The new house, now reverting to the name 'Ludgrove', was sold by Paris in 1830 to David Bevan of the bankers Barclay, Bevan, Tritton & Co, who bought it for his eldest son Robert.

David Bevan himself was then living in a nearby house called Belmont – formerly known as Mount Pleasant – designed by Inigo Jones and occupied for a time by Elias Ashmole, the noted antiquarian who was to give his name to the world-famous Ashmolean Museum in Oxford. In the 19th century Belmont was itself to become a preparatory school called Heddon Court. A long-standing rival of Ludgrove, it was finally demolished in 1934[6].

Ludgrove stood next to Trent Park. This splendid estate had been owned in the 18th century by a famous physician, Sir Richard Jebb, Bt. (1729-1787), who had been personally granted its lease by George III in recognition of Jebb's role in saving the life of the King's younger brother, the Duke of Gloucester. The Duke had fallen ill at Trento in the South Tyrol, after which the house was named.

Trent Park

This too was acquired by David Bevan at auction in 1833, from its then owner, a London merchant named John Cumming. It is delightfully – but probably fictitiously – recorded that David Bevan had attended the auction with the sole intention of buying some wine. While waiting for this lot to come up, it is said that he fell asleep, nodding as he did so, and woke to find that his nod had been taken as a bid for the whole Trent Park estate, of which he then became the unwitting owner. In 1837 he transferred ownership of Trent to his son Robert, who lived there until his death in 1890.

The Bevans were not only good bankers but a deeply-committed Christian evangelical family. On Sundays Robert frequently preached in the local chapel, and there are reports of his son Francis and his wife entertaining haymakers on summer evenings at Ludgrove "to tea and hymns". The Bevan family were dedicated to good

Francis Bevan 1840–1919

works in support of the local community. In 1839 Christ Church, Cockfosters, was built at Robert Bevan's expense. He also provided for a girls' school and, in 1859, founded Trent Boys' School, part of which still stands next to Cockfosters underground station.

The third vicar of Christ Church was the Rev. Robert Tabor, who lived in the cottage next door to Ludgrove, and to whom Francis Bevan and his brother Wilfred were sent as pupils. In 1855 Tabor received a loan from Francis enabling him to purchase Cheam Preparatory School in south London. The school had been moved there in 1665 to avoid the Great Plague, and he took over as Headmaster, with the aim of rescuing it from the near-oblivion into which it had fallen. Typical of the Bevans' way of thinking, the terms of the loan required that it was to be repaid only if the school succeeded. Succeed it did, becoming one of the foremost prep schools in the country. (Lord Randolph Churchill was a pupil there under him). Tabor was a fearsome man, of whom an old boy wrote:

> Cheam hung upon the assumption that a bevy of young imps had been handed over by Providence to Mr Tabor so that he might shake them up in a big bag until they had lost their horns and tails.[7]

Robert Tabor was succeeded at Cheam by his son Arthur, who became famous as the founder of the Association of Preparatory School Headmasters in 1892.

Tabor's old cottage at Ludgrove was subsequently acquired by Arthur Dunn, and became the residence of Ludgrove's bachelor masters, known as 'the Masters' Cottage'.

Robert Bevan died at Trent Park in 1890, whereupon his son Francis moved out of Ludgrove Hall into the main house. Two years later Arthur Dunn opened his school

Old Ludgrove School in Barnet, in about 1900

there – probably with much the same financial help from Francis as his father, Robert Bevan, had given to Tabor. It was to be the second time in two centuries that Ludgrove had served a scholastic purpose.

PIONEERING DAYS

Arthur Dunn was 32 when he founded Ludgrove in 1892. His motivation for leaving Elstree, where he had been so happy, so free to follow his own athletic pursuits in parallel with his teaching career, was ostensibly to move away from a school that sent boys mainly to Harrow, so that he could run one where boys could be prepared for his beloved Eton. He clearly had all the goodwill and support that the Rev. Lancelot could give him. Ludgrove was located with the help of Katherine Sanderson, known as 'Mrs Kitty', wife of the Elstree Headmaster. Arthur was doubtless also encouraged by his great friend and fellow-Corinthian Norman Malcolmson, who lived nearby, and whose sister, Helen, would become Arthur's wife in 1892. (The other Malcolmson sister, Laura, married Bertrand Bevan a year later.)

There is no record of the terms on which Dunn leased Ludgrove Hall from Francis Bevan, but there can be no doubt that this bold venture into the unknown from the security of his tenure at Elstree could not have been made without the help of others. Funds had to be found from every source available. His father backed him with a certain amount of money, and the Old Etonian Football Club presented him on St. Andrew's Day 1891 with a silver bowl and 100 guineas (in today's terms about £5,000)

> in recognition of his invaluable services to the Club of which he had been the leading spirit for the last seven years.

The new school took the colours of dark blue and white (which have remained its colours ever since), and opened its doors for the first time in May 1892. It was all done on the slenderest of resources. As Helen Dunn recalled in later life, Arthur was so poor that he had to go round to his future father-in-law, who lived nearby, to borrow table-cloths, spoons and forks for the first meals.

For the first few weeks of that first term, there was but a single boy – Theodore Pelly – whose name lives for ever on the Honour Board at Ludgrove today as the founding pupil of the school: "Ludgrovian Number One". Pelly subsequently became the only

Theodore Pelly

Ludgrovian old enough to serve in the Boer War. But soon Arthur had four more pupils: Gerald Gurney, and, surprisingly, three American boys, Robert McCormick (whom we shall meet later), his brother Medill, and Charles Hoadley. It

is recorded that Dunn was "hugely chuffed" when he brought his entire school over from Ludgrove to Elstree in a dog-cart. We can imagine the delightful picture of a young, smiling Dunn arriving at his old school with his horse-drawn cargo, and showing off his new charges to the plaudits of his former headmaster and the colleagues who had given him such a promising start in his new life.

In that first summer, the

Late Victorian personal transport

number of his staff – one assistant master Henry Hale, the matron Nurse Broom and two maids, as well as Helen and himself – equalled the number of boys in the school! It seems that there was also a multi-talented gardener who supplemented his horticultural duties by bowling to the boys in the nets and playing in the Salvation Army band at weekends. But new entrants were on their way. It is no coincidence to find that three of the next five boys into the school were from one of the famous founding families of Barclays Bank: Trevor, Hugh and Knyvet Buxton.

Their arrival was a considerable relief, not only financially, but also matrimonially, since Arthur's father had forbidden his marriage to his beloved Helen until he could secure their family and professional base by having ten boys in the School. It seems that the tenth pupil took time to arrive: for weeks the School roll contained only nine names, and the nuptials were accordingly postponed. But finally the tenth boy, Nicholas

Ludgrove school group, July 1892

Woods, arrived in the middle of the summer term, no doubt little appreciating the rejoicing and relief which his appearance caused.

Arthur's marriage to Helen proved to be one of unalloyed happiness. Helen Dunn gave her husband the strongest possible support, producing for him three children – John, Margery and Mary – and providing a home of love and security amidst the whirlwind of activity that he imposed upon himself in the ten short years that he still had to live.

Pupil numbers did not 'explode': in the whole of 1893 only seven new boys appeared. But it was now that the enormous circle of friends whom Dunn had acquired in his soccer and cricketing career at Eton and Cambridge proved valuable. By 1895, when Pelly left the School, Ludgrove had 36 pupils, and had become an established part of the preparatory school landscape of southern England. By that time Arthur Dunn had gathered round him a team of masters of remarkable ability. They included two other outstanding soccer internationals in Gilbert Oswald Smith and William John Oakley, who were close friends of Arthur's in the Corinthian and England soccer teams of the late 1880s and 1890s. It was said of those early years that when England was playing an international soccer match, Ludgrove dispensed with three of its six masters for the day.

Ludgrove masters, July 1897. Back (l to r): G.O. Smith, C. Sharp, W. Oakley
F. Crabtree, H. Crabtree. Front: (l to r): T. Weatherhead, A. Dunn, H. Hansell

The character of the school

What sort of school did Arthur Dunn wish his new foundation to be? He ran it on a number of principles which were central to his philosophy of life, and which – while they may seem obvious today – represented an altogether different approach to running a preparatory school at the end of the 19th century. His founding tenets still underpin the School's philosophy in the 21st century.

First, he was tireless in cultivating an excellent rapport between himself and the staff, and between staff and pupils. He held that unless people got on well together, they could not give of their best to each other. While the Rev. Sanderson at Elstree had also subscribed to this approach, it was by no means in keeping with the custom of the times, when masters were not encouraged to mix with the boys outside the classroom, nor to be on familiar terms with their headmasters, who reigned supreme in the isolation of their position and lodgings. But at Ludgrove the masters were Arthur's friends, the staff was a well-knit group of talented and like-minded individuals from similar backgrounds, and they were welded into a team by the inspiration of Arthur's unquenchable enthusiasm. It was a happy and united ship, and this spirit communicated itself to most of the boys at the School, one of whom referred to his time at Ludgrove in the mid-1890s as "this delectable life".

Secondly, he believed that school should be pleasant rather than painful, and that boys should be encouraged rather than terrorised. It is hard, from the perspective of the 21st century, to appreciate the radical nature of this philosophy, against the background of bullying, beating and general brutality of the regimes on which private education was based in the 19th century. "The Hosts of Misery" were prowling around everywhere. The Rev. Dr. Leopold Bernays, whom we met at Elstree in the early part of the century, was no isolated scholastic Captain Bligh. The beating of boys was rooted in a system in which headmasters were tyrants and acted the part with relish, and where physical punishment was seen as a duty by those who administered it.

Rev. Dr Bernays,
Headmaster of Elstree
1845-1861

Winston Churchill's descriptions of his prep school days in the 1880s at St. George's, Ascot, under the savage Rev. Herbert Sneyd-Kynnersly, are well-known: one of the duties of the head boy was to hold down other boys by force while they were being beaten. Even simple academic errors, such as (according to one headmaster) following the Latin conjunction *ut* with the indicative instead of the subjunctive verb, received ferocious chastisement.

When the boys of Haileybury decided to join the national outburst of joy at the relief of Ladysmith in February 1900 by marching to Hertford waving Union Jacks, the Headmaster, Canon Lyttleton (later Head Master of Eton) gave the entire upper school six of the best – being applauded afterwards by the boys on his way back to his house for this remarkable feat of physical exertion. The atmosphere of constant fear is vividly captured by a pupil's description of the headmaster of one prep school in the 1890s as:

> a terrifying personality which seemed to hover over the school like some obscene vulture over a flock of lambs. The rustling of his wings was forever in the air. At any moment he might pounce. He was like the Angel of Death stalking through a plague-stricken city. No-one was immune from that dreadful summons.[8]

Such men seem to have been commonplace. It was said that the appalling food at preparatory schools in those days gave the boys just sufficient nutrition to survive the constant floggings which they had to endure.

But Arthur Dunn was of an entirely different mind. Rewards were more plentiful at Ludgrove than punishments; and punishments, when they came, were largely confined to detention, or to drills in the school yard under the instruction of Sergeant-Major Everett – a custom which continued up to the 1950s. While the cane may have been used, there is no mention of it in any writings that have survived about

Old Ludgrove dining-room

Ludgrove class-room, early 20th century

Ludgrove in the Arthur Dunn years. Sir Shane Leslie, who came to the school in 1895, records that he once decided to run away to London to see what it was like, to smoke his first cigarette and look for a job as a shop-assistant. He was discovered and returned to Ludgrove. It is daunting to imagine what might have been Leslie's penalty for such an offence in most other prep schools of the day. But at Ludgrove his punishment was simply to write a letter of apology to Arthur Dunn, which was read out to the whole school. He was then taken back on condition that he undertook to work hard for his Eton entrance exam. Leslie recalled later that "the effect was instantaneous: for I gave up interest in games and became a bookworm", and in the next year he took Remove at Eton, the highest form into which a new boy could enter the school.

In reading the records of those times, one has the clearest impression of Dunn as a kind and caring man, who considered that part of education should be for the enjoyment of boyhood, and who respected equally those boys for whom games meant nothing or who were stronger in intellectual than athletic disciplines. He believed that discipline should be enforced more by the spirit of the place than by chastisement, by giving boys a clear knowledge of the boundaries of right and wrong, and that the atmosphere of the school should be supportive and pleasant, rather than harsh and repressive. Robert McCormick, who was

Sir Shane Leslie

24

the second boy into the school, would have spoken for most when he said of him fifty years later: "He was kindly, and a good influence on the boys. I have always remembered him with affection"; declaring that his days there were among the happiest of his life.

Finally, Dunn's style of leadership was the embodiment of his favourite saying *"Whatsoever thy hand findeth to do, do it with thy might"*. He was one of life's natural enthusiasts. He led by example, and expected the same enthusiasm from everyone with whom he came into contact, whether men or boys. One of his early pupils, Lord John Hope (who subsequently became Lord Linlithgow and Viceroy of India) personally told Helen Dunn in later years that this verse had profoundly influenced his own life – an example of the direct influence of Ludgrove on the development of Empire. It was said of Arthur Dunn that "he taught Keenness as a subject", and everyone fell under the spell of his phenomenal energy. Sir Shane Leslie said of him that

> he was born keen, and keen he remained as a burnished razor until the end. He was keen on sport, keen on games, keen on music, keen on singing, and keenest of all on his friends, colleagues and pupils. His short life was lived on the edge, partly owing to his proverbial keenness and partly to his magnificent fitness.

If someone's keenness fell below a certain level, he could be classified as a "scug" and sent off to a distant corner of the school yard, kept and named for the purpose. But everyone was fired up by his presence – by his leadership if you were a master, by his inspiration if you were a boy, by his loyalty if you were a friend. Arthur Dunn comes across the pages of time as an inspiring personality of boundless energy, who never-theless always had time for people, who inspired devotion by his example and who became a legend in his own lifetime through his selfless dedication to the cause he had embarked on, and to which in the end he was literally to give his life.

So Ludgrove flourished virtually from the start under the guiding hand of its tireless Headmaster. The early records provide proof of ceaseless activity, of success both in the classroom and on the games field, and an environment of constant endeavour and achievement.

School life – 1892-1902

Arthur Dunn was determined that progress at his new school should be fully recorded, and he bequeathed the practice of writing School Notes at the end of each term, which was continued by successive headmasters until replaced in the 1980s by the School Magazine. The Notes – especially in the early days – formed a remarkably complete record of life at the school for over three-quarters of a century.

The first term of which we have a record is the Lent term of 1894, by when the school had grown to two masters (T.C. Weatherhead and H. Hansell) and 17 pupils; by

Ludgrove cricket XI, 1894

the following term a Mr George Field had joined the staff and there were 24 boys. Thereafter the build-up was remarkably swift: 35 boys in the Spring Term of 1895, 43 by Christmas that year, 54 by the end of 1896 and 61 by the summer of 1897, by which time there were six staff. That remained the approximate number at which Dunn considered the school 'full', and 60 was to remain the average number of boys at Ludgrove until the 1940s.

There are interesting signs of the school's build-up from its standing start two years previously. Summer 1894 was recorded with pride as being the first term in which cricket matches were played against other schools – two games were lost against Northaw and Elstree, and there was great disappointment that the last three matches of term had to be abandoned because of chicken-pox.

On the academic side, Dunn was clearly pleased with the expansion of the Library "which now contains 300 books, and is under the charge of Mr. Hansell who makes it his chief endeavour to recommend books to boys, and to encourage those who show little aptitude for reading". Mr. Hansell (another of life's enthusiasts) also gave a lecture that term on Germany, where he had been educated for a time, and delighted his audience with what must have been a very vivid description of duelling in German universities – of which he had clearly had first-hand experience. At the end of that summer term of 1894, the first boys left Ludgrove for their Public Schools – E.H. Buxton to Harrow and H.C.H.W. Moffat to Wellington. How strange that his first leaver should go to the very school which Arthur Dunn had left Elstree to avoid!

The great winter of 1894-5 was the year the Thames froze over, the traditional ox was roasted on the ice and the Grenadier Guards marched across the Serpentine. At Ludgrove, football gave way to ice hockey as everything froze for weeks (unheard of today when boys usually go through their entire school careers without even seeing snow), and the school was in the grip of "the frost fiend". But when football did resume, there was a triumphant victory against Elstree, undoubtedly the highlight of the term and one of the best moments since the foundation. It must have given Arthur Dunn immense pride to have beaten his old school, and his delight knew no bounds – "a great game and brilliant victory…we need only say that we are proud of our champions". Elstree must have smarted over this: the following year they defeated Ludgrove by 12–0, nine of the goals being scored before half-time!

The early staff

Arthur Dunn sought to recruit staff who met as nearly as possible his criteria of 'the Scholar-Athlete' – men from either Oxford or Cambridge who were able to show substantial academic achievement; if combined with demonstrable ability on the games field, so much the better. By 1894, the staff consisted of Messrs Henry Hale, T.C. Weatherhead, H. Hansell and George Field. We will return to the first three later. Field had taken a Second in Classics and a Third in History from Trinity College, Oxford, had also been in his Football and Cricket XIs at Uppingham, and had won a Cricket Blue. He was followed the next term by Mr F. Jones of Magdalen College, Oxford "who was in the Sixth Form Select for the Newcastle Scholarship at Eton in 1888".

In the same year the music teaching was put into the hands of an outstanding master, Mr Cecil Sharp, who was later to become famous for his rediscovery of English folk music and dance, and as the most important 20th century collector of British and American folk-songs.

In 1895 Mr F.L. Crabtree, a former King's Scholar at Eton and an Exhibitioner at King's College, Cambridge joined the staff; to be followed in 1897 by his brother Mr. H. Crabtree, who had been a scholar of both Charterhouse and Pembroke College, Cambridge, from where he had graduated as a Wrangler. Both Crabtrees had been in their school and college Cricket and Football XIs.

In between, he appointed Mr. G.O. Smith and Mr. W.J. Oakley, just down from Oxford and both English international footballers, of whom we shall hear much more later. These appointments were followed in 1896 by the arrival of two more masters: Mr A.N. Brown (known as 'Bunco'), an Exhibitioner of Queen's College, Oxford who was "placed high in the Second Class of Honour Moderations and Litterae Humaniores" and had for ten years previously been first classical master at Mortimer School; and Mr. W.P. ('Willie') Blore, nicknamed 'Bluff', a classical scholar of Marlborough and Christ Church, Oxford, also with Second Class Honours in Mods and Greats.

In later life Mr Blore recalled that "in the letter that Arthur wrote to me offering me a post at Ludgrove he added nothing more than this: 'There is only one thing that I think I need mention, and that is that I am most anxious that we masters should be punctual for early school and for breakfast on Sundays". Blore adds that for 35 years he carried out this injunction "religiously"!

The last of Dunn's 'great' appointments was Mr. W.F.H. Stanbrough, who succeeded Mr F. Crabtree in the spring of 1900. Walter Stanbrough had been in the football and cricket XIs at Charterhouse. He won his Football Blue at Cambridge, where he gained a Second in Classics; and went on to play football for England in a South African tour in 1897. For the six years since coming down he had taught the scholarship class at

F. Jekyll, top King's Scholar

another prep school, Horton Hall. He was to remain on the staff at Ludgrove for 34 years. Smith, Oakley, Brown, Blore and Stanbrough were to be the backbone of the Ludgrove staff for over a third of a century.

As far as their pupils were concerned, the three cleverest boys in those early days were C.M. Palairet (subsequently the last British Minister to Vienna before the Second World War), Norman Chamberlain (a cousin of Austen and Neville), and F.W. Jekyll who, in the summer of 1895, came first in the list of those elected to King's Scholarships at Eton. This achievement has remained without parallel in more than a century of Ludgrove's history to date. The whole place seems to have erupted with delight at the news. It was considered an achievement of such brilliance that Arthur Dunn gave the entire school a day's holiday and took them to London Zoo to celebrate it! Jekyll subsequently lived up to every academic expectation in his career at Eton, which he left in 1901 as an Exhibitioner to Balliol. The School Notes record with pride that, among many other prizes during his Eton days, he won the Jelf Prize, the Latin Prose Prize, the College Prize, the Prince Consort's Prize for French and the Newcastle Scholarship in 1900.

Sports

One of the prime purposes of the School Notes was to record the football and cricket matches. Dunn writes with great enthusiasm about the games. It is clear that for him Triumph and Disaster were by no means to be treated "just the same". His pen almost runs away with him in recording a victory, as in the case of that first win over Elstree in

Ludgrove Football XI, 1896

1894; and he was always ready to praise and encourage - thus, in reviewing the winter term's matches in 1896: "Wiggin was *wonderful* (Dunn's italics!) and his example of hard play was well followed by Aspinall and Lacon. Nearly all played well". But in defeat he could be highly critical, writing after one match that "a little more pluck and dash might have lessened the score enormously"; and again "a great want of dash was shown by our side in this match."

On some occasions he was merciless, for example in 1898:

> Little can be said of the game, for it was practically a bombardment of our goal all through…the half-backs were only fair, and the forwards disgraceful. These latter did nothing, and seemed to prefer inglorious inaction to any effort that might possibly entail some injury. It is impossible for the Eleven to do any good while some of its members persist in these funking tactics.

and again in 1901:

> The first game against Cholmeley House this term ended in a pointless draw; neither side ever looked like scoring. The second was won by the visitors, a result mainly due to the lamentable weakness of the Ludgrove centre forward who missed three inexcusable shots.

"Dash" is one of Dunn's favourite words – "The forwards occasionally pressed well, but there was a lamentable lack of dash throughout the line" – and he considers this a sporting quality which boys should acquire above all others. The football reports are peppered with it. One can imagine the presence of the Headmaster, by then England's football captain, on the touchline during these matches, willing his boys to take advantage of the openings which he could spot so clearly himself, and to seize the chances and half-chances that a little more "dash" would put within their reach.

One of the major projects of those early years was the levelling of the hillside near the house to make the new football pitch. It was stony ground, and the task of clearing it was carried out, stone by stone, by Headmaster, masters and boys alike, often working for long periods on their knees. The fixture lists expanded rapidly after 1894, and regular matches were played against Elstree, Northaw, Cheam, Heddon Court, Sandroyd (recently founded by Dunn's former colleague at Elstree and the England Football XI, C.P. Wilson), Sunningdale, King's College Choir School (the 'away' matches there followed by hearing their opponents, changed from shorts into surplices, sing Evensong in King's College Chapel), Aldenham and Gisburne House – and the matches which Arthur Dunn enjoyed the most, against the Old Ludgrovians who came back from Eton to play, as they still do to this day.

The boys also had the unique opportunity of witnessing football played on their own school ground at the highest level in the land - between the Old Etonians and other

Fives-court at Ludgrove, 1920s

Old Boys teams, and also in what Dunn called 'Masters' Matches' between his own selected sides against the Corinthians, and the university teams of Oxford and Cambridge. In the Ludgrove sides in these games there were seldom less than four or five England international players of the day – G.O. Smith, W.J. Oakley, R.E. Foster, C. Wreford-Brown, C.P. Wilson, R.C. Gosling and of course A.T.B.Dunn himself, playing with all the "dash" of a 20-year old until he was forty. These sides were supplemented by members of the staff, notably H. Hansell in goal, W.P. Blore and W.F. Stanbrough, all experienced footballers. For all the distinction of their opponents, throughout the 1890s his side was seldom defeated.

In the winter term of 1897, a new Eton Fives court was completed, as a result of the first appeal that Ludgrove made. Many parents and most of the staff appear to have contributed. It was said to have been "an exceptionally fast and true court, and there could hardly have been a better court in England". Coaching was in the hands of Mr. H. Crabtree, and was a success from the outset. Ludgrove has been associated with excellence at Eton Fives ever since.

Health

After the disruption of so many fixtures by chicken-pox in the winter of 1894, whooping-cough came in 1895 to decimate the cricket fixture list for the whole of May and June, to be rapidly followed by measles later in the term, when only one match could be played in July. The school was reduced to playing a series of three matches against a Miss Buxton's XI which consisted entirely of ladies. (Sir Shane Leslie remembers that "they wore long, swishing skirts with which they could cleverly but unfairly impede the ball, for in those days a lady's ankle could only be seen unswathed in the pantomime.").

The Malcolmson cricket team at Ludgrove, with ladies in attendance, c. 1900

In the following winter term of 1898 Dunn writes that "the long list of matches arranged for the term had to be scratched because of the outbreak of measles"; and in the summer term of 1899 it is recorded that "with a First XI of exceptional strength, it was doubly disappointing to have to own to an outbreak of chicken-pox towards the end of May; for 8 weeks we remained under a cloud, only relieved by a match against another 'chicken-pox school.'"

Health issues were of enormous concern to preparatory schools in those days. While

Female staff at Ludgrove, 1898

illness was of course endemic, the onset of a major epidemic could virtually close a school, with a consequent loss of income for its headmaster and livelihood for its staff. While boys were expected to get such illnesses as measles, whooping-cough, chicken-pox, scarlet fever and mumps, there were more serious ailments in the wings: typhoid, tuberculosis, diphtheria, typhus, smallpox – and even cholera.

The Ludgrove School Notes between 1894 and 1908 record no less than six heart-rending "In Memoriam" notices of Old Ludgrovians who had died from such diseases while at their public school – James Worrall in 1898, Cyril Abel-Smith in 1902, Vincent Corbet in 1903, Ronald Hunter in 1905, and Guy Hoare and Hugh Charrington in 1908. A magazine of the day called *The Private Schoolmaster* wrote that

> outbreaks of even mild epidemics have proved so disastrous for schools – public and private – that the mere suggestion of measles and scarlet fever is enough to instil fear into the hearts of all [...] Sanitary conditions are now as much desired by Principals as examination successes.

Schools felt helpless in the face of such potentially lethal threats. Robert McCormick recalls how

> in 1889, while we were living in London, there was a cholera epidemic. No one knew how it was carried. The only protective measure that I recall was spraying a mixture of carbolic acid and water on the curtains. Migration to the Swiss mountains by those who could afford it was a successful escape.

A school's reputation as a healthy environment was one of the most important assets it could have. This put a high premium on rural locations like Barnet, which was then far

Ludgrove's garden staff, 1898

from the metropolitan sources of disease. But in those days most schools paid relatively little attention to hygiene, and for all its splendid location Ludgrove's standards of sanitation were dreadful by comparison with the present day, with freezing cold washrooms, very public 'thunder-box' lavatories until the 1930s, and boys given baths only twice a fortnight.

> During the summer holidays of 1900, an installation of electric light was carried out. We now have the advantage of light in every room and passage in the house, cottage, laundry and carpenter's shop.
>
> *School Notes*

Music

This was another area of school life in which Arthur Dunn showed himself to be far ahead of his contemporaries in his conviction of what the essentials of a boy's education should contain. With the notable exception of Uppingham under its great headmaster Edward Thring, who did introduce music as a compulsory subject into his curriculum, most public schools of the 19th century had little interest in music teaching. Music therefore had no bearing whatever on the preparation of boys for entrance to their public schools, and consequently preparatory schools also gave it the lowest priority in their curricula (except at the choir schools), treating it as a mere 'extra'. They held that it was an activity best suited to girls (a prejudice which survived to the middle of the 20th century), and confined any spare-time teaching of it to the techniques of learning an instrument of some sort rather than developing any wider ability to appreciate music for its own sake.

Cecil Sharp with 'music boys' 1893

It is all the more impressive, then, to see the central importance that Arthur Dunn himself attached to musical education in his new school – inspired no doubt by his own singing ability, and by his mother's upbringing. Most nights he made time to sing for an hour with the Masters' Quartet in preparation for school concerts. And above all, he had the prescience to recruit a music master of genius who was subsequently to become world-famous: Cecil Sharp.

Immediately on arrival in 1895 Sharp instituted Ludgrove's first Music Prize. That same term the combined enthusiasm of Sharp and Dunn put on a concert for the boys by visiting musicians which included string and piano works by Bach, Handel and Haydn. It was followed by the following inspiring notice in the School Notes:

> The Concert was an experiment designed to illustrate in a practical manner the truth of the theory that the appreciation of the beauties of Art should form an essential factor in all schemes of true education; and that this power of appreciation is one which can be taught and developed like every other faculty. It was also eminently successful as an entertainment. 'Classical Music', that bugbear of the youthful mind, is for the nonce held in high estimation at Ludgrove.

Later in the year a splendid organ was presented to the school to accompany evening prayers and other occasions. It was a gift from F.C. Arkwright of Cromford, Derbyshire, father of F.G.A. and R.A. Arkwright (1894), and the forebear of no less than eight Arkwrights at Ludgrove between 1894 and 1923. They were descendants of the 18th century textile magnate and inventor, Sir Richard Arkwright, who had made a fortune a century earlier, by revolutionising thread-spinning. This organ added a vital dimension to the musical life of the school, which was in the uniquely qualified hands of Cecil Sharp, probably the most outstanding of the teachers whom Arthur Dunn summoned to his banner. They were clearly like-minded people, and Sharp was subsequently to dedicate his famous *Book of British Song* to Arthur Dunn in the following testimony to Dunn's personality:

> Arthur Dunn, by placing in my hands the management of the singing classes at Ludgrove School, gave me the opportunity of teaching boys to sing in the way I had found best. [....] By his originality of mind and sympathetic energy, he rarely failed to exercise a permanent influence for good on those who came into contact with him; and those who had the privilege to work with him will understand how much we owe to his knowledge, enthusiasm and kindly encouragement.

Religion

Sir Shane Leslie says of Arthur Dunn: "Religion lay old-fashioned at the back of Arthur's mind…his creed was evangelical, interpreted by the code of a gentleman". He taught the stories of the Bible under the subject headings of Old Testament History and New Testament History, as they are still called at Ludgrove, rather than 'R.E.' or 'R.S.'. He would undoubtedly have subscribed to the Ten Commandments as summarising the behaviour expedient for a stable and ordered society. He promoted belief in a simple Christianity, as the basis of the values and standards of behaviour that he sought to impart to his pupils: integrity, decency, reliability, telling the truth, keeping your word, good manners, and of course (in keeping with his favourite saying) trying as hard as possible at everything.

In 1898 Francis Bevan of Trent Park paid for a major project to enlarge the nearby Christ Church at Cockfosters to cater for the whole school. Dunn notes:

> We now have permanent sittings for the whole school, most of them in a side aisle…Stained glass windows, a new Pulpit, Font, Lectern and many other beautiful gifts have…improved the Church almost beyond recognition.

Every Sunday without fail the whole school would wend its way in a crocodile through the Bevans' Trent Park estate to the nearby church for Matins. Arthur Dunn would bring the collection plate round. During one service one of the Barclay boys proffered what he thought was the usual penny, only to see with horror at the last minute that it was a florin (2 shillings or 10p). He realised his mistake, hastily withdrew it, saw Arthur staring at him impatiently down the row, proffered it and withdrew it again – and finally, with huge reluctance, dropped it into the plate "with a groan". His small friends all around were "reduced to suppressed hysterics" by the pantomime.

School lectures

Many notable lectures are recorded on a wide variety of subjects. The Winter term of 1901 gives a good insight into their number and variety, with no fewer than eight taking place on such subjects as "Pompeii", "The Mission to Seamen", "The Sea Life of Lord Nelson", "St. Paul's first two missionary journeys", "Birds and their ways" (which was followed by the formation of the Ludgrove branch of the Society for the Protection of Birds, with Mr Stanbrough as Secretary), "The Library through history", "The Order of Knights Hospitallers of St. John and Jerusalem" and "Our Fleet today".

In 1900 the Ludgrove Branch of the Navy League was formed, under Mr. Brown's supervision. The League existed to promote the 'Senior Service' throughout the land,

Osbert Sitwell in about 1903

and since the Royal Navy then sought cadets from the age of 13 to enter its training establishments, preparatory schools saw it as their calling to prepare boys for the Navy as well as for the Public Schools. Every term a representative of the Navy League came to lecture, and on occasion a party of boys would go down to Portsmouth to be entertained to a wide-ranging programme of ship visits, gunnery practice and lectures.

Osbert Sitwell, who was at Ludgrove in 1902, recalled one episode involving this side of school life:

[My friend] Clive possessed a sense of humour with a certain spirit of audacity. We talked of the trouble in which, as the result of a joke, he had recently found himself. In all schools of this sort the Navy League used to indulge in propaganda: lectures used to be given, and each term the boys received printed forms with the request that they should enter against one enquiry the sum of money they wished to give to the institution. In a fit of high sprits, Clive had written down "Two Million Pounds" against his name, and had sent it off: a form of exaggeration not appreciated either by the Navy League or by schoolmasters..."[8]

COMMON-ROOM CHARACTERS

It is a testimony to the personal qualities of Arthur Dunn that he succeeded in attracting to the staff of his new school a remarkable group of masters, no fewer than four of whom – Cecil Sharp, 'Bunco' Brown, G.O. Smith and W.J. Oakley – made their names on stages far wider than the confined world of the Ludgrove Common Room.

The first to join his staff was Henry Hale. Little is known of him except that, while there, he fell in love with Mrs Dunn's sister Laura. When she rejected his suit, he immediately emigrated to Australia, where he worked for a time as a missionary before becoming headmaster of a school near Hobart, Tasmania.

In the first year of which records exist, there were just two masters to teach the 17 boys in the school, in addition to Arthur Dunn himself: Mr T.C. Weatherhead and Mr H. Hansell.

T.C. Weatherhead

He took the First (top) Division for Classics and the bottom one for Mathematics. He had a "sandy-peaked beard, contemptuous little eyes and the quickest of tempers" and was apparently "full of sarcasm and asthma". He was a brilliant versifier in Latin, of which W.S.Gilbert's *Bab Ballads* were among his favourite targets for rendering into hexameters, and considered that skill in this art "as exquisite an accomplishment as petit-point embroidery or timing the cricket ball". He was nick-named "the Feather" for obscure reasons. He

T. Weatherhead

left Ludgrove in 1898 to become headmaster of Glenarth preparatory school in Cheltenham. Arthur Dunn considered his departure "a great loss…since he has been successful in every way here, and has contributed very largely to the many creditable performances of Ludgrove boys at Public Schools".

Henry Hansell

Henry Hansell was a fine-looking, six-foot-four giant of a man, the son of a Norfolk squire, who was likened to Gulliver in Lilliput, with the boys swarming around him. Hansell taught everything – Classics, Mathematics, French and New Testament History. Schoolmasters come in two categories: those of predictable temperament, who you know where you are with, for better or worse; and those who are unpredictable, by whom you may be considered out of line even when you believe you are not. Mr Hansell fell into the latter category. Sir Shane Leslie recalls that:

H. Hansell

[Hansell] believed that it was his duty to entertain his class whenever he was not losing his temper. Arthur Dunn placed Hansell's class between his own and Weatherhead's to keep an ear on what was going on. On one occasion his class fell into an ominous hush, and when Dunn entered he found, to the apparent merriment of all, that Hansell was asleep. […] Mr Hansell was not a scholar…but

he was a splendid goalkeeper, prancing with his
6 ft 4 ins into the air between the posts. On the
whole he was an exciting master, and to him I
owe my first impulses in English literature.

Through a curious chance, Hansell subsequently
became tutor to the royal princes, the sons of the
Prince of Wales, who succeeded as King George V
in 1910. It came about after two Ludgrove boys,
Roger Coke and Evelyn Barclay, chose to run away
to London – without any cause, it would seem,
other than to purchase a cage of white rats. Mr
Hansell was sent in pursuit. Subsequently the boys
were spotted and detained by a retainer of Coke's
father, the Earl of Leicester. Interviews were then
conducted between Mr Hansell and the families
and it was thought he would make an ideal

Hansell as goalkeeper

private tutor. So he left Ludgrove and began a new career as a tutor to the great and the
good, moving through a number of posts until he reached the Royal Family.

In 1902 he was employed by the Prince of Wales as tutor to his sons, Edward (later
Edward VIII and Duke of Windsor) and Albert ('Bertie'), later George VI. Subsequently,
Hansell also tutored the other brothers, Henry (Duke of Gloucester), George (Duke of
Kent) and John, who was epileptic and died in 1919, aged only fourteen.

"Absolutely straight but very broad-minded," Lord Derby wrote of Hansell. "I can
imagine no man better able to guide rather than drive a boy." The Prince of Wales
agreed: "I always think his judgement is good." However, Hansell does not seem to have
distinguished himself in royal service. He has been described as having a "humourless
solemnity", and to have been "more qualified by muscle than by mind" for his new
responsibility.

One shortcoming of Hansell's methods came to light when the Prince of Wales
discovered that his eldest son Edward, aged eleven, could not calculate the average
weight of the stags shot by his father at Balmoral during the previous season.

The same Edward, as Duke of Windsor, wrote of Hansell:

> On looking back over those curiously ineffectual years under him, I am appalled
> to discover how little I really learned. He could scarcely be said to have possessed
> a positive personality. If he harboured strong views about anything, he was careful
> to conceal them. Although I was in his care on and off for more than twelve years,
> I am today unable to recall anything brilliant or original that he ever said.[8]

This judgement does not appear to have been excessively harsh. Kenneth Rose, in his biography of George V, writes:

> Hansell clearly recognised the inadequacy both of his own talents and of any attempt to educate a future sovereign by private tuition alone. He repeatedly warned the Prince of Wales that if the boys were to hold their own at Naval College, they ought to exchange the seclusion of Sandringham for a well-managed preparatory school. There, he urged, they would benefit not only from a specialised curriculum but also from the friendship and rivalries of communal life. The Prince would have none of it. "My brother and I never went to a preparatory school," he told Hansell. "The Navy will teach David [Prince Edward] all that he needs to know."
>
> [...] The Prince of Wales also harboured…doubts about the wholesomeness of boarding-schools. [...] [He] feared the perils of a fashionable preparatory school. He would keep his children at home until they were old enough to join a well-supervised and morally aseptic naval establishment[9].

At Osborne Naval College, Prince Edward emerged from his first year "not far from the bottom", and Prince Albert was 68th out of 68. Their younger brothers, Prince Henry and Prince George, were sent to St Peter's Court, in Broadstairs. Their father did not choose Ludgrove, although the future Queen Mary's two nephews, the Princes George and Frederick of Teck, both went there.

The future Duke of Gloucester, at least, seems to have remained on cordial terms with his former tutor. Kenneth Rose tells us:

> Henry did, however, surprise his parents by passing the entrance examination to Sandhurst [from Eton] halfway up the list. Basking in a rare message of congratulation, he wrote to his old tutor, Henry Hansell: "Mama and Papa are delighted. They think rather more of Eton than they did before."

John Sessions as Hansell

In 2003 Henry Hansell was portrayed by the actor John Sessions as the rather exasperated tutor to the young princes, in the television documentary drama, *The Lost Prince*, about George V's youngest son John.

Cecil Sharp

One might think that a prep school music master whose name was 'C sharp' would have stood little chance of credibility in such a merciless arena as a prep school. But Cecil Sharp was no ordinary music master. He was to become famous as the most important

Cecil Sharp

collector ever of English folk-songs, and for his rediscovery of English folk dance. At the same time as being on the staff at Ludgrove he was also Principal of the Hampstead Conservatoire, both of which posts he held from 1893 until he left in 1910 to found the English Folk Dance Society.

Cecil Sharp was born in 1859 and educated at Uppingham (a beneficiary of the priority given to music by its Headmaster Edward Thring) and Cambridge, where he read law. As a lawyer he emigrated to Australia where he became assistant to the Chief Justice of South Australia. But in 1889 he changed to a musical career, becoming assistant organist of Adelaide Cathedral and Co-Director of the Adelaide College of Music. He returned to England in 1892 and became the music master at Ludgrove from 1893.

This was some years before his interest in folk song was revealed; but in 1901 he published the first of a series of five volumes of *Folk Songs from Somerset* and *The English Folk Song*. These publications led to a widespread revival of interest in the country in English folk music. In 1905 he also began to collect English folk dances. He launched the teaching of folk song and dance in English schools through his Vacation School of Folk Song and Dance, at Stratford-on-Avon. Probably his most famous exploits were the three visits he made to the Appalachians in the USA between 1916 and 1918 to collect songs of English origin. He became a legend in his lifetime: in 1930 Cecil Sharp House was founded in his honour, near Regent's Park, London, as the home of the English Folk Dance and Song Society, and there it thrives to this day.

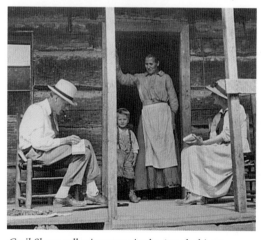

Cecil Sharp collecting songs in the Appalachians

Cecil Sharp gave many vivid lectures to the boys on the origin and meaning of English folk songs, and of his approach to rediscovering them. G.O. Smith wrote in 1907:

It is impossible to hear Mr Sharp without being impressed by the interest and importance of the work upon which he is engaged. He has now completed four volumes of songs from Somerset alone, and he shortly intends to explore other counties.

And again in 1909:

> To us at Ludgrove, who for many
> years have followed Mr Sharp in his
> work with great interest, the lecture
> showed what progress he has made in
> his field since he last addressed us;
> and we most heartily wish him
> continued success in collecting and
> handing down to future generations
> English folk songs which, but for his
> labours, would otherwise be lost and
> forgotten.

Girls folk-dancing in Stratford-on-Avon, c.1912

As previously stated, Cecil Sharp had an enormous respect and affection for Arthur
Dunn, whose inspiration it had been to attract him to Ludgrove in the first place. He
had been moved by his Ludgrove experience to (as he said) "put this musical heritage
of England within reach of every home and schoolroom", to which end he published his
Book of British Songs in 1902, dedicated, as we have seen, to Arthur Dunn. It contains
78 songs from every era of British history, including the "Song on the Victory of
Agincourt", written shortly after the battle in 1415 and which Sharp believed to be the
oldest English patriotic song in existence.

A.N. ('Bunco') Brown

Arthur Neville Brown was born in 1864 at Nayland in Suffolk, the
eldest son of the Rev. J.T. Brown. He was educated at St. Edmund's
School, Canterbury and won an Exhibition to The Queen's
College, Oxford, where he was a classical scholar. He taught
Classics at Canon Lovett Cameron's prep school at Mortimer in
Berkshire until 1898, when Arthur Dunn appointed him to take
charge of Classics at Ludgrove. He retired from Ludgrove in 1923.

His most famous pupil, Alec Douglas-Home, who was prime
minister in 1963–4, wrote of him:

A.N. ('Bunco') Brown

> The master to whom I and countless others were most indebted was a non-
> games-playing teacher of classics who for some forgotten reason we christened
> 'Bunco' Brown. He was rather a forbidding figure, invariably dressed in a
> greenish-brown herring-bone tweed suit and a stick-up collar which, with a large
> drooping moustache and plastered-down hair, produced a portrait of unrelieved
> gloom. But as an interpreter of Virgil and Ovid, Homer and Plato, he was a
> genius. He could even bring alive the interminable campaigns of Caesar. As a

politician, where above all an accurate use of
language matters, I gladly acknowledge my debt
to 'Bunco' Brown. He roused in me a love of
learning for its own sake which has stood me in
good stead ever since.[10]

"a love of learning…"

In addition to his teaching duties, 'Bunco' Brown
was in charge of the Ludgrove section of the Navy
League, and of the Library, gave numerous lectures
and used to work the complicated 'magic lantern'
for visiting lecturers. But Brown's interests went far
beyond his school duties – further perhaps than any
Ludgrove master who has ever taught there, for his main interest lay in astronomy.
When his work was done, he used to spend several hours of the night observing stars
with his 5-inch telescope. In this field he achieved the very highest level of national
distinction. According to the British Astronomical Association, A.N. Brown was one of
the most distinguished of British amateur astronomers of the first part of the 20th
century. His speciality was variable star astronomy, on which subject he communicated
more than 40,000 observations of the heavens in his lifetime, and published no fewer
than 17 papers to the British Astronomical Association, of which he was elected a Fellow
in 1907. He served on the Society's Council for many years, and was a member of the
National Committee for Astronomy.

After his retirement, as doyen of the Variable Star Section of the BAA, the
Association wrote that "he kept up a lively correspondence with members of the
Section, especially beginners. All those who received his friendly advice and clever hints
will have admired his masterly grasp of variable star observing, which was founded
upon many years of hard work in the open at all hours of the night, without shelter."

Again, Ludgrove possesses many fascinating summaries of the lectures given to the
boys by this distinguished astronomer throughout his years there until his retirement
in 1923.

G.O. Smith

Gilbert Oswald Smith, who joined the Ludgrove staff with Bill Oakley in 1895, was
universally known as "G.O." By that time his name as a footballer was so famous that,
in company with "W.G." (Grace), he was one of only two public sporting figures in the
late Victorian era to be known to the general public by his initials alone. Writers of that
time refer to football "in the G.O. Smith era", and many consider that his skill as a centre
forward has never been exceeded.

G.O. was the fourth son of Robert Smith of Godalming, and after prep school at Branksome followed his three brothers to Charterhouse in 1887. His sporting achievements there were extraordinary even by the standards of those times; he played in the school cricket and football XI's for four years between 1889 and 1892, and captained both for the last three. In 1892 he amassed the highest score ever made in a school match at Charterhouse, 229 against Westminster (the whole school was allowed out of lessons early that day to see the completion of the second century); *The Carthusian* celebrated his feat as only school magazines from those days could do:

G.O.Smith

> *The Westminster boys, they can bowl, bat and field*
> *And they thought they would win, but they found they must yield*
> *For a certain G.O. he can drive like G(eh)U,*
> *For his cutting is clean and his timing is true*

and so on for five idolising verses. He followed that innings a month later with 109 against Wellington.

From Charterhouse he went on to Keble College, Oxford where he read Classical Moderations and History. He played football for the University in all four years he was there, and gained Cricket Blues in 1895 and 1896. While at Oxford he was selected to play football for England, and over his career gained 21 international caps, including several as the England captain. He also played cricket briefly for Surrey on coming down from Oxford in 1896.

G.O. has been dubbed by history as "the greatest of all centre forwards". A spectator in a Corinthian match described him as "a three-way player – the opponent one way, the ball another, and G.O. another"; and the Sheffield United international half-back Ernest Needham said of him "I am a good player when playing behind him, but only a medium player when playing in front of him". A sense of his virtuoso abilities is instructive – for it is what the boys would have seen when he came to Ludgrove in 1895. This was especially true in the 'Masters' matches played on the reclaimed upper field against the Universities, the Corinthians and the Old Boys' sides, who came each spring term to challenge (and usually lose) to the sides which Arthur Dunn assembled under the Ludgrove banner. This is how the great C.B. Fry described G.O.'s skill:

> The secret of his consummate skill in football, his adroitness in trapping and
> controlling the ball, his mastery in dribbling, his precision in passing and deftness
> in shooting, was an altogether uncommon faculty of balance and…neatness of
> foot. It was by his balance that, without being a sprinter, he moved so quickly; his

"G.O.Smith tricks the northerners." Cartoon from a report on the North v. South match at Crystal Palace in 1899

speed on the field with a ball consisted in quickness in starting, in turning, in stopping and in changing his paces. [...]His neatness of foot gave him his more obvious virtues – cleverness and quickness; a foot so light in running, so heavy to drive his shot. [...]He'd eyes all round his shirt, had G.O. Most unselfish of players, he got most of his own many goals by his own individual finishing effort. Just his own final turn of the ball made good the chance...and no forward was ever more artfully adept at drawing his opponents before passing.

G.O.'s cricket was not the equal of his football. But in his four innings for Oxford against Cambridge between 1893 and 1896, G.O scored 222 runs at an average of 74 (a record not surpassed until R.W.V. Robins averaged 78 in the seasons 1926–28; the Nawab of Pataudi exceeded even this at 91 between 1928 and 1930). His greatest cricketing exploit came in 1895 when he played one of the most celebrated innings in the whole history of Oxford v. Cambridge matches either before or since. In their second innings, Oxford had to score 330 to win, a target never previously reached to win a Varsity match. They lost their first three wickets for 60; but from this almost hopeless position, G.O. took Oxford to victory by 4 wickets with a wonderful innings of 132. In the words of the *Daily Mail*: "As if by magic the whole of the ring dissolved and melted into one swarm of shouting, cheering, jostling partisans who rushed to the pavilion after the departing cricketers, loudly calling for Smith". The innings subsequently moved Sir Pelham Warner, in his book *Lord's 1787–1945*, to write:

> As long as there is a history of Oxford and Cambridge cricket, the name of G.O. Smith will be emblazoned on its rolls

In later years, G.O. wrote:

After the Varsity match I played a few matches for Surrey, but with no success, and as I knew I could not play serious cricket after that year, I refused to go on with the county. Arthur Dunn had asked W.J. Oakley and myself to join him at Ludgrove, and that meant no serious cricket in the future, though both Oakley and myself played football until Arthur Dunn's death.

Ever modest, he omitted to say that he did play that year for Surrey against the Australians at the Oval, although (as he himself had predicted) he made nought in both innings. Thereafter his cricket was played mainly for the Charterhouse Friars until the beginning of the First World War.

And so, flush with such outstanding success on the sports fields of Oxford and England, G.O. went down from university in 1896 with a Third Class Honours degree in History, to join the staff of Arthur Dunn's new school at Ludgrove. In Edward Grayson's words:

> Today he is regarded as the greatest centre-forward in the history of Association Football; and at Ludgrove he played his full part in the growth of the school to its present stature as one of the country's outstanding preparatory schools in the nation's educational framework.[11]

And yet, for all his legendary prowess as a sportsman, G.O. Smith was a reserved and nervous man. One of his fellow-Carthusian soccer colleagues at Oxford said of him:

> Both as a boy and a man, G.O. was distinguished for his modesty, and perhaps handicapped to a slight extent by his diffidence and shyness.

Given G.O.'s shy and retiring nature, it is just as well that in accepting Arthur Dunn's summons he was joined there by a strong, decisive and outgoing man and one of his closest friends from the Oxford and England football stables from which they both came, W.J. Oakley. Together they were to lead Ludgrove to new heights of fame through the first 22 years of the 20th century.

W.J. Oakley

Bill Oakley was born in 1873, the eldest son of William Oakley, a farmer of Lea Hall, Shropshire and a Burgher of Shrewsbury. His son was at Shrewsbury School from 1884 to 1892, where he made his name as one of the finest all-round sportsmen and athletes that Shrewsbury has ever produced. In athletics he won the 100 yards, quarter-mile, half-mile, mile, steeplechase, hurdles, high and long jumps and throwing the cricket ball at Junior and Senior level in almost every year of his

W.J. Oakley

career there. Two of his 1892 school records of 10.5 seconds in the 100 yards and 2 minutes 4 seconds in the 880 yards (both run on grass) were not beaten until 1955 and 1961 respectively. In one year he won the Inter-House Sports Cup for his house single-handed, no other boy in the house scoring even a single point in the process.

In addition to this athletic record, Oakley was in the School Football XI for five out of his six years there; he rowed in the school VIII for three years; and gained his school cross-country running colours. In his last year he was Captain of Football, Boats and Huntsman (cross-country running) – and it is thought that he would probably have been in the school Cricket XI as well (for which he played once or twice) had he not been so busy on the river.

He went up to Christ Church, Oxford, in 1892 to read Mathematics and Natural Sciences. During his university career he continued to enjoy the same astonishing success as during his school days, representing Oxford against Cambridge in the 120-yard hurdles, long jump, shot-putting and throwing the hammer – and winning many of them. He ran the 100 yards in 10.35 seconds, the 120 yard hurdles in 16.15 seconds, and could jump over 22.5 feet. He was Amateur Long Jump Champion of Britain in 1894, when he also rowed in the OU trial eights; played for the OU football team against Cambridge for all three years; was President of the OUAC in 1895; and represented England in the Long Jump and 120 yard hurdles in an international athletic match against the USA in New York in 1895. On going down from Oxford he played his first international match for England against Wales in 1895, and went on to gain 16 international caps against Ireland, Wales and Scotland in his football career.

He played at full back, in which position he established his reputation as one of the finest exponents of the age. He was clearly a mighty man of valour on the football field:

Oakley in 'Football', from the Badminton Library

on one occasion playing for England against Scotland, he collided with two other players and was knocked out, with blood flowing from his nose and mouth. In spite of his concussion he played on, and on returning to the dressing room after the game was obliged to ask, "Who won?" One of his team-mates said afterwards that he simply couldn't understand how a man could have played so well in such a state. C.B. Fry wrote of him:

He had great pace, was a strong, sure tackler, and kicked accurately and powerfully to his forwards. No professional of his time could outpace him. [...] He had a magnificent physique – tall, long-limbed and sinewy. With his grey eyes and unvaryingly quiet voice, he was notably cool and collected, and capable of intense effort… Give me Oakers in a rough and tumble, and you can have any other man in England except Sam Woods.

G.O. himself wrote:

His qualities as a football player illustrate what he was in life – absolutely reliable and never ruffled. He was indeed an English gentleman in the best sense of the word.

In all, Arthur Dunn had assembled a team of men possessed of gifts beyond the ordinary, committed to the cause which he himself represented with such infectious enthusiasm, and all devoted to their Headmaster as a friend, an athlete and a leader whose "sympathetic energy" inspired them all.

SOME EARLY PUPILS

In the spring of 1901, T.R. Pelly, "Ludgrovian Number One", visited his old school on a short break to recover from wounds in the Boer War. Arthur Dunn had a great affection for Pelly – together they had started the school – and the Notes keep their readers regularly informed of his progress through the ranks of Haileybury and the Army. His return to his old school must have been emotional. It is clear that Pelly returned to active service in South Africa shortly thereafter, since later that year Dunn records that "in July T.R. Pelly received the South African Medal with three clasps, from the hand of the King."

We have already met one or two of those pioneering boys at Ludgrove – Pelly, Palairet, Chamberlain, Jekyll. Others who entered the school in those early years included four Bowes-Lyons, brothers of the late Queen Mother, three Barrington-Kennets, who would all be killed in the First World War, and many whose names were to become familiar to generations of Ludgrove boys as their sons, grandsons and great grandsons were to become Ludgrovians also – Abel-Smith, Baxter, Charrington, Cornwallis, Douglas-Pennant, Hart-Dyke, Worsley, Wyndham-Quinn. Of the boys in

Ludgrove has taught four generations of Baxters (l. to r.): George, Normile, Angus and Robert

the school in 1900, no fewer than ten had descendants there in 2003: Abel-Smith, Baxter, Bevan, Bruce, Boscawen, Cobbold, Gibbs, Hoare, Holland-Hibbert, and Wiggin.

Two early deaths

Two boys from those early years met their ends in tragic, if spectacular, fashion. One, Knyvet Barclay, who was among the first ten boys to enter the school in 1892, was mauled to death by a lion on his father's Norfolk estate. The other, Julian Hall (1895-1900), was shot in bed by an actress, in a desperate frenzy of thwarted love. It happened in 1913, when Hall was in his mid-twenties.

The murder became headline news because the "extraordinarily beautiful" actress, named Jeannie Baxter, was defended by the brilliant barrister, Edward Marshall Hall, in one of his most celebrated court performances. Julian Hall (no relation) was a "young pioneer of the air, magnificently built", but a violent man, given to unpredictable outbursts when in drink, who on one occasion broke a strong oak table with his bare hands.[12]

He met Jeannie Baxter in a night-club; they fell violently in love, and Julian saw off her current beau by challenging him to a pistol duel (which the latter sensibly declined). Jeannie grew to love Julian "better than anybody in the world," as she later told the court. But his drinking and violence destroyed their happiness: indeed Julian would sometimes fire his revolver into the ceiling during their violent quarrels.

Although marriage was planned, and Julian's will was drawn up in Jeannie's favour, he began, under the influence of "a constant male companion", to grow cool about the whole thing. Early one morning, when Julian was in bed with a hangover, Jeannie came to visit him at his Soho flat. It seems that they then formally agreed to marry. But a little later, according to Jeannie's evidence, Julian said: "It's no good – I can't keep my promise. It's better to finish it. The drink is killing me!" Then a maid outside heard six shots, and Jeannie ran out of the room sobbing: "I've shot him…he dared me to do it!" Julian had received two bullet-wounds and died shortly afterwards.

At the Old Bailey Jeannie Baxter had a difficult case to answer. But Marshall Hall put forward an ingenious hypothesis in her defence: that Julian in his drunken stupor had teased her by threatening suicide; had played with the revolver by pointing it at his chest, daring her to pull the trigger; that she refused, but tried desperately to take it from him; and that during the struggle he himself had involuntarily pulled the trigger twice before she wrested it from him. She then fired the other four bullets into the ceiling and ran to get help. As the great advocate's biographer wrote: "Marshall Hall was always at his best when his case had a strong romantic interest." The jury found her guilty only of manslaughter, for which she received a 'light' sentence of three years' imprisonment. As the beneficiary of Julian's will, Jeannie Baxter later became the subject of a decision by the Court of Appeal, that "no person who feloniously causes the death of a testator can benefit under that testator's will." It was a landmark judgement for, although the principle had already been established for murder, in the Crippen case, it had not hitherto been applied to manslaughter.

A loss to athletics and academe: Gerard Anderson

Among the brightest and best of the Old Ludgrovians of the late 1890's was Gerard Anderson. He gained a First in Mods and Greats at Oxford, followed by a Fellowship of All Souls, and represented Great Britain in the Stockholm Olympic Games in 1912 as a hurdler, when he became known as "the man who fell at Stockholm". In practice he had broken the world record, and won his first heat with ease. But in the second heat he fell when leading easily, after landing on a hole in the track made by a starter in the previous sprint race. Tragically he was killed at Ypres in November 1914. According to his obituary, "Anderson was the best man over the sticks we have ever had in England, and the unluckiest." His great friend and rival at Ludgrove, Victor Barrington-Kennett, would also be killed in the Great War.

Careers of distinction: Robert McCormick and Daniel Jones

Two of the earliest Ludgrovians who achieved world-wide fame in vastly different ways were Robert McCormick and Daniel Jones. McCormick, an American, entered Ludgrove in 1892 with his brother Medill as Ludgrovians Numbers Three and Five, the sons of an American diplomat in London. Robert was to become the sole proprietor and editor of the *Chicago Tribune*, and one of the towering fig-

Robert McCormick

ures of American journalism of the 20th century. We shall hear more of him later.

One of his contemporaries was Daniel Jones, whose father was one of the founders of the All-England Tennis Club at Wimbledon. Jones' mother was the sister of Richard D'Oyly Carte (the impresario of Gilbert and Sullivan). Daniel himself became one of the 20th century's foremost authorities on phonetics. In particular, his influence on the pronunciation of

Professor Daniel Jones

English was worldwide, and he published pioneering research on languages as diverse as Cantonese, Russian and Bantu. He was Professor of Phonetics at London University from 1921 to 1949; and for forty years held the offices of President and Secretary of the International Phonetics Association. It is said of him "He was a most gentle man whose complete devotion to his work is rarely encountered today. There can be little doubt that in the history of British phonetic studies, his name dominates the century."

A BOLT FROM THE BLUE

But in this prospering, expanding environment, on the night of 19th February 1902, a thunderbolt struck the School. At the height of his success and fame, Arthur Dunn suffered a massive heart attack and died. He had not felt well the day before, when playing ice-hockey up at the Bevan's home in Trent Park. But there was no hint of the blow to come, and he spent the day of his death making his first visit to the House of Commons with a parent, Col. Kenyon-Slaney MP. On his return, he briefly visited G.O. who was ill in the Cottage – one England Captain saying farewell to another, though neither could have realised the finality of their meeting. He was feeling unwell, and went to bed early. Helen Dunn said later that around 11.00 pm she went to open the window; and in the short time it took her to do so, he sighed deeply and died.

Ludgrove, Eton, his friends and the world were stunned. His personality and strength had seemed indestructible. Two days after his death, the Varsity football match was played; he was to have acted as linesman. In an unprecedented show of respect, the entire Cambridge team and the Captain of Oxford wore black arm-bands in his honour.

The *Times* said of him: "It would be difficult to find another man of his age and position whose premature loss has been more widely or more genuinely mourned"; and the *Morning Post* wrote: "If Old Etonians had been asked a few days ago to name half a dozen people who embodied and carried out the traditions of the school in the best manner, there can be little doubt that Arthur Dunn would have found a place in every selection". Appropriately, it was the *Eton College Chronicle* which best captured what Arthur Dunn meant to his contemporaries and how keenly his loss was felt:

> His success when he started at Ludgrove was immediate and almost phenomenal. He collected around him a staff as devoted as he was to their work. Any visitor to the school was impressed by its home-like atmosphere, and of the wonderfully intimate terms on which the boys were with their masters, without any loss of respect or discipline. [...] It was known how earnestly he tried to raise everything to the standard of the best. He was always trying to improve the work, and always ready to entertain any scheme that might lead to greater efficiency. When school was over and it was a question of play, the same intense desire for efficiency was

The last school picture before the death of Arthur Dunn

found.; and here his experience in all matters athletic was devoted to producing the best. […]

Transparent simplicity and unfaltering firmness were combined in him with a singular power of inspiring affection: and the secret of his success was his genuine and absorbing interest in boys. […]

Of his private life and its intense happiness this is hardly the place to speak. All we can do is to offer our sympathies to those he has left behind, and to assure them that their sorrow is shared by all men who knew Arthur Dunn as boy or man, and by the boys to whom he devoted his life. By them he will never be forgotten.

Arthur Dunn's name lives on today, immortalised both in a memorial plaque in the Eton College Chapel unveiled to him by the Provost of Eton nine months after his death; and by the foundation in 1903 of the annual inter-school Old Boy football competition known as the Arthur Dunn Cup. Its centenary was celebrated in 2003, when the competing finalists were the same two sides – Charterhouse and Shrewbury – which contested the first final in 1903. How pleased he would be to know that in that 2003 final, the captain of the Charterhouse side was an Old Ludgrovian, Tom Walker!

In the writings of the time there are phrases about Arthur Dunn by his contemporaries whose impact is still felt long after they have been read. One such is Cecil Sharp's comment on "his originality of mind and sympathetic energy"; and another, the judgment of 'Pa' Jackson, founder of the Corinthian Casuals, that "he was not only a perfect footballer but a perfect man". But in the end, it is still Arthur Dunn's own favourite saying that best sums up a great Victorian whose legacy so richly inspired his own and future generations:

Arthur Dunn and his family

*"Whatsoever thy hand findeth to do,
do it with thy might; for there is no work, nor device,
nor knowledge, nor wisdom in the grave whither thou goest."*

Chapter III

STRENGTHENING THE
FOUNDATIONS: 1902–22

*"They will strive to advance in that direction to which their beloved
master and friend would have pointed."*

School Notes

T he School itself embraced fully the philosophy that "Life must go on", of which
no-one doubted that Arthur Dunn himself would have been the strongest
advocate. The attitude is reflected in the notice that appeared in the School
Notes at the end of that terrible Spring term of 1902:

> It seemed as if Ludgrove without Mr. Dunn was an impossibility. But the grand
> old motto "Think and Thank" is well illustrated by such a case as this, and during
> this period of trial there has been much for which to be thankful. Second
> thoughts suggested that such a work, begun and developed but not nearly com-
> pleted, must be continued. So Ludgrove is still to go on, always depending on
> what had been so well described in a letter from a parent as 'the Arthur Dunn
> Tradition'. With masters, boys and members of the household all combining to
> keep the machine in motion, and encouraged by masters and Old Boys at Eton,
> time has been afforded for arrangements to be made …
>
> Beautiful appreciations of Mr. Dunn have appeared. There is no necessity to
> add more; but this is perhaps a fitting opportunity for expressing the sincere and
> heartfelt thanks of all at Ludgrove for the ever-ready, helpful, tactful kindness
> shown to them by Mrs. Dunn. It is their fervent wish that she should in due
> course receive comfort, and they feel that no greater solace could be afforded to
> her than the knowledge that they will strive to advance in that direction to which
> their beloved master and friend himself would have pointed.

Little could Helen Dunn or any Ludgrovians of the time have realised how fully that
charge was to be fulfilled by the succeeding generations to whom responsibility for the
school's fortunes was to be passed.

It had very probably been Arthur Dunn's express wish that G.O. and Bill Oakley

The newly appointed G.O. Smith flanked by Bill Oakley and C. Beavis (far left) and 'Bunco' Brown and W. Stanbrough (far right). Back row: l. to r. G. Hignett, W. Blore, C. Sharp

should in due course succeed him. At all events, through discussions and arrangements of which there is sadly no record, it was at once decided that they would take over his mantle. No doubt sums were agreed and settled to buy the partnership from Helen Dunn. Arthur ('Bunco') Brown also assisted in this process with financial support, thereby becoming a co-partner with Smith and Oakley, although he did not subsequently seem to play any directive or administrative role in the life of the school. G.O. was the titular Headmaster (Oakley's name appears in Division Lists throughout these years as an Assistant Master), but the reality was an equal partnership between them. G.O.'s sister, Katherine, agreed to come and live at Ludgrove to provide the female dimension so essential to a school run by two bachelor headmasters, and she remained there – loved and respected by staff, parents and boys alike, a key figure in shaping the domestic and pastoral life of the school – until G.O.'s retirement in 1922.

In this way Arthur Dunn's successors managed a seamless transition from the old regime to the new. There were now 61 boys in the school. The period of the Smith-Oakley tenure was to last for twenty years, and would establish Ludgrove firmly among the leaders of English preparatory schools.

THE PARTNERSHIP

There had never been any doubt that Arthur Dunn was in sole command at Ludgrove. The baton was now passed to a duumvirate. Partnerships are notoriously difficult to keep on a steady course over the long term. How would this one work – especially given such vastly differing characters as the two men who formed it, one sensitive, shy and retiring, the other bluff, extrovert and gregarious? It is clear that, in spite of these differences of character, Smith and Oakley made a marvellous team. They were close personal friends, men of integrity and fair dealing, each holding the other in the highest regard, sharing the same values and a common commitment to Oxford, Ludgrove and Football.

G.O. and Bill Oakley c. 1910

Their personalities were complementary, and they knew each other's minds.

Apart from their teaching experience together, they were also joint-secretaries of the Corinthian Football Club. In this capacity they collaborated in 1898 to produce a well-known book, the Badminton Library volume on 'the Association Football Game'. This book occupies an important place in the Story of Ludgrove, and is worth closer examination for the insight it provides into the authors' friendship and co-operation, and as a guide to many of the principles they held, which were to prove the backbone of the school for a nearly a quarter of a century.

The Badminton Library

The Badminton Library on Sports and Pastimes is a late 19th century encyclopaedia of sport written to instruct the citizens of the Empire in the history, rules and etiquette of all the main sports and games which made up the panoply of English leisure activities in that era. The volume on the Association Football Game is written in alternating chapters by Smith and Oakley. One can imagine them, two of the greatest football players in the world at the time, working at Ludgrove throughout the spring and summer of 1898, discussing the shape of the book in the Common Room; writing their chapters in between lessons, in the evenings and through the holidays; exchanging and commenting on each other's drafts; and bouncing their ideas off Arthur Dunn, their Headmaster and England's Captain.

In the first two chapters, Oakley describes the foundation of the Football Association and Smith the development of the game. The chapters then pass alternately from author to author, with G.O. writing on 'The Attack', 'Referees' and 'The Effects of Professionalism', and Oakley on 'The Defence' and 'The English Cup and Cup Ties'. The book concludes with a marvellous chapter by G.O. on 'Captaincy' – notable not only for its economy of style but as an evergreen piece of advice on the management of men, as wise today as it was then for anyone aspiring to lead a football side, a school or an enterprise of any sort where people come together with a common purpose. He expounds three basic tenets:

- First, the Captain must have a thorough knowledge of the men that form his eleven. He should know their characters off by heart, and should have accurately gauged their failings and good points...
- Secondly, he must be able to make a quick judgment as regards altering the position of his men on the field. An occasion often arises during the game when the shifting of an inside forward to an outside position may have a great effect on the result of a match, and it is here that a Captain has scope for proving himself a good instead of an indifferent leader...
- Thirdly, and above all else, he must remember to set a good example and to play an absolutely fair game himself. This is the most important duty of a Captain, the performance of which has the most wide-spreading *[sic]* effect on the welfare of the side in general. [...]. He must therefore be above suspicion, and resort to nothing that is in the slightest bit shady; if he is an unfair player his side will probably become so too [...] and unfairness, if once begun, will extend in all probability to each member of the team [...]

There follow what he calls 'one or two points of minor importance', such as: "Do not shout too much to or at your team – a Captain should talk very little: more attention will be paid to an occasional order than to a perpetual flow of directions". And again "There should be but one Captain in a side, who must lead and not be led."

And he concludes with these masterly words:

The Captain then must rigorously perform the duties we have laid down, and remember too that besides this he must be very careful about his own example – if he is enthusiastic, he will in turn inspire enthusiasm; if slack and despondent, he must not be surprised to see these faults mirrored in others.

These simple, wise words would be as much at home today in a Leadership course at Harvard Business School as they were in 1898 in the pages of the Badminton Library. On reading these passages, one could not but be confident of entrusting the upbringing of one's offspring to two such men, who exemplified in their own lives those arts and skills of which they both wrote so well.

Then one summer afternoon in 1898, when it was all done, they changed and headed off for the Ludgrove playing field with all the other masters and the boys, to take up

(1) Before the pass (2) The middle of the pass (3)After the pass. In the first picture, G.O has the ball, with Oakley far left.

the various postures and formations for the book's photographers, demonstrating Dribbling; Passing; Heading; a Low Volley; Saving a High Shot; and such delights as: "A Selfish Player robbed of the Ball"; "the Goalkeeper – Too Late"; "Misjudgement in Goal"; "a Foul"; and "Charging Down after Racing for the Ball" – all under the approving eye of Arthur Dunn, who took vigorous part in the photographic tableaux himself.

The result of that afternoon's work is a richly-illustrated volume full of action shots of friends and colleagues led by three great international footballers. Sir Shane Leslie was a boy in the school at the time and vividly recalled the whole process in a hand-written note in the flyleaf of the volume of the book now kept at Ludgrove:

> I watched the illustrations [for this book] being taken in the summer of 1898 at Ludgrove on the cricket field. The Ludgrove masters of the time were all there: A.T.B. Dunn, G.O. Smith, W.J. Oakley, T.C. Weatherhead, H.P. Hansell, H. Crabtree. The first three were internationals. None ever equalled their records, and the photographs recall their poise and grace as I remember them.

Osbert Sitwell

Sitwell in 1953, photographed by Norman Parkinson

Nearly all who have written of the school in these early years – especially Sir Shane Leslie, on whom I have depended extensively for his accounts of this period – expressed happiness and pleasure in recalling their days at Ludgrove, "this delectable life" as one boy had put it. But not everyone was so contented. A year after Arthur Dunn's death there arrived, in the Spring term of 1903, a boy who was to become famous as a writer, traveller and scourge of all philistines, and who, in the second of his five volumes of autobiography, included an excoriating memoir of his days at Ludgrove.

This was Osbert Sitwell (1892–1969) who, with Edith and Sacheverell, was one of the celebrated children of the eccentric Sir George Sitwell (Bt.) and the glamorous Lady

Ida, of Renishaw in Derbyshire. His recollections, written at the height of his powers, bring all his force and acrimony to bear on this place of "trimensual internment". Although he was only at Ludgrove for four terms, Sitwell's memories are expressed so vividly and eloquently that they form an integral part of the story of Ludgrove, whether or not one considers (with his biographer, Sir Philip Ziegler) that his judgments might have been a trifle exaggerated. I therefore quote them at some length. All the following extracts are from *The Scarlet Tree*, the second volume of his autobiography, published in 1946.

The first edition of The Scarlet Tree

Sitwell first describes the process by which Ludgrove came to be selected for him by his parents:

> My father and mother had succeeded in picking out a school they thought suitable for me, and one which was known to pay much attention – by means of the generally accepted combination of brutality, boredom and slow torture – to preparing pupils for their time at Eton. The boys were not mollycoddled, that was the great thing everyone agreed, and the school team was notorious for its proficiency at football, which was held out in some mystic manner to be – I could never make out why – supremely important. In London I heard my father discussing this school with my mother; that which finally converted them to it, I had gathered, was their discovery that the Headmaster "was the most famous dribbler in England". This recommendation bewildered me, because I had never hitherto observed that dribbling was considered a meritorious accomplishment at home. [......] My Mother liked the school because the Headmaster's sister seemed so fond of flowers.

It is only with difficulty that he brings himself to begin writing about his memories of Ludgrove :

> With an insuperable repugnance I face, in writing about it, the prospect of going to school for a second time....The sensation amounts almost to physical nausea, to the feeling of being lost, isolated, of waking up in a strange place and wondering who and where you may be, of being utterly confused and disoriented in the world of the senses, so that what you touch and see is not what your neighbours touch and see, your north is not their north, nor your south their south.
>
> So bad was the atmosphere of those days, so hopeless and lonely, that it becomes almost impossible for me to write about them without seeking to protect

myself by ridiculing them…. In short, so strong is my aversion from contemplat-
ing these long months struck by Medusa into stone that…I shall avail myself of
every possible escape from school, and make the fullest use of every exeat or afternoon off in the account of it that follows, no less than in real life.

He then describes how his mother took him to Ludgrove for his first term, evoking that
awful feeling of dread which so many generations of boys have felt on going to a new
school:

> The morning of that macroscian day which I had dreaded for so long…I see in
> my bedroom for a week or so beforehand that terrible play-box (how ironical a
> name!) of white wood with – painted on it plainly and immensely in black, as if it
> were tarred and feathered upon it – those impersonal initials 'F.O.S.S.' I see the
> preparations, the fussy packing and consequent unpacking….
>
> I see too the badges of my degradation, the hideous garb laid out; and the
> things intended to compensate one for it in the imagination, the supplies of
> oranges, biscuits, Suchard chocolate in slabs – all purchased in accordance with
> the rules laid down in the encyclical.

They arrive by train from London at Barnet station:

> In the darkness we only knew which station it was because the masters and school
> officials were bouncing up and down the stained, damp platforms, barking orders
> and asking names. There followed a drive through wet darkness in a rolling
> cab…We arrived: a bright maid in a white apron and a cap shaped like a petrified
> blancmange opened the door and ushered us into the drawing room…The
> Headmaster's sister, a most charming woman, gave
> us a kind welcome: but the enormous heads of the
> chrysanthemums – a flower which seems to thrive
> on winter as carrion on offal – communicated to
> the air a subtle scent of camphor, comparable to
> that which would issue out of a cupboard wherein
> hang the clothes of a man who has been drowned
> these many years.

There followed the traditional tea for the boys and
their parents, at the end of which

> my mother got up to leave in order to catch her
> train back to London…Suddenly she began to cry. I
> felt this in a thousand different ways. I could not
> comfort her, or attempt to comfort her, in front of
> the other four new boys – unknown quantities – or

Osbert's mother, Lady Ida. "Extravagant and self-indulgent", she was said to be an illegitimate descendant of George IV.

in the restraining presence of the Headmaster's sister. My mother was the only parent who cried, and I perceived that the rest of them disapproved of it. Her sobbing was something that I could remember long after she left. I courageously or obstinately refused to weep…dry-eyed I faced my weeping mother…Now she was at the door, had left…that moment was here, that moment which in its solemnity and terror only death can rival…The Headmaster's sister turned towards the boys and said "Now dears, I'll take you through into the school".

What lay behind the door of the drawing-room, to which Miss Smith was now moving?

She led the way from her comfortable, rather overcrowded room – outpost of civilisation – to a heavy red-baize door that blocked the passage…She opened it and we were in a different world. The air was full of an astounding clamour, as loud with cries and yells and clatter as any madhouse in the 18th century. We saw

W.S. Cornwallis, Ludgrove, 1903

a vista of bare corridors and of class-rooms with bare floors, reformatory benches with ink-stains, inkstands and iron clamps…. Boys of various ages were milling around the rooms, shouting, screaming, singing and hitting. A calm fell as Miss Smith was seen.

"Cornwallis" she cried. "Act as shepherd for Sitwell".

This injunction sounded comforting in a biblical way. But no sooner had the door clanged behind her than the din started again, and I was surrounded by a mob of small boys who bore down upon me like a cloud of locusts to devour my self-esteem. This was the moment….and as for my shepherd, he seemed to be leaning on his crook; indeed at moments, he took a leading part in the Inquisition. As I looked around and tried to answer – though one was shouted down before it was possible to say a word in reply – the terrible knowledge came to me that I hated school, loathed the boys and – though I could not be sure of this until the next day – abominated the masters.

So began Osbert's life at Ludgrove. How was one to begin to make friends in such an environment? Osbert describes his first attempt at friendship:

I recall walking down a dripping avenue in a large park on the first Sunday, a few days after arriving at the school…I was at the very end of the school crocodile, and beside me trudged another new boy…I think my companion liked the weather, for he was homesick, plainly, audaciously homesick for some haunted Irish fastness which he had left for the first time only three or four days previously; homesick with the frankness unabashed of a child who as yet has developed no guile and thinks no ill of his fellows…Presently he stopped crying and thrusting his hand into mine said: "Let us be friends. Let us promise…" I was inexpressibly touched, though I scarcely knew how to show it. It was such a friendship as might have sprung up between two early Christians in the arena; but it was not destined to prosper or endure. We were not in the same form, and slept in different dormitories, though they were next door; and that term I could often hear the sound of his being beaten at night for being a cry-baby.

Sitwell's biographer, Philip Ziegler, notes that Ludgrove was "only a couple of miles from the lunatic asylum at Colney Hatch, a coincidence which gave much innocent pleasure to the boys who assumed that most of the masters had recently escaped from that neighbouring establishment. The asylum caught fire a few weeks after Osbert arrived; the boys stood on the lawn to admire the flames and speculate gleefully on the number of the dead".

But the actual location of the school – somewhere near London – remained a mystery to Sitwell:

Colney Hatch asylum at the time of its opening in 1851. It closed in 1993 and was converted into flats.

I never mastered the topographical place of my internment. The surroundings were so laden with bitterness for me that their whereabouts seemed scarcely to matter. I knew certainly that the place was in Hertfordshire near Barnet; that we were on the edge of a forest called Hadley Wood, in which, very regularly it seemed, the bodies of murdered women were discovered – but that was all. Beyond these fragments of knowledge, I was ignorant of the locality. Similarly Hell has a climate but no situation; it lies in the spirit, and not in space.

The masters proved to be little better than the boys:

> I hated the masters – with one exception: the music master who happened to be
> Cecil Sharp, and only visited the school at intervals

Sundays were no better:

> Sunday nights were not different from ordinary nights. Long after the sounds of
> beating and sobbing and restless whispering had subsided, I used to lie awake lis-
> tening to the trains as they hooted and pounded along the route to Scotland.

There was little solace to be found in the bosom of the Matron:

> The Matron, with her white cap tied under her chin, and her sallow complexion
> that seemed to draw attention to her curative systems, her salves and boluses,
> would look in from time to time, and say with a certain acerbity coating her
> native kindness (for she believed in 'hardening' the boys) – "Fussing again, Sitwell,
> I suppose. You are an old crock". And then she would hurry out because she had
> to dispense continually the various but sparse and Spartan remedies of her 18th
> century pharmacopoeia: iron, castor oil, liquorice and Gregory powder – and of
> course there was always rhubarb, an immense shadow in the background.

However, there always seemed plenty for her and the nursing staff to do:

> Cases of severe illness were comparatively few, nor do I recall a single instance of
> an inmate dying. Of colds there was of course a continual and abundant supply –
> just colds in the winter, 'summer' colds in the summer, 'spring' colds, I suppose, in
> the spring. And infectious diseases in this, as in all similar establishments,
> occurred with distressing frequency and regularity and formed almost a school
> tradition.

The only purpose in life seemed to be waiting for the next visit of his mother:

> I lived for my mother's visits, and she responded and came to see me, no doubt
> more often than was good for me, in the sense that it was difficult for me to "set-
> tle down", as the Matron said, or – to put it another way – to acquiesce in my own
> misery….Often my mother would arrive by a later train than she had named, for
> she was extremely unpunctual…Trains were the rule, rather than motors, for
> these were too recent an innovation to be used as yet except by a very few, the
> exceptionally rich, the daring or the go-ahead.

In the summer term the school went every year to watch the Eton and Harrow match
at Lord's. No haven of happiness seems to have been found there either, but Sitwell
paints an indelible word-picture of the upper classes of England at their leisure at the
turn of the 20th Century:

The upper classes in full dress at the Eton v Harrow match at Lords

One had to sit there for hours, clad in Eton suit and top hat, watching the cricket. I used to observe with interest the smug-faced crowds, the happy families that promenaded in the intervals, keeping in clumps, across the ground. As they walked through the glowing, spangled air of summer, it was their clothes rather than their faces which held the attention: the waisted gowns, the high lace collars, the frills, the richness and weight and yet lightness of these full July clothes, the feathered boas, ethereal as dusting brushes, the hats plumed as though they were bright fowls about to take wing, or flowered as though they were full summer baskets from a rectory garden.

I liked to watch the crowds and enjoyed the intervals, the meals, better than the game itself. Even my family's connection with cricket – my uncle, like his father before him, was President of the MCC, and sat in a box with the band playing to him – even WG's sponsorship of my name at birth for that august body, even such glories availed me nothing. I was hopeless at cricket and hated watching it. On the other hand the ices and cider – especially the cider – during the interval were a great pleasure to me; and I now suspect, looking back, that the slight sense of exhilaration without reason which I then experienced may have been due to that initial encounter with alcohol.

In the end, another epidemic at Ludgrove persuaded his parents to take him away at the end of his fourth term:

For over a year I dwelt in so dark a valley, lived in so deep an abyss of spiritual misery, that the physical collapse ensuing at the end of it should have offered no matter for wonder to parents or masters. Illness did however come to my aid. It freed me. During my second summer term, a mysterious and novel epidemic, said to be of pleurisy, broke out and introduced an element of variety into the usual curriculum of school diseases appropriate to the season: colds, influenza, pink-eye, chicken pox (German and Empire), scarlatina, scarlet fever, whooping cough (or "whoppers" as it was familiarly known), mumps, boils, blains and ringworm. Since cases continued to occur we did not again re-assemble after the customary exeat for the Eton and Harrow match, and my mother decided to take me to Scarborough where for once I found no regular tutor in ambush for me.

Throughout his time, Sitwell never rose much above the middle of the class – except History in his first term (taught by Mr. Stanbrough) in which he came top with 176 marks to the next boy's 139 – though this seems to have confirmed the Headmaster's conviction that "Osbert has not been trying at subjects that absorb him less".

He left after the summer term of 1904. And so to his final verdict:

The fashionable school where I had been sent bore the reputation of being a very good school, among the best of the period. The parents felt, I believe, that so long as they had to pay a great deal of money to keep their boys there, it must be a good school.

I had been just ten when first sent to that fashionable place of internment for the sons of the rich. I had gone there, a tall, well-made boy with a strong temper, high spirits and possessed of a naturally sociable disposition…and "somewhat serious" for my age….In return for the large fees received, the school restored to my parents a different boy, unrecognisable, with no pride in his appearance, no ability to concentrate, with health impaired for many years, if not for life, secretive, with no love of books and an impartial hatred for both work and games, with few qualities left and none acquired, save a love of solitude and a cynical disbelief, firmly established, in any sense of fair play or prevailing standards of humane conduct.

On my leaving his flock, the Headmaster wrote a letter to my mother which contained the sentence "I am sorry for Osbert, as he will lose all his friends, and it is not very nice to have to start all over again." But indeed it was. I lost my enemies as well as my friends.

He moved to another prep school, St. David's, Reigate, in Surrey (where he seems to have been much happier – or perhaps "less actively miserable") as a prelude to entering Eton.

THE GRATITUDE OF PARENTS

How representative were Sitwell's views of the nature of the school and the character of its famous Headmaster? For all his shy and retiring nature, and in contrast to the unchanging solemnity of his photographs, G.O's Headmastership was marked by the affection and trust he won from most of the boys, the close friendship he enjoyed with the staff, and the confidence and support which he gained from the parents. The clearest evidence of this is supplied in the many warm letters of thanks and appreciation that he received from grateful parents throughout his tenure. These still survive in Ludgrove's archives, a counterbalance to the maledictions of Osbert Sitwell, and evidence of the essential happiness of the school during these years. A brief selection of these gives their flavour:

Linton Park, Maidstone
Dec 10, 1905

My dear Smith,

I need not tell you how grateful we are to you, Oakley & all your staff for their kindness to the boys during these many years: I hope they will always do Ludgrove credit: and on the other side to Miss Smith: nobody could start life with better impressions and guidance than those they have received from Ludgrove.

Yrs. sincerely,

Stanley Cornwallis
(who sent three sons to Ludgrove)

Presdales, Ware.

Dec. 22, 1907

My dear Joe,

I hardly know how to begin to write to you. I have put off this letter for some days as I rather dreaded writing it. Poor Oliver* is so distressed at leaving Ludgrove that we have said very little about it. He feels it very much & so do I.

I am glad indeed to think he ended up so well.

When I tell you that I know he owes everything to you & all of you at Ludgrove I think I have said all there is to say.

Will you give Miss Smith every good wish from my wife & myself & tell her that if I don't write to her it is because I find it very hard to do it.

I hope I shall never lose touch with Ludgrove.

Yours ever

L.A. Leese

* For an account of Oliver Leese's distinguished army career see Chap. 7

37, Chester Square, S.W.

July 19th, 1907

Dear Mr. Smith,

Would you kindly send Terence up by the train which leaves New Barnet at 9.38 when the holidays begin.

I am very sorry to think he won't be going back to you any more, & I must thank you so very much for all you have done for him while he has been with you. I know how happy he has been with you, which has made me so much happier parting with him – and I know he himself will be very sorry to leave. I hope you will always take an interest in Guy & him & that they may never lost your friendship. I know they will often go & see you.

G.G.B. Nugent and O.W. Cornwallis, Ludgrove, 1906.

Yrs. very sincerely

Isabel Nugent

Eildon Hall, St. Boswells.

29 March, 1909

Dear Mr. Smith

It is a great and gratifying surprise that Billy has taken Remove and says a lot for his instructors. He seems very surprised himself.

Now that Billy is leaving may I say how delighted I have been with Ludgrove in every way and for the trouble you and Miss Smith have taken with my boys. Though I think they have both been very well taught what I have always most appreciated is the tone of the school as, although it is an advantage if boys take good places, in my opinion character at that age is more important than learning and I think Ludgrove excels in making them gentlemen and straightforward, and at the private school age boys are so impressionable.

The credit is of course due to you both for the way you manage the boys and in the selection of your masters. I don't think you could have got a better set of men and I have never had a moment's anxiety whilst the boys have been with you.

Yours sincerely

Dalkeith

There are nearly 50 such letters in the Ludgrove archives, and these are no doubt a small fraction of those G.O. received during his twenty years as Headmaster. They are his finest testimony.

> British Legation, Lisbon
> April 16, 1922
>
> Dear Mr. Smith,
>
> It was a great pleasure to me to receive such an excellent report on James for his last half with you. I am so glad that he has done credit to you by taking Remove at Eton. He is very sad at leaving Ludgrove where from the beginning he has been so well and happy. I feel that I owe you and Miss Smith a great deal for all that you have done for him and I am most grateful to you for the grand start that under your care and influence he has made in life. May he keep up at Eton his high Ludgrove standard and be as successful there in lessons and games as he was with you. I wish that I had another boy to send you!
>
> Believe me,
>
> Yours very sincerely,
>
> Lancelot D. Carnegie

SCHOOL LIFE 1902-1914

Sport

During the first summer term after Arthur Dunn's death, he would have been proud to have noted the first Old Ludgrovian to have represented Eton at Lord's against Harrow: P.F.C. Williams. It was not until 1905 that another old boy – E.G. Williams – became the first Ludgrovian to row in the Eton VIII at Henley.

The Headmasters continued the style of Arthur Dunn in their reports on school matches. In 1903, massive defeats occurred on the football field, the first match of the season being lost to Stanmore Park by 11 goals to nil; the second, against South Lodge, by 10-1, after which the reporter writes "there is little to be said about this match, in which the result was due absolutely to the general slackness of the Eleven, and their slowness in getting the ball…it is hoped that Ludgrove will show more determination and energy in the return match". A subsequent game against Stanmore Park was again heavily lost, and the writer has no compunction in saying that "after half-time our forwards seemed utterly to go to pieces, and beside doing nothing right, lost all dash and spirit". It could have been Arthur Dunn himself writing. A victory against Northaw in 1907 shows how hard it was for the Ludgrove football team to earn praise from their

distinguished Headmasters, who comment that "the shooting in this game was distinctly poor, and many chances of scoring were lost in rather a ridiculous manner".

The following summer, 1904, there was again something to cheer about – the remarkable batting record of W.A. Worsley (later Sir William Worsley, Captain of Yorkshire, President of the MCC and father of the present Duchess of Kent) who scored 579 runs in the season, with a top score of 125 and an average of 64.3. This performance is described as "a truly wonderful record", and was not bettered for thirty years. In 1904

W.A. Worsley, Ludgrove, 1903

R.O.R. Kenyon-Slaney took 29 wickets in the season for an average of 6.58 – an analysis bettered in 1907 by J. Heathcoat-Amory who achieved 45 wickets for an average of 5.44 runs. In 1905, in the 2nd XI match against South Lodge, C.A. Carnegie took all 10 wickets in dismissing them for 38, a record which was included in Wisden. No mention of this remarkable feat is recorded in the School Notes. The closest a Ludgrove boy came to this in subsequent years was in 1964 when D.W.R. Jack took 9 for 20 against St Neot's.

In 1907 Ludgrove defeated Sunningdale by an innings and 53 runs, after making only 81, since Sunningdale in their two innings scored 18 and 10(!), with E.T.N. Grove for Ludgrove taking 14 wickets for 14 runs in the match. (Another of Grove's particular distinctions was to have set a new school long-jump record in 1905 of 13 ft 5ins, a record which still stands to this day.) That year Arthur Dunn's son Johnny captained the side, and the Ludgrove XI recorded 9 wins and 2 draws. G.O. wrote with pride:

> The First Eleven have gone through the season without a single reverse, and have thus accomplished a feat which has never before been equalled in the annals of Ludgrove cricket.

C.A. (later Lord) Carnegie with his younger brother in 1905

But in the world of prep schools, as in all walks of life, Hubris is inexorably followed by Nemesis, and in 1909 the Notes record:

> It is a long time since we have had such a disastrous cricket season as the one that has just ended.

Music

When Cecil Sharp left Ludgrove at the end of the summer term 1910, G.O. Smith wrote:

> He has been connected with the school practically since it started… and it is indeed almost impossible to estimate the debt that is owed to him for everything that he has done here.

He was succeeded by Mr. G.J. Wilkinson who ran the music until his departure for Flanders in 1915, when his successor was another famous English musician, Henry Balfour Gardiner. A friend of Gustav Holst, Balfour Gardiner was a nationally-known composer of church anthems and his music still features widely today in the repertoires of our cathedral choirs. He taught music at Ludgrove for one year, before he too went off to the war. However, the impact of this great English composer in the short time he spent at Ludgrove was considerable: on his departure G.O. wrote:

> We are greatly indebted to him for all he has done here. He threw himself heart and soul into the life of the school, and took endless trouble over the interests of the boys. We shall all miss him very greatly.

Balfour Gardiner's enduring legacy to the school was the music of the Ludgrove school song "A Song for Supper Night", which he composed to words by Willie Blore. His talent lives on today through his great-nephew Sir John Eliot Gardiner, who is a conductor of world stature.

"Play up for Ludgrove!" The Gardiner-Blore collaboration.

Charles Kennedy-Scott with the music boys in 1925, flanked by the Earl of Hopetoun (l.) and Lord John Hope

He was succeeded in turn by Charles Kennedy-Scott, the third Ludgrove music-master to be a distinguished musician in his own right. After teaching at Ludgrove until 1927, he went on to become a noted conductor, composer and expert on the English madrigal.

The Lectures

The most remarkable feature of the School Notes of the Smith-Oakley years is the marvellous summaries they contain of the lectures given to the boys. Almost certainly written by G.O., they are graphic, eloquent and astonishingly complete records of almost everything of note said in Ludgrove school lectures for over 20 years. Whether one is reading about lectures on "Pond Life", "the Horse", "the Life of Christopher Columbus", "the Wonders of the Sky", "Personal Memories of the Indian Mutiny", "Folk Song collecting" or "Corsica, the Land of the Vendetta", one cannot but find these masterly summaries of absorbing interest in themselves. A good example is a lecture given in 1904 by the Rev. E. Jameson Wood, on the subject of "the Spider":

> Mr Wood said that the hunger of a spider can only be described as ravenous.
> It has been calculated that, if a spider were as large as a man, he would eat a fat
> bullock for breakfast, another bullock and five sheep for lunch, and two bullocks,
> eight sheep, four fat pigs and four barrel-loads of fish for dinner at the end of the
> day…

and so on, for over 1000 words. One of the best known of the lecturers was the Rev. Theodore Wood who lectured on the natural world every year for over 20 years. He too seems to have focused on the topic of gargantuan animal appetites:

> He dwelt at length upon the robin. It is a savage and greedy bird. A French naturalist had recently found, by carefully weighing a robin and giving it more or less food as it lost or gained in weight, that one bird needed 14 feet of earthworms every day to keep it up to its normal weight – and to demonstrate this, Mr Wood stretched out a red cord 14 foot long, and said that he had calculated that a man weighing 12 stone and eating with the same voracity as a robin would need to consume 420 lbs of solid food a day, or the equivalent of 2,520 sausages a day.

The theme of Empire was ever-present in the lecture programme. At the time that the European powers were falling over themselves in their 'Scramble for Africa', a lecture was given in 1903 on the "beneficial results" of the French occupation of Algeria and Tunisia, emphasising that "Englishmen, who are justly proud of the splendid results of the British occupation of India and Egypt, should view with special sympathy and appreciation how our friends the French are civilizing countries which only 100 years ago were as badly governed as any in the world".

We have seen that in 1900 'Bunco' Brown set up a branch of the Navy League at Ludgrove. In the Spring term of 1904 Brown gave a talk on "Our Fleet Today", which he described as "by far the most splendid navy in the world". For the first time the rise of Germany as a naval power was noted – a theme which was to be revisited with growing urgency in the years that followed. Brown concluded with the hope that "it will be a very long time before our ships have to confront an enemy in battle," and that the Royal Navy might "continue for many years its peaceful patrol of the oceans that surround the shores of the British Empire".

HMS Conqueror, *and three other battle-cruisers, all of which fought at Jutland.*

Staff in 1910: Front row (l to r) Frank Henley, 'Bunco' Brown, G.O. Smith, W.J. Oakley. Back row (l to r) W.P Blore, Wilfred Bird, A. Bowmar-Porter.

Yet within 14 years, no less than 15 of the boys listening to the lecture that night would lose their lives in the First World War, and one of them – J.S. Dunville – was to win Ludgrove's only Victoria Cross.

The Staff

In the summer term of 1905 it was announced that a new master would be joining the Ludgrove staff the following term, Mr. Frank Henley of Oriel College, Oxford, who had represented Oxford against Cambridge at Lord's. Frank Henley was to become Joint Headmaster with Bill Oakley after G.O. Smith's retirement, and when Oakley retired in 1934, was sole Headmaster of Ludgrove for three years. He himself finally retired in 1937 after 32 years of service to the school. His arrival at Ludgrove was followed in 1906 by that of Mr Wilfred Bird, who had been educated at Malvern and New College, Oxford and had captained Oxford against Cambridge at Lords that year. Sadly, Wilfred Bird, a popular and talented man, was killed ten years later in the Great War.

SOME LANDMARKS OF THE EARLY SMITH-OAKLEY YEARS

These are a few of the events recorded during this period:

- In 1905 Astronomy was introduced into the Ludgrove syllabus as a formal subject, taught by Mr Brown.

- The same year, Eton instituted the Victor Ludorum Cup in School Sports for the first time; its first three winners were all Old Ludgrovians – A.E.D. Anderson, G.H. Benson and G.R.L. Anderson.
- In 1907, Johnny Dunn, the son Arthur was so proud of, left Ludgrove for Eton, having fully justified his father's expectations of him at Ludgrove by being School Captain of Football and Cricket, and winner of the school 200 yards

Johnny Dunn (r.) with J. Heathcoat-Amory in 1905

race and the high jump. Tragically Johnny Dunn was among those to lose their lives in the Great War.
- In the summer of 1908 a new cricket fixture was instituted against A Parliamentarians' XI (all parents of boys) in which the opponents innings was opened by a noble partnership between the Duke of Devonshire and the Earl of Dalkeith, who put on 35 for the first wicket.
- In 1910 every football match of the Spring term was cancelled owing to an outbreak of whooping-cough followed by one of measles.
- In February 1914 the tragic death occurred in a hunting accident of Robert Austen Bevan, who was at Ludgrove from 1899 to 1904. He was one of the grandsons of Francis Bevan, owner of nearby Trent Park, from whom Arthur Dunn had acquired Ludgrove in 1892.

Prelude to war

As concern about the international situation mounted, a lecture was given in 1911 on the Battle of Sedan, in the Franco-Prussian War of 1870-71, with dramatic descriptions of the Prussian attack on the French stronghold. Boys were instructed to carry coloured flags representing the Prussian and French armies, with the final attack being made on a large table (Sedan) beneath which crouched several boys – the French army of 130,000 men! – exposed to devastating fire from the heights opposite. The bravery of the defenders, the horrors of the doomed town and the humiliation of the surrender were all vividly described – and the boys were exhorted to learn from this example and, in later life, not to neglect the defence of their country.

THE GREAT WAR, 1914 – 1918

When the Archduke Franz-Ferdinand, heir to the Austrian throne, was assassinated in Sarajevo in June 1914, the European summer was filled with sabre-rattling, and war became inevitable. Austria declared war on Serbia, Russia leapt to Serbia's defence and Germany supported Austria. Germany declared war on Russia's ally, France, on 3rd August and invaded neutral Belgium. Britain formally declared war against Germany on 4th August and quickly despatched its Expeditionary Force to Belgium and northern France. After weeks of skirmishing, it engaged in the first and bloody battle of Ypres in October and November. This led to a stalemate that was to last four terrible years. But those early days were full of moral certainty about the rightness of the cause, and the hope that it would all last long enough for everyone to volunteer to do their bit for freedom.

Two members of staff, Wilfred Bird and G.J. Wilkinson, joined up immediately and Bird would not return. They were soon joined by many Old Ludgrovians.

Two unknown O.L. officers revisitng G.O. in 1915

Ludgrove's records include many letters to G.O. Smith from former Ludgrove boys now fighting at the front, and from their parents, revealing the horror of war, death and bereavement in the most direct and poignant way. Four of these letters are shown here; a fuller selection is included in Appendix 5.

The first letter received at Ludgrove was sent by three boys who had left only five years earlier. It was full of high spirits and optimism:

On His Majesty's Service, France
Sept 23, 1914

Dear Mr. Smith

We three thought you might like to hear from us out here. We are all fit & well, & things are going much better now: at first we had a very hard time, as we were left unsupported by the French, & had to retire before very superior forces of the Germans: but the Army effected its retreat in very good order, though the infantry suffered very severely. The French have now joined us, & we expect a big battle very soon, & we ought certainly to win, as the Germans seem discouraged by their heavy losses, & are not so formidable as at first, and I think we have superior numbers, though the battle-front is so long that we know little or nothing of events except in our immediate area. I have seen Charles Norman, Rex Benson & Bill Bailey lately, & all are quite fit: Cornwallis mi. has been hit & is on his way home, but is doing well. We have been lucky in the regiment (XI Hussars) so far & have had few casualties, though we have been constantly in action. I hope we shall continue as fortunate. We hope you are all well at Ludgrove & not affected by the war. Please remember us kindly to Miss Smith & the rest of the staff. With best wishes

Yours ever

Arthur Curtis – Richard J. Lumley – Sackville Pelham

And there was re-assurance from the wounded –

The Cottage at the Crossways,
Hoe Benham, Newbury   Oct. 2nd 1914

Dear Mr. Smith,

It was so very kind of you to write to me about Jim. He was wounded on the 8th Sep: had a bad time getting to hospital at Le Mans – two and a half days in a cattle truck – nothing but sips of water from 4 a.m. on Tuesday to midday Friday – as they thought he was shot in the stomach – added to which the man on each side of him in the cattle truck died on the journey. He was wounded by shrapnel bullets – 3 in right arm & one in chest – low down on left side – mercifully the latter did not penetrate – it must have hit a rib & come out again by the same hole it went in! He has been x-rayed twice & no bullets can be found.

After Le Mans he was sent to hospital at St. Nazaire & landed in England on 20th – in pyjamas & a dressing gown lent him by hospital as all his kit had been stolen! A week in King Edward VIIs Hospital & then we brought him down here – at least he is really at Benham as we have no room in this tiny cottage. But we are very near. It's quite marvellous how quickly he is getting well now. His wounds are nearly healed & he is losing the dreadful haggard look he had first. His eyes still show a little of what he has been through. But I fear he will have to return at end of this month for certain....

What fearful days we live through & yet how proud we are of our youngsters – Jim has done very well I am glad to say & proved himself a very gallant soldier.

Yours very sincerely,

Nina Ashley

But then came the first of the many tragedies which were to follow: a letter at the same time proud, tragic, brief and confident in the rightness of the cause for which so many were now dying. Little could Mrs. Barrington-Kennett have known that she would lose all three of her sons before the war was ended.

19 Cheyne Gardens, S.W.
Oct 12th/14

My dear Mr. Smith

Thank you so very much for your most kind letter of sympathy with us in our loss, which is an irreparable one, of our dear Aubrey. We thought you would like to see the enclosed from the Colonel of his regiment and the Captain, also one from Basil, another of your old Ludgrove boys. They give a few interesting details of what happened, and we had some copies made to give to friends. It is a great happiness to us in the midst of our grief to know he died so bravely & that he was thinking of others, not himself, up to the end. Aubrey grew up all we would wish a son to be. Home will never be the same without him but we are proud he gave his life in England's righteous cause.

Again thanking you very much & with kindest remembrances from Colonel Kennett.

Believe me

Yours most sincerely

Elinor Barrington-Kennett

Aubrey Barrington-Kennett

The letter the family had received from Aubrey's commanding officer was enclosed:

21st September 1914
My dear Colonel Barrington Kennett,

You will, long before this letter arrives, have had the sad news of your poor boy's death.

British and German wounded at a British first-aid post on the Western Front.

I thought you would like to hear from me something about him. It was just an unlucky shell that caught him. We are in a place that is liable to be shelled at any time, and it was after shelling had begun that he was moving from one part of the position to another when he got wounded by splinters chiefly in the jaw and neck.

He was very plucky about it, would not allow the two men with him to carry him to a safe place, but in order to save them from being hit ordered them each under cover and remained in the open himself till the brunt of the shelling was over. This was a very brave act, especially as he must have been suffering from the shock of his wounds. The men offered to carry him in but he would not let them.

When he was brought in he was very cheerful. He kept wonderfully cool over it and was in quite good spirits.

We got him away in an ambulance the same evening, and everyone hoped he would make a good recovery, but yesterday to our great sorrow we heard he had died of his wounds.

I cannot tell you what a loss he was both personally and as a soldier. He had done so well all through the hard times we had, always cheerful, and everyone liked him.

We shall miss him very much and remember him always. You may indeed be proud of the way he died. It was a very fine thing indeed to refuse assistance himself, and to save the men with him, and the way he bore his wounds made everyone admire him. You will be glad to know that I do not think he suffered great pain. It was I think chiefly shock and discomfort.

Whatever he felt, he bore it marvellously well.

Yours very sincerely,

H.B. Davies

And this was followed a fortnight later by a letter from Aubrey's brother Basil who had tried so hard to find him on the field of battle. Basil wrote of him, and the cause for which he died, in moving terms –

In the Field
28.IX.14

My darling Father and Mother,

I got Vi's letter yesterday afternoon, sent by air, and letting me know the sad news about poor old Aubrey. I got leave to-day to go out to try and find what had happened. I searched all over the place, trying every hospital, and at last I came upon the right one – a pretty old farm house in a village called Vieil-Arcy about 12 miles E. of Soissons. This farm is being used as a temporary field hospital and I saw the Colonel in charge of it.

Aubrey was taken in to this farm on the 19th with a very bad wound in his side (right) and a nasty cut on the head – the result of being hit by a shell in the trenches.

He was buried with about 30 others in the orchard belonging to the farm. They had put up a little wooden cross with his name painted on it in black letters. There were some flowers on the grave. I just picked 2 little heads which I now send you, as I thought you might like them.

Poor old Aubrey – he was one of the best and I'll bet he carried himself all through this War as he always did – a perfect stamp of English gentleman; quiet, good tempered, kind hearted, as brave as a lion, and one of the most unselfish fellows I ever met. It is horribly sad and I can't really get it into my head yet, except that so many good fellows are being killed every day.

I can't tell you how sorry I am for you as I know you are feeling this blow as only a Father and Mother can feel it. We must cheer up though, as he died a soldier's death and there's none finer. I long to hear all about Aubrey's life and how he was getting on in the 52nd and I hope before long to get up to them. I will extract every little bit of information I can, you may be sure, and will write it all to you at once. Also I will go out again and take a photo of the grave. It is in such a quiet peaceful little spot, though shells are bursting all round it. Four shells burst within 100 yards of it while I was standing there. I wish I could be with you, if only for a few moments, to help cheer you up, but you have Victor and Vi – Vi loved him as much as we did.

Goodbye my darling Father and Mother. God help us all to bear this blow. It is after all the finest sacrifice you can make for your Country and it won't be thrown away, as we are bound to win in the long run.

God bless you both,

Basil

I am putting this letter into Sir J. French's bag, so I hope you will get it in good time. Under the circumstances I think he will let it go.

Tragically, Basil himself and his younger brother Victor were also to perish with Aubrey in the Great War.

Basil Barrington-Kennett (middle row, far right), in the Ludgrove First X1, 1898

LUDGROVE DURING THE GREAT WAR

Little is revealed of school life at the beginning of the war to hint at the climactic events which had now burst upon the outside world. But from the termly recitation of Old Ludgrovians serving, killed or wounded, and the departure of Wilfred Bird and the Music Master Mr G.J. Wilkinson to the front – to be followed by Henry Balfour-Gardiner (Wilkinson's successor) and Frank Henley in 1916 – everyone knew that Ludgrove, too, was playing its full part in the country's struggle. Death struck quickly in the autumn of 1914, with the casualty lists of old boys; and then in the summer of 1915 came the news of the death of Wilfred Bird, killed instantly on 9th May while leading his men over an exposed 300-yard stretch of no-man's-land. G.O. wrote:

It is not possible to express in words what a terrible blow the
School has sustained by the death of Wilfred Bird at the
front… He died, as he had lived, just doing his duty…. His
loss here is irreparable…

and a parent wrote: "He stood for that enthusiasm and sense
of duty which drove English gentlemen from all they loved
best to take up arms."

When the war started there were 65 boys in the School, and
190 Old Boys serving in the armed forces; at its close five years
later there were 68 in the School and 250 serving. Regular lectures
were given to the boys on the progress of the war, albeit with
considerable 'massaging' of the real facts as they later emerged.

Wilfred Bird

*It is clear that Henry Hansell also served King and Country, and revisited Ludgrove in a startling variety
of uniforms.*

A loss unconnected with the War occurred in March 1917 with the death through
illness of G.A.F. Byng, who had left Ludgrove only three months previously. He had
been near the top of Division I for most subjects, a School monitor, a member of the
cricket XI and captain of football. Amidst all the carnage of the War, the news of Byng's
early death was shattering to his former friends and teachers. G.O. wrote:

> He was so recently here and so much endeared to us all… It seems inexpressibly
> sad that a life so bright and sunny and so full of promise should be brought to
> such a sudden close… We all here share his family's grief and mourn with them.

Three Eton scholarships were won during the war years, by O. St. M. Thynne in
1915, and by A.B. Money Coutts and N.W. Hoare in 1916. The number of school

matches was reduced from ten to three by the end of the war. Music flourished under the distinguished guidance of Henry Balfour Gardiner and Charles Kennedy Scott who replaced him in 1916. New teachers arrived – Mr Sharpin, Mr Poole and Miss Rowe (who came in 1915 to fill a gap in teaching the youngest boys, and stayed until the 1930s). The curtain was finally lowered on those war years by a lecture on 'Aircraft in the Great War' by Miss Gertrude Bacon, a famous aviatrix of the day, concluding with a general discussion of "what the War has taught us". Sadly, her views are not recorded.

PEACE RETURNS

The Great War ended during the Michaelmas Term 1918. The mood at Ludgrove during that immense conflict is perhaps best reflected by the Head Master of Eton, the Rev. Cyril Alington, in a moving invocation to the "School at War" which appeared in the *Eton College Chronicle* of 1914, and which G.O. kept by him throughout the fearful struggle:

> We don't forget – while in this dark December
> We sit in schoolrooms that you know so well
> And hear the sounds that you so well remember,
> The Clock, the hurrying feet, the Chapel bell;
> Others are sitting in the seats you sat in;
> There's nothing else seems altered here – and yet
> You know we don't forget.

> We don't forget you – in the wintry weather
> You man the trench or tramp the frozen snow;
> We play the games we used to play together
> In days of peace that seem so long ago:
> But through it all, the shouting and the cheering,
> Those other hosts in graver conflict met,
> Those other sadder sounds your ears are hearing
> Be sure we don't forget

> And you, our brothers, who for all our praying,
> To this dear school of ours come back no more,
> Who lie, our country's debt of honour paying –
> And not in vain, upon the foreign shore;
> Till that great day when on the Throne in Heaven
> The books are opened and the judgments set,
> Your lives for honour and for England given
> The School will not forget.

J.S. Dunville (r.) with J Burbury and F Marchant in 1906

Ludgrove has never forgotten the 255 Old Ludgrovians who fought in the War; of those no fewer than 64, or one in four, were killed. Among their number were the three Barrington-Kennett brothers, two Boscawens, and Arthur Dunn's only son, Johnny.

The names of Ludgrove's fallen are inscribed on the Roll of Honour in the School Chapel. They include one Victoria Cross, won posthumously by Lieut. J.S. Dunville of the Royal Dragoons in 1917.

Other Ludgrove decorations included 17 DSO's; 26 Military Crosses; 49 Mentioned in Despatches; numerous *Croix de Guerre* and *Légions d'Honneur*, together with the Order of St. Stanislas (Russian), the Order of the Crown (Rumanian), the Serbian White Eagle and the Order of the Nile. As a permanent mark of the School's respect, a new Cricket Pavilion at Ludgrove was erected in memory of Wilfred Bird, to which over 100 of his friends and pupils contributed. Eight years later its clock was dedicated "*To the memory of Dick Howey, late Coldstream Guards, killed in a motor accident at Boulogne Aug. 26 1926 aged 29. Ludgrove 1905–1910*". Both pavilion and clock were later moved with the School from Cockfosters to Wokingham in 1938, and remain in full use to this day.

The Bird Memorial Pavilion with the Howey clock, in the late 1920s

Down the years Ludgrove has remembered its dead through the annual Chapel Scout Parades; and today, during each Remembrance Day service attended by the whole school, a boy reads from the pulpit some extracts from a few of those tragic and heroic letters which are Ludgrove's most direct link with the Great War. In this way Ludgrovians of every generation remain aware of the sacrifices made on their behalf all those years ago, and keep faith with the undertaking that "Ludgrove will not forget".

1919–1922

The winter of 1918–19 brought global devastation with the Spanish 'flu epidemic, which killed some 20 million people around the world – more than had died in the whole of the Great War itself. Many schools, such as the Dragon School, Oxford, were obliged to close completely as a result. At Ludgrove no-one died from it, but its ravages wiped out every single school soccer fixture. The following term, due to severe frost and snow, only one match could be played.

Clearing snow, 1919

Despite these privations, school life resumed its even tenor – the continuity being particularly marked in the soccer and cricket XIs of 1919, which included many traditional Ludgrovian names such as Pilkington, Hill-Wood, Arkwright, Montagu-Douglas-Scott, Grenfell, Buchanan, Head, De Zoete and Gosling.

It was the era of the Hill-Woods: the brothers D.J.C. and C.K. Hill-Wood were in

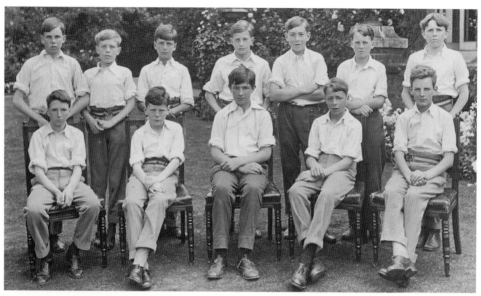

1920 First XI Cricket

both the XI's at Ludgrove in 1919 – and both subsequently gained their cricket Blues at Oxford. Their elder brother W.W. Hill-Wood opened both the batting (with G.O. Allen) and the bowling for Eton against Harrow at Lords, making 43 in Eton's first innings, and taking 5 Harrovian wickets in each innings. He and C.H. Gibson took every single one of the 20 Harrovian wickets that fell in that game, bowling them out for 76 and 41 in the two innings. With their eldest brother Basil, all four Hill-Woods played cricket for Derbyshire in the 1920s and '30s, and W.W. made 100 against Victoria for A.C. Maclaren's MCC side, which toured Australia and New Zealand in 1923. But the all-round 'star' at Ludgrove in that first post-war year was E.F.P. Gage, who was Captain of the School, won the Classics, French and History Prizes, captained the Soccer and Cricket XIs, won the Fives and Fielding Cups, and was subsequently elected an "Oppidan" Scholar at Eton.

Few boys at Ludgrove before or since have assembled such a glittering array of both academic and sporting achievements. In athletics, though, he yielded to his contemporary Trotter, who won the senior athletic cup that year and was responsible for one of the more startling entries in the School Notes:

> The High Jump was quite the best we have ever had at Ludgrove, 3 boys (Trotter, J. Pym and Renshaw)

E.P.F Gage

all clearing 4 ft. Trotter would probably have equalled the school record, but was hurling himself over the bar in such a dangerous-looking way that to avoid possible broken bones it was thought better to stop when he had won.

Echoes of the Great War continued to resound. In 1920, Frank Henley delivered a lecture on his wartime adventures with the 60th London Division: through France to Salonika, Eastern Europe and thence to join Allenby's forces in Palestine. He was involved in one of the most famous events of the war outside Europe – the capture of Jerusalem from the Turks. The keys of the city were formally handed over to the commanding officer of the 60th Division on 9th December 1917. From there Henley went on to describe the fall of Jericho, Haifa, Damascus, Homs and Aleppo, before the conclusion of the campaign with the Turkish armistice in October 1918.

THE TECK CONNECTION

Among the boys at Ludgrove in the closing days of the war were two cousins of German origin: Prince Frederick and Prince Rupert of Teck. Rupert's father, Prince Alexander of Teck, was the younger brother of Queen Mary and, like the Battenbergs who became Mountbatten, had changed his alien name to Cambridge, and adopted the title of Earl of Athlone. He was later to become a much respected Governor-General of South Africa

The Earl and Countess of Athlone (Prince and Princess of Teck) with their children. Rupert is on the left.

(1923-31) and of Canada (1940-46). His wife Alice was the daughter of Prince Leopold, Duke of Albany, who was the youngest son of Queen Victoria. Rupert of Teck came to Ludgrove from St. George's Choir School, Windsor, but he was not a robust child, suffering from the royal affliction of haemophilia, which dogged him all his short life.

Alexander of Teck must have applied to Ludgrove when his son was little more than eight months old, as this letter indicates:

4 Devonshire Place, W.
May 18th 1908

Re: Prince Rupert of Teck.

May 1917.

Dear Sir,

I hear from my brother that you are full up till the end of 1917, but I hope you will be able to take in our little boy in September of that year.

I enclose a form, which I have filled in.

Believe me,

Yours truly,

Alexander George of Teck.

In 1916, Prince Alexander was still hoping for a summer admission for his son:

British Military Mission with the Belgian Army.
Sept. 23rd, 1916

Dear Mr. Smith,

Can you take in our boy Rupert at the beginning of the Summer Term 1917? I hear my brother is sending his boy at that time.

Rupert has been at St. George's Choir School as a day boy since he was 7 years old, so I hope he has learnt to work with other boys.

He will be ten in August 1917, and I think it will do him good to get away from home.

Believe me,

Yours sincerely,

Alexander of Teck

Six months later, Rupert has clearly been accepted for the Summer term and his mother writes to Ludgrove, revealing a remarkably enlightened attitude to her son's education, and also something of her formidable personality.

Henry III Tower, Windsor Castle

17.IV.1917

Dear Mr. Smith,

I am so sorry there has been no opportunity of meeting you & having a talk about Rupert, but my house has been full of measles & I am now going to take both children to Eastbourne for a change before the term begins.

I am enclosing some of Rupert's reports, as they explain a certain amount. In the earlier ones he was only a day pupil & came home for French with the French governess before lunch. The last two he was quite [i.e. wholly] at school, which may not have been so good for his French, but which improved him enormously. He is quite an intelligent child, but unless the utmost is expected of him he does not try, & like so many boys is very lazy if he has the chance.

I am very keen indeed about languages, & he has quite a facility for them. I don't know if German is taught as an extra, if so I would like him to continue with it, unpalatable as it may be for the moment; he knows quite a lot of it. Could you make a point of his mathematics, as he is keen to go in for engineering as a career.

I have given him most of his religious instruction myself, & I fear he may be found lacking in exact knowledge of Bible stories, altho' I have tried to impress upon him the broad lines & great main facts of our faith. And I think he has a good grasp of what that means & of the very real presence of God in us & around us.

As to his health he is sturdy enough beyond the one weakness I have mentioned, & which I am thankful to say he is outgrowing, altho' a sprain of any kind takes on a much more serious form with him, & is a more lengthy business, as it necessitates laying up if it is a leg, as the only remedy. However let us hope this tiresome eventuality will not occur in term-time.

I put down the violin as an instrument, but so far he has only begun the piano, his music-master thinking it best to begin like that, so I leave entirely to your music master's discretion what he does now, & I don't care if he only goes in for piano, as I doubt his being good enough to take up the violin.

I hope he will do well, & be a good boy with you at Ludgrove. He looks old, but is a great baby still & in very many ways.

Believe me

Yours sincerely

Alice of Teck

In his first term, it appears that Rupert's proneness to bleeding had become a problem and G.O. Smith was clearly alarmed at the responsibility of having a boy in the school who at any moment might suffer a minor cut which could prove fatal. He sought professional advice, and the next letter is from a solicitor who confirms his concerns while endeavouring to reassure him in respect of any liability should disaster befall the Prince.

28, Queen Anne Street, Cavendish Square, W.
Confidential
May 1917

Dear Mr. Smith,

If the Mother did not know of the risks attaching to this condition, I certainly think that whoever is their ordinary medical adviser should inform her.

….I think you are entirely exonerated from any special responsibility.

In my judgement it would be best to keep the boy at school taking all reasonable precautions.

If another haemorrhage occurs, and is of any severity, it would give you the opportunity of getting Dr. Moore's authority to point out to the Mother that bleeding is sometimes serious in such a condition. But even this much is perhaps of doubtful expediency, for both Dr. Scott's statement & the family history make it I think probable that the Mother takes the view that it is no use spoiling the boy's life by keeping him, so to speak, in cotton wool, although she realises that his life may come to an early end through haemorrhage.

Personally, I think it is most unwise to send such a boy to school.

For your comfort, however, I may say that these children survive many haemorrhages, & that the fact of his having had 'bad nosebleeding' several times & yet surviving shows that, in him, the bleeding is not entirely uncontrollable.

With kind regards,

Yours sincerely

Geo. F. Still

In June Princess Alice arranged to visit her son at Ludgrove for the first time:

Henry III Tower, Windsor Castle.
10.VI.1917

Dear Mr. Smith,

Thank you so much for your letter about Rupert. I am very glad he made a good start, if only he will keep it up. You soon discovered his inattention & slowness; we have always been fighting that, but I hope in time when his ambition is awakened he will get over it, for it is a dreadful hindrance.

We hope to come & see him next Wednesday 13th if it is all right, he wrote saying it was a good day.

Believe me

Yours sincerely

Alice

Late in 1918 the Spanish 'flu epidemic struck Ludgrove and, predictably, Prince Rupert was an early victim:

Henry III Tower, Windsor Castle

27.X.1918

Dear Mr. Smith,

Many thanks for your letter, which I was scarcely surprised to get, as Rupert generally develops a heavy cold this time of year & now of course it has turned to Influenza. I am thankful he is in such good hands, tho' I feel awfully sorry for you having so many boys down with it & other people's children are such an anxiety.

I won't worry you with coming down to see Rupert, tho' perhaps when he is first up you would kindly let me know, & I might run down & see him.

Yours sincerely

Alice

Later, Rupert's father was the first person to suggest to Ludgrove that the school should set up a Scout Troop.

Henry III Tower, Windsor Castle.

Feb. 6th 1920

Dear Mr. Smith,

As you say the [Scout] movement ought not to be so necessary for our children, but it will be useful in after life as, knowing something about Scouts themselves, they will be more likely to take an interest in, & to encourage the movement amongst others. I did not suggest the idea to Rupert! He belongs to a Troop in London, so he has not really had the proper training in Scout-craft. I shall be interested to see whether he will have the determination to carry on with the present idea of forming a Ludgrove Troop or not.

I am very glad Rupert is a dormitory monitor & I hope he will become a little more responsible for his actions. I also find that he must have someone near at hand and, like I heard a German trainer say to a baboon during a performance at a circus, to say to him: 'Verliere nicht den Kopf'! ["Don't lose your head"]

Yours sincerely

Athlone

Prince Rupert later became Viscount Trematon. Sadly, he died in a car accident in 1928, aged 21.

ROLAND PYM LOOKS BACK

Roland Pym in Alexandria in 1944

Roland Pym followed his elder brother John into the school in the Michaelmas term of 1919. Their great-uncle was Sir John Lubbock (later Lord Avebury), the famous naturalist, writer and friend of Charles Darwin, and their two uncles Roy and Alan Lubbock had been at Ludgrove under Arthur Dunn. It is through Roland, who was aged 94 when interviewed for this book, that we first come into contact with Ludgrove's living history. His personal recollections of Ludgrove's life in the immediate post-Great War period give the authentic flavour of the school as it then was. He has also brought to bear his remarkable draughtsmanship, developed over a lifetime as a painter and muralist, theatre designer and illustrator of many well-known books, to depict vividly remembered scenes and events from his time at the school. Let him now take up the story.

I never really liked leaving home. My Mother used to read books to us, including David Copperfield, which describes a boy at a terrible school while his mother is dying, and this gave me the idea that she might die while I was away at school – indeed she did do so while I was at Eton, when I was 16.

My number at Ludgrove was 59; I have never forgotten that, and throughout my life it has always been propitious for me. I remember very clearly going back there each term – Mr Oakley used to meet us off the school train from King's Cross at New Barnet station, and then lead us wearing our straw boaters and caps under the railway bridge, past the gas works, through fields of gloomy cabbages up to the school football fields and into the school.

"Back to school"

Mr Oakley was a huge, hearty man, like a giant, and a bit intimidating, especially on that first day of term when we all sang "Oh God our help in ages

"Miss Smith reads on Sunday"

past" and he sang it particularly loudly, which I rather disliked. He always seemed to wear a Free Foresters tie. G.O. Smith was a tall, angular man and was reputed to have been the best "dribbler" in England – I didn't really understand at the time what was meant by this. G.O's sister, Miss Smith, is also very clear to me – I remember that she said "grasp" as in 'asp' and "demand" as in 'bland'. She was very nice, and always wore a very large hat, a relic of Edwardian times, I never remember her without her hat, and she used to read to us in the evenings in her drawing room.

The dining room walls carried the school boards with the names of everyone who'd been at the school – I remember seeing my uncles' names there from the early 1900s. The food wasn't too bad; I particularly remember that at every meal there was plum jam on the tables, which also had huge aspidistra plants on them, and boys used to pull down the aspidistra leaves into the jam at meals and then let them spring back again! And if you were given something you didn't like – gristle for example – you put it into the aspidistra bowl, and that wasn't cleaned out for ages! It used to be quite a common occurrence to have fights behind one of the arches in the dining room!

I recall that one morning we came down to breakfast, and one of the leaded panes of glass in the dining hall windows had been removed by a burglar and all the School's silver sports cups were stolen. He just took the lot and was never seen again – I remember seeing his footprints in the flower-bed outside the window.

"Behind the arch"

In the dormitories there were 5 or 6 to a room. We had baths all together, with three people having the same water before it was changed. One of the boys in my dormitory was called Garret Moore who one day at the school became Lord Moore; later in life, as Lord Drogheda, he became Chairman of the Financial Times, Chairman of the Governors of the Royal Opera House, Covent Garden,

"Night watch for the kidnapper"

and a Governor of the Royal Ballet. His parents had just been divorced and somehow the rumour went around that he was going to be kidnapped in the night. There was a keen sense of anticipation about what might happen, and five or six of us took it in turns to stay up through the night to watch for the kidnapper. Of course we saw nothing, and in the morning the atmosphere of the previous night had quite evaporated – although it seemed to us that his slippers had been strangely moved from where they were the night before, and a wire which had been seen hanging across the window the evening before was not there in the morning. This episode was of course wholly imaginary, but its atmosphere remains a vivid memory.

The masters were mostly very nice – Mr. Henley was very kind, he used to wear an I Zingari tie, and once asked me to do a drawing for him of Norsemen landing from their ship, which I did. He was athletic and good looking; and Mrs Henley was nice-looking too, always smiling – she was related to the Lyles of Tate & Lyle, I believe. In his classroom there was a loose board or two beneath which you could store things. I remember one birthday keeping my presents down there.

Bunco Brown was a master of whom I have the clearest memory – he was very strict and quite a frightening-looking person with a huge walrus moustache and a very old-fashioned 1870s-style suit of thick ginger-brown tweed with a high stiff collar: he looked a bit like Crippen the murderer, and rumour had it that he was once arrested because of it! He pronounced "Breakfast" like "Breaf-kast" which we always tried to make him say so that we could laugh about it. He was a brilliant teacher of classics, and was also a very keen astronomer with a large telescope which he kept in the Masters Cottage nearby, overlooking the school yard. One day in the yard I did an imitation for my friend William Douglas-Home of Bunco Brown looking

"Bunko brown, astronomer, mocked"

"Mr Blore's division and scribings"

through his telescope – and then suddenly realised to my horror that he was looking right down at me, he'd been watching the whole thing from the garden next door. I got hauled in by him and punished for it in some way, I don't remember how.

Mr Blore was very nice too – he had an aesthetic side with a wonderful talent for calligraphy, he would give you a prize of an inscription drawn like a mediaeval manuscript, and once gave me a drawing in an illuminated capital letter with a tiny mediaeval tree-filled landscape, I was so pleased with it.

The drawing-master himself was Mr Bowmar-Porter, and the music was taught by Mr. Kennedy-Scott who was quite a well-known composer of songs.

Of the boys, I remember the Gilliats – Martin in later life became personal aide to the Queen Mother for which he was knighted, but his brother Anthony was killed by a tiger in Bengal. Denis Browne, later the Earl of Sligo, was a sculptor and we were at the Slade together. There were two Princes too, Prince Rupert of Teck and his cousin Prince Frederick of Teck, and two Douglas-Homes, Henry and William. William and I became good friends and in later life I

designed the set of one of his plays, *Master of Arts* (although he was unaware of my involvement). He became famous during the Second World War because he was imprisoned for refusing to obey an order to fire on one of the German-occupied Channel ports in France.

Everyone wore knee-breeches or knickerbockers all the time, except of course for games. I was in the Cricket 2nd XI, and particularly enjoyed playing against Lockers Park when I made 25 and hit the winning run – Mr Henley was there in his IZ blazer, and I remember that Garret Moore's sister Patsy was watching too, who I thought was most attractive.

I also got into the School Football side,

"Second Eleven cricket"

"Midnight adventure to the clock"

and was terribly proud of getting my 1st XI colours, the blue and white striped shirt, and the red stockings – you probably never win anything in later life that you enjoy quite as much as winning things at that age: nothing in life comes up to it really! I also won the drawing prize most years I was there, and remember going up at Supper Nights to collect my prize.

We were only allowed out of the school to walk in Trent Park next door. There was this great wood, Hadley Wood, nearby, which had a stream at the bottom where it was rumoured that someone had once hanged themselves from one of the trees, so it was a bit sinister. Beyond the Wood was another prep school called Heddon Court, although we never played them in school matches.

The things I especially enjoyed were not so much to do with the routines of the school as getting away from it all to other places around it – for example I made a hole in the fence of the cricket ground through to the garden next door, and used to go through it to a secret hiding place I made in the shrubbery. And sometimes I used to meet a boy from another dormitory at midnight and go up inside the school clock, where we would have a feast of various things we'd collected for the purpose. That was pretty high up, I don't really know now how we managed to do it, and we'd certainly have been beaten if we'd been caught!

The school had a lovely garden with lawns on two levels leading down to a pond at the bottom. In the summer the whole school would sit out in the garden with our rugs, and I used to go down by the pond at the bottom where I enjoyed studying the newts, sticklebacks, frogs and other forms of aquatic life which started an interest which has lasted all my life.

I was very interested in Nature studies, because we had wonderful lectures on that,

"Pond life"

"Rev. Wood's Saturday lecture"

which I used to look forward to so much. They were given by the Rev. Theodore Wood, a well-known naturalist, who was fascinating – he used three blackboards on which he used to illustrate his talks with coloured chalks: I particularly remember him drawing a bat on one occasion, and from that moment on I've always been able to draw bats in full, with their bone structure displayed like birds just as he did.

As for the school, there was no swimming pool and no chapel. We walked every Sunday to Cockfosters Church, up by Philip Sassoon's house at Trent Park.[1]

I was happy at Ludgrove – as far as I recall there was no bullying and very little beating there (unlike Eton later) – and it was a good atmosphere. Perhaps I derived my happiness from things which weren't at the heart of the school life – and of course perhaps too one conjures up memories and tells oneself stories which become fixed and may perhaps have become exaggerated with time – but they are all none the less real for me today!

It will not surprise the reader to know that Roland Pym won the school drawing prize no less than seven times while at Ludgrove. It was a skill which was to lead him to his subsequent career as a painter and muralist. (For over 3 years he painted the murals in the Grand Saloon at Woburn Abbey for the Duke of Bedford; and also those of Buckland Abbey, the home of Sir Francis Drake, for Lord Astor). He was also a theatre designer and illustrator of books – and in that context too he recalls the Ludgrove connection:

> I was interested to know that the Duke of Devonshire had been at Ludgrove; I knew his wife Debo, and illustrated two of her sister Nancy Mitford's books, *Love in a Cold Climate* and *The Pursuit of Love* for the Folio Society. And one of my best friends was Bryan Guinness who was Diana's first husband before she married Oswald Mosley. Another Ludgrove connection is the Sitwells – I painted shell decorations for Osbert's dining room, and also illustrated one of Edith's books, *The English Eccentrics*.

It is a happy chance that one of the most senior of Old Ludgrovians is also one its most artistically talented – and that those talents, still remaining as sharp today as ever, have been lent to this history to bring alive once more those sights and scenes of the old School as it was over 80 years ago.

THE STORY OF H.M.S. TARA

The programme of lectures already mentioned continued through these post-war years, and were comprehensively and elegantly summarised in the School Notes. G.O. must have spent hours of work on these – and the last one he records must be one of the most exciting the boys can ever have heard. A Captain Gwatkin Williams described an extraordinary adventure during the Great War. In G.O.'s words:

> Captain Williams was the commander of H.M.S. *Tara* which was torpedoed and sunk on 15th November 1915 by a German submarine off the North Coast of Africa, a little to the east of the Egyptian-Tripoli frontier. The survivors of her crew, 92 in number, were handed over by the Germans to the wild Senoussi tribe, with whom they had to march nearly 180 miles into the Libyan Desert, where they were treated with the greatest cruelty, being compelled to work like slaves on a starvation ration, lashed with rhinoceros-hide whips and when ill, left to die. Captain Williams gave the most thrilling account of these adventures of his unfortunate ship's company and of the terrible sufferings which he and they had to endure during their captivity. He himself finally resolved to escape, and succeeded in stealing away by night, but after many days of wandering and hardship in the desert he was taken prisoner by roaming Bedouins, who eventually gave him back to the Senoussi. He vividly described how, by an almost miraculous chain of coincidences, the whereabouts of himself and his men became known to the British Forces in North Africa, and how these at last succeeded in reaching the prisoners. The survivors of the party were eventually rescued on 17th March 1916 by an armoured car squadron under the Duke of Westminster.

The Senussi were not a tribe but an extremist sect of Islam who, led by the Mahdi until his death, controlled much of North Africa in the 19th and early 20th centuries. Their hatred of the infidel was fierce and fanatical. However, in 1914–18 they sided with Germany and its Turkish ally, against Britain and France. Left: A local Senussi governor in 1920. Right: Senussi in the Libyan Sahara.

G.O AND MISS SMITH RETIRE

In the summer term of 1922, the School heard with sorrow of G.O. Smith's retirement due to ill-health. He had been a great Headmaster. One of the many appreciative letters he received towards the end was from Violet Pym, mother of John and Roland – referring to the wise guidance G.O. provided when writing to boys just *before* the start of their first term at public school.

> Foxwold,
> Brasted,
> Kent   September 20th 1921
>
> Dear Mr. Smith,
>
> Only a line to tell you that Jack went off to Eton this morning with his father in very good heart.
>
> It was so kind of you to write to him. Of course the start at a public school is a plunge into life that mothers must rather dread – but I do feel, and with such thankfulness, that Ludgrove has been a very real preparation for it, and am more than grateful for all that you have done for him (not least for the help and advice that you have now given him).
>
> We have never found anything but improvement in him since he came to you, and with such a start I hope and think that he should get the best out of Eton too.
>
> With kind regards to Miss Smith
>
> Sincerely
>
> Violet Pym

But with his shy and nervous disposition, G.O. had become worn out by his unceasing dedication to the school. So he decided to retire, and his devoted sister Katherine retired with him. He left at the end of the summer term 1922, and his old friend and partner Bill Oakley marked his departure with these words:

> All who have had any connection with Ludgrove will learn with deep regret that, owing to ill health, Mr Smith has been obliged to give up his work. After 26 years' work here, during 20 of which he was Headmaster, such a parting must needs be a sad one.
>
> He has been wrapped up heart and soul in the boys and in his work. Inspired by his example, Ludgrove will enter on the new chapter in her history full of hope that the reputation which she has earned in the past will be fully maintained by future generations.
>
> Nor must we forget the part played by Miss Smith during all these years. Her life has been entirely given up to the best interests of the School, and many an Old Boy on returning to Ludgrove years afterwards has recalled incidents in the

G.O. and his sister Katherine

books she used to read on Sunday evenings. She also has a great facility for devising games and amusements for boys in the sick room, and has made things much easier for them by her cheerfulness and interest in their doings. New boys especially had their first days at Ludgrove made happier by her unfailing tact and sympathy.

All Ludgrovians past and present will unite in expressing their sympathy with Mr and Miss Smith at this time, and their deep sense of gratitude for all that they owe them, and will wish them many years of health and happiness in the future.

A seemingly contented G.O., at the time of his retirement

Chapter IV

THE ROARING TWENTIES

Of Oakley: *"He found little difficulty in retaining our attention as he picked up the story of Goliath and raced towards the goal"*
Of Henley: *"Their eyes absorbed his blazer, and their ears his kindly enthusiasm"*
William Douglas Home

Frank Henley joined Bill Oakley as Joint Headmaster on G.O's retirement in the summer of 1922. Henley had arrived at the school in 1905, and – together with Bill Oakley, G.O. Smith, 'Bunco' Brown, Walter Stanbrough and Willie Blore – he formed the nucleus of those long-serving masters who had joined the school in the first fifteen years of its life and were to provide its backbone for over a third of a century. Henley's wife Margaret assumed the vital domestic role which Katherine Smith had played so ably throughout the Smith-Oakley years, including the traditional reading to the whole School on Sunday nights which had first been started by Helen Dunn.

In 1922 there were 64 boys in the School, a number virtually unchanged since the turn of the century. One of the early pupils to enter Ludgrove under the new regime was Roland Pym's friend William Douglas-Home, who went to Ludgrove in 1923, following on the heels of his two elder brothers Alec and Henry. He later became famous as an author and a playwright. Here William Douglas-Home captures what it really feels like as a small boy to leave the security of home for one's first day at boarding school:

Frank Henley as Headmaster in the late 1920s

*Sir Alec Douglas Home …   his brother William …   and his son David …
were all at Ludgrove, and David, the present Earl of Home, sent his son there.*

I had heard about school from Alec and Henry. Not only of Eton, where they both
resided at this date, but of a mysterious place called Ludgrove where they had
both started their scholastic careers…From their conversation, Ludgrove seemed
to be peopled with inhabitants bearing strange names such as 'The Bug'
(Stanbrough), 'Po' (Oakley), 'Billy Bluff' (Blore), and 'Bunco' Brown. In the nights
previous to my deportation…these figures passed like nightmare ogres through
my agitated mind…

After saying "goodnight" to my father and mother on the night before I left
home; after lying in bed with the tears soaking into my pillow;…after waking in
the cold morning light, with red-rimmed eyes and a feeling of cold despair in my
heart, I bade farewell to my familiar spirits and drove to Berwick-on-Tweed with
my father, en route for what I imagined would be hell…But as always my father
was there with his impersonal and sympathetic understanding, and his
conversation about something which he called "next holidays", but which to me
seemed scarcely less elusive than the after-life…

Now on the train to London it was my father's turn to put sugar on the pill
and ease it gently down my throat. And this he did – with tact and understanding,
and a sense of humour which held back my tears and even made me smile…

Then came the dreaded moment when my father replaced his teacup on Mrs
Henley's table and announced his departure. I suppose I took his hand and said
"Goodbye", but if I did the action was instinctive and not visual because my eyes
were blind with tears.

And when he had gone, even the maternal smile of Mrs Henley – and what
smiles are more maternal than the smiles of the wives of joint headmasters? –
failed to dispel the sense of utter desolation in my wretched little heart. I thought
of my father driving in his freedom back to London with his pipe alight; of my
mother up at the Hirsel, sitting at her writing table, writing possibly to me; of
Rachel sitting at the schoolroom table at the elbow of dear, kind Miss Pattenden

and of Mr Collingwood whose farewell smile had been my last view at the front door of my home. And finally I thought of me – poor orphan child, in exile from my Scottish hills and rivers, standing helpless in the land of 'Billy Bluff' and 'Bunco' Brown.

Later, William draws a penetrating portrait of the different personalities and teaching styles of the extrovert Bill Oakley and the meticulous Frank Henley:

> Divinity was always the subject of early school at Ludgrove. Usually it was taken either by Mr Henley or Mr Oakley. The former was a keen and competent cricketer, the latter had played football in his day for England. Their methods of teaching Divinity – though both excellent in their way – were different and characteristic.
>
> Mr. Henley loved to deal in different coloured chalks. It was rare for the names of Isaiah or Abraham or Solomon to be written on the blackboard by Mr Henley without the assistance of three or four coloured chalks. By the time he had outlined the family tree of the House of David, the board resembled nothing so much as the I Zingari blazer which he sported on the cricket ground with such an excellent effect on small and keen-eyed boys. To Mr Henley went the credit for instilling the desire to play and the ability for playing cricket into tiny boys whose hands were still too small to clasp a full-sized cricket bat. Their eyes absorbed his blazer and their ears his kind enthusiasm, and in later years he sat in pride and watched a very fair percentage of them carry out his teaching on the cricket ground at Lord's.
>
> But Mr Oakley was the footballer. Not for him the airy tinsel of the cricket ground, the cotton dresses of the women-folk, the different coloured chalks. To 'Po', Isaiah was a character portrayed in total white. Yet what he lacked in decoration he made up in punch, determination and sincerity. The man who so often in the past had held a breathless crowd in tense excitement while he took a penalty found little difficulty in retaining the attention of a dozen little boys as he picked up the story of Goliath and raced towards the goal. He had us with him all the way.

In the summer term of 1923 another great Ludgrove career came to an end with the retirement of 'Bunco' Brown, that stern, learned, rather forbidding man with the old-fashioned suits and high collars, for whom the Classics and Astronomy were his life, and to whom so many boys had paid their tributes down the years for the genius of his teaching and "the love of learning" they gained from him – the greatest legacy a schoolmaster can give his pupils. Bill Oakley wrote of him:

> The School incurs a great loss this term through the departure of Mr A.N. Brown, who came here from Mortimer in September 1898. Mr Brown has done an

enormous amount of hard work during the last 25 years, and a great many Ludgrove boys owe him a large debt for the way in which he has prepared them for the Entrance Examination. He never spared himself, and during his time here, no fewer than 70 boys have been placed in Remove at Eton, a record of which he may well be proud. He will be very much missed, and takes with him all our very best wishes for a happy time in his new home at Bucklebury near Reading.

As we have seen in an earlier chapter, it was in his retirement that Arthur Brown consolidated his reputation as one of the country's leading amateur astronomers; his contributions to our knowledge of the stars is acknowledged by the British Astronomical Association to this day.

His successor as Head of Classics was Mr G.C.B. Johnson, a Classical Scholar of Dulwich School and Trinity College, Cambridge, who came from being senior classics master at Winton House School, Winchester.

The departure of G.O. brought to an end one of the treasures of the Ludgrove story, namely the masterly recording in the School Notes of the lectures given to the boys each term. G.O. seems to have enjoyed writing these as much as anything he did at Ludgrove

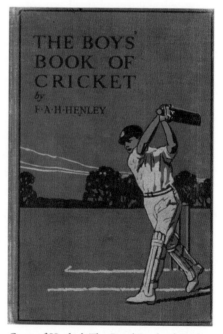

Cover of Henley's The Boys' Book of Cricket

– he could not otherwise have recorded them in such entertaining and profuse detail – but it must have required enormous effort to capture so completely and eloquently the essence of so many lectures on so many subjects throughout his time. It has only been possible to include a fraction of these summaries in this history, but they form an integral part of Ludgrove's story, and from now on there is an 'emptiness' in the School Notes without them.

Like G.O., Frank Henley was a keen cricketer, a former Oxford Blue and the author of a widely acclaimed manual *The Boys' Book of Cricket*, published in 1924 with an introduction by Sir Pelham Warner, President of the MCC. It is a compendium of coaching advice, illustrated by photographs of a Ludgrove boy, Nigel Gibbes (who was killed in the Second World War), demonstrating all the 'Right' and 'Wrong' positions of batting and bowling.

The introduction begins with an intriguing statement:

'Right' and 'wrong' shots from The Boys' Book of Cricket

Mr. F.A.H. Henley took part in the historic University match of 1905, and he has not failed to draw attention to the burning lesson which that match taught, viz. that it is essential to hold a 'kit inspection' before an XI takes the field. Had such an inspection taken place, it is more than probable that Oxford would have won on that occasion.

What could Sir Pelham be referring to? The dry record of that match shows merely that Cambridge made 218 and 264 in their two innings, and Oxford 319 and 123, thereby losing by 40 runs. In what mysterious way did the state of Oxford's kit intervene to change the fortunes of that far-off and "historic" match? In his book, under the heading "A Warning to Remember", Henley tells the story: Oxford had achieved a lead of 101 on the first innings, and Cambridge lost 6 wickets for 77 runs in their second innings. The match then seemed to Oxford to be "as good as over", since the Cambridge side had a long 'tail'. But at this point Oxford's star bowler, W.H.B. Evans, who had taken 5 of the 6 Cambridge wickets up to that moment, burst one of his boots. Another pair was

A member of today's Ludgrove staff, George Hughes-Games, illustrates the offending boot.

found in someone else's bag, but evidently they did not fit. Evans could not bowl comfortably in them and the Cambridge batsmen, recovering confidence, began to 'take him apart', hitting the Oxford bowling to all parts of the field to end the innings on 264, a lead of 163 against which Oxford in their fourth innings could only score a total of 123, thus losing the match by 40 runs. Henley comments: "Had that wretched boot been seen before the match began, Oxford would have been packing their bags all smiles on the second day. *Be sure that you inspect your boots and all your kit very carefully before a match begins.*"

The book concludes with a simple list of 'Do's' and 'Don'ts' which – as Sir Pelham says in his Introduction – "could with advantage be hung on the wall of every cricket pavilion throughout the British Empire". It is not exaggerated praise: many of our test and county cricketers today would gain from reading such a succinct summary of all the best advice that a cricketer could ever receive on the arts of Batting, Bowling and Fielding. It shows convincingly the observation and mastery with which Frank Henley must have coached his boys and inspired them to excel. His Do's and Don'ts are included in Appendix 8 to this book.

Unlike G.O., Frank Henley had a splendid singing voice, and he and Bill Oakley invariably sang together at the end of the Supper Night Concerts, giving renderings of well known folksongs from the store bequeathed by Cecil Sharp. These concerts, organised by the music master Charles Kennedy-Scott, had always been a central part of the Ludgrove tradition, each programme closing – as Arthur Dunn had ordained – with the *Carmen Etonense*, 'Auld Lang Syne' and the National Anthem. The concert of 1925 was designated "one of the most successful we have ever had", being notable in that two boys – the Earl of Hopetoun, who was School Captain of Cricket, heading both the batting and bowling averages, and holder of the Senior Boxing Cup; and Lord John Hope, who won the Classics, Scripture and Music Prizes and the Senior Athletics Cup –

CONCERT.—The following Programme was performed on "Supper Night." Mr. Kennedy-Scott is to be congratulated on the high standard attained, and Hopetoun and Hope were chiefly responsible for the success of a large number of the items :—

1.	A Song for Supper Night.		
2.	Piano Solos	(a) "March" (*Curse*)	R. D. Dale.
		(b) "March of the Men of Harlech"	P. W. Marsham
3.	Unison Songs	(a) "Flowers of the Heather" (Welsh)	
		(b) "Kitty of Coleraine" (Irish)	
		(c) "Row dow dow" (English)	
4.	Piano Solos	(a) "Song of the Reapers" (*Schumann*)	P. Arkwright
		(b) "Minuet" (*Mozart*)	C. B. M. Cokayne
5.	Unison Song	"Glad Hearts Adventuring" (*Martin Shaw*)	
6.	Piano Solos	(a) "Valse Petite"	Earl of Hopetoun
		(b) "Minuet in G" (*Beethoven*)	Lord John Hope
7.	French & English Songs	(a) "En revenant d'Auvergne"	
		(b) "Sir Eglamore"	
8.	Trio	"Three Little Maids from School" ("*Sullivan*")	
9.	Piano Duet	"Air de Ballet" (*Curse*)	Mr. Kennedy-Scott & Lord John Hope
10.	Chorus	"Ave Verum" (*Mozart*)	
11.	Quartette	"God be in my Head" (*Walford Davies*)	
12.	Song	"Who is Sylvia?" (*Schubert*)	Lord John Hope
13.	Piano Duet	"Hejre Kati" (*Hubay*)	Mr. Kennedy-Scott & Mr. Blore
14.	Sea Chanty (with chorus)	"Let the Bulgine run"	Mr. Johnson
15.	Song		Mr. Wood
16.	Duet		Mr. Henley & Mr. Oakley

"**Carmen Etonense.**" "**Auld Lang Syne.**"
"**God Save the King.**"

The 1925 School Concert Programme featuring Hope and Hopetoun

*The Earl of Hopetoun and
Lord John Hope together*

were responsible between them for two piano solos, one piano duet and a solo song. Seldom since the days of Arthur Dunn had the musical life of Ludgrove been so enhanced by the school's leading sportsmen. Later, in his career at Eton, Lord John Hope was to become Victor Ludorum, winning the Mile, Half Mile and Quarter Mile in 1931, and in due course served as an MP and Minister of Works under Harold Macmillan (1959-62).

Ludgrove continued to enrich the long line of musicians who featured in the records at Eton during these years. In one year C.M. Janson won the Pianoforte Prize, C.M.B. Cockayne that for the flute and K.F. Malcolmson won an organ scholarship to Exeter College, Oxford. He would later become Precentor of Music at Eton. There remains however an impression that the foundations of Ludgrovian cultural life of the time were less deep than these achievements might suggest. This comes in the notice of a lecture given in the Michaelmas term 1925:

> Mr C.F.Cook lectured to us on "Some British Painters". *This does not seem at first sight a very suitable subject for boys of preparatory school age (author's italics)* – but Mr Cook was most interesting….and succeeded in keeping the full attention of even the smallest members of his audience.

The writer's astonishment is scarcely concealed: how *could* Mr. Cook have interested the boys in such a subject as British painters? It must have been a triumph on someone's part that an invitation had been extended to him at all to lecture at Ludgrove on such a subject. The School was no doubt more at home the following month with a lecture by Commander Adams who was second-in-command of Shackleton's first expedition to the Antarctic in 1907-09, which got within 90 miles of the South Pole.

Eton Connections

Close contact continued with Old Ludgrovians at Eton, and in 1926 their exploits made significant contributions to most parts of Eton's academic and sporting life:

Eton v. Harrow at Lord's	M.H.de Zoete, M. de S.C.Ward, C.K.Hill-Wood
Rowing VIII	Viscount Tiverton
Loder Declamation Prize	A.W.Baird
Science Prize	J.R.S.Arkwright
Asst. Masters' Science Prize	H.A.F.Hohler (the next year he won the Cockerell Prize for Imperial History and Geography)
Drawing Prize	J.Pym
Prizeman in Trials	Viscount Moore

This is indeed the first time that we have seen Ludgrovians acclaimed for achievement in both Art and Science.

Triumphs and disasters

Epidemics of scarlet fever, whooping–cough and measles continued to take regular hold, leaving in their wake a raft of cancelled school matches. And in the spring term of 1924, infection caused an event of which there is no parallel in Ludgrove's long history: the total destruction of the school library. It was a heart-rending event: the school doctor concluded that the source of a scarlet fever epidemic, which had taken hold in the Michaelmas term of 1923, had not been eliminated by the beginning of the Spring term, and he formed the view that its germs were still lurking in the pages of the School's books. So he instructed that the entire Library – over 1100 books, many very valuable, built up through gifts of leavers, masters and parents since the time of Arthur Dunn over 30 years previously – should be consigned to the flames. One can well imagine the despair of masters and boys as they watched this happen.

George Hughes-Games recreates the burning books episode.

But Ludgrove was able to deploy its greatest asset in a rescue, namely the unlimited goodwill of all who knew the school. An appeal was quickly organised under the Chairmanship of one of the parents, Lord Home, who personally wrote to every fellow parent, and from their contributions "a very handsome sum" was collected to replace the lost volumes. Through this generosity the Library was largely reconstituted by the beginning of the summer term.

Illness remained ever-present in these years. In 1926, the 1st Cricket XI went through the season undefeated, including a memorable victory over Lockers Park in which Ludgrove scored 121 runs in 58 minutes to win, with a century partnership between Beaumont and Goschen. But the following summer, 1927, whooping-cough wiped out every single fixture, so the record could not be defended; and in the Michaelmas term not one football match was played as a result of German measles. Again, three years later, in the summer of 1930, the record mourns:

We shall not readily forget this term. With a side which was certainly above the ordinary in ability and keenness, it was cruelly hard luck to be robbed of all school matches owing to a prolonged visitation of mumps. The side have never allowed their disappointment to show itself, but through the term have worked hard and successfully to inspire general enthusiasm.

Epidemics were always a vast imponderable in determining the shape of the School's life – and indeed sometimes beyond the school: in the autumn of 1927 another tragic 'In Memoriam' notice tells of the death through illness during the summer holidays of Robin Bell, who had left that summer term to go to Dartmouth Naval College. The school was shattered by the news, and Oakley wrote in moving terms about someone well known to all who had so recently been among the outstanding boys at the School:

> Robin's loss will be deeply felt by all who knew him…he made friends wherever he went, and his bright and sunny nature won for him the deep affection of everyone with whom he came in contact. It is impossible not to feel the greatest sorrow that a life so cheery and full of promise has been brought to a close so quickly. But, through it all, it is the greatest comfort to know that nothing in his short life called for regret.

No illness appeared in 1928 to disrupt the sports fixtures, but the sporting disasters which befell Ludgrove's teams that year were of a magnitude without precedent in the school's history. In the summer the Cricket XI suffered its worst defeat in the School's history at the hands of their old enemy Elstree. Elstree made 63, a modest score even by prep school standards; but in their two innings the Ludgrove side scored a combined total of 23 – with no fewer than 8 ducks in the first innings and 5 in the second.

2nd Match. v. **ELSTREE.** Played at Elstree, June 13th.			
LUDGROVE.			
1st Innings.		2nd Innings.	
M. R. Arkwright b Simpson..............	0	c Catlow b Simpson	0
J.-Paterson ma c Graham b Martin......	0	b Martin	5
Birkbeck ma b Simpson....................	0	b Martin	4
Parker b Simpson...	0	c Duveen b Simpson	3
Tabor b Simpson......	0	b Simpson	0
Scott c Simpson b Martin	1	b Simpson	0
Marsham c Wetherby b Martin	3	c Barton b Gold ...	0
M-Hinds c and b Martin..................	0	b Duveen	0
Cokayne b Simpson...	2	c Martin b Duveen	1
H-Hunt not out......	0	not out	3
Adams c How b Martin....................	0	c and b Simpson ...	1
Total ...	6	Total	17

The dire performance recorded for posterity

The official record speaks only of "the debacle at Elstree on June 13th". The next term Ludgrove's Football XI followed their cricketing colleagues into oblivion by losing their away match to Elstree by a record score of 1–12, the margin of defeat also being unrivalled in Ludgrove's annals. Again the School Notes commentator merely sighs: "The less said about this match the better". These two matches of the 1928 sports season occupy a special place in the mausoleum of Ludgrove's sporting disasters; like the consecutive defeats of the Romans by Hannibal at Lake Trasimene and Cannae in 216 and 215 B.C., the corpses of Ludgrove's cricketing and footballing reputations that year lay scattered by these two battles all over the Elstree grounds.

Lord Burghley – Olympic athlete

Ludgrovian sporting success was to come from a source other than its own teams that year. Everyone at Ludgrove would have taken a vicarious pride in the summer of 1928 in the news – only hinted at in the School Notes – that at the Olympic Games in Amsterdam an Old Ludgrovian had won a Gold Medal in the 400 metre hurdles, at the same time setting a new world record for the event. This was Lord Burghley, the greatest and most famous of all Ludgrove's athletes. Burghley (later Marquess of Exeter) had been at Ludgrove from 1914 to 1918.

During that time the promise of his athletic prowess was not obvious: in his last year he had only come third in the 100 and 200 yards (though he did win the high jump and long jump), and was not even placed in the hurdles at which he was later to excel. But Bill Oakley had spotted his potential, and it remained one of his proudest boasts until the end of his life that, as a former international hurdler himself, he had coached the great Lord Burghley.

At Eton Burghley developed his talents to outstanding effect – he was the first hurdler to put match-boxes on each hurdle and then try to knock them off with his leading foot: a trick from Oakley's own repertoire, perhaps? – and from there went up to Magdalene College, Cambridge, where he won every athletics honour available to him. He also caused a sensation throughout the University by running around the Great Court at Trinity College in the time it took the Trinity clock to strike twelve.

Following his Olympic triumph of 1928, he was elected to Parliament in 1931, and went on to captain the British athletic team at the Olympic Games in the Los Angeles Olympics in 1932, where he won a Silver Medal in the 400m relay, and was placed 4th and 5th in the 400m and 110m hurdles respectively.

Lord Burghley was a colourful character: on one occasion he set an unusual record by racing around the upper deck of the Cunard liner *Queen Mary* in 57 seconds in his ordinary clothes. For over 40 years he was President of the British Amateur Athletic Association, and a member of the International Olympic Committee. Probably his greatest achievement came in 1948 as Chairman of the Olympic Organising Committee when, having only two years in which to do it, he organised the staging of the highly successful Olympic Games amidst the ruins of post-war London.

A completely distorted account of the Trinity quadrangle feat was presented in the film "Chariots of Fire" when it was wrongly attributed to Harold Abrahams. Lord Burghley, then aged 76, reportedly refused to watch the film of his exploit being performed by another. It was on Burghley himself that the film's character of Lord Lindsay, played by Nigel Havers, was based.

Lord Burghley

Robin Milford – musician extraordinary

In the summer of 1927 Charles Kennedy-Scott gave up teaching music at Ludgrove "owing to pressure of work". He was succeeded by Robin Milford, then aged 24, the brother of the amateur rackets champion of England and the fourth music master at Ludgrove who would go on to make a national reputation, after Sharp, Balfour Gardiner and Kennedy-Scott himself. When Milford came to Ludgrove he was already a composer of importance, of whom none other than Sir Ralph Vaughan Williams once wrote (in a letter to Sir Adrian Boult):

> If I wanted to show an intelligent foreigner something worth doing which could only possibly come out of England, I think I would show him some of the work of Robin Milford.

Milford had trained under Vaughan Williams and Gustav Holst, and was a personal friend of the composer Gerald Finzi. During his life his musical output was prolific, much of it composed while he was at Ludgrove – concertos for orchestra, violin, piano and organ, innumerable songs and anthems for choirs and soloists, ballet music, an opera for children (*The Shoemaker*, based on one of the stories of Beatrix Potter) and also a large scale oratorio, *A Prophet in the Land*, which was performed in Gloucester

Cathedral as part of the Three Choirs Festival in 1931. Some of the most distinguished conductors of the day performed his works including Sir Ralph Vaughan Williams, Sir Malcolm Sargent and Sir John Barbirolli. Milford composed as if his life depended on it – which in the end it literally did. He never recovered from the tragic death in 1941 of his 5-year-old son Barnaby in an accident which occurred when running an errand for his father. Milford was plunged into a deep depression, later exacerbated by self-doubt, poverty and career worries; and in December 1959 he took his own life. He has been called a composer "whose musical charm and

Robin Milford with his wife Kirsty

sincerity never fail to please all those who listen". His works live on, and in the music world the centenary of his birth was celebrated in January 2003.

The close of the Twenties

The winter of 1927 also saw the departure of the Classics master (Mr Thorne), and of Miss Rowe, who had arrived on a temporary basis during the War in 1916 to help out with teaching the juniors, and stayed to educate four generations of Ludgrove boys. Three other masters also departed at this time – Mr. Wood, Mr. Downey and Mr Beckwith – and among their replacements it was announced in the summer of 1928 that Mr. T.W. Shaw of Shrewsbury School and Christ Church College, Oxford, would be joining the staff the following term.

Tim Shaw was Bill Oakley's nephew and godson. He was also an outstanding oarsman, having rowed for Oxford three years running and having been President of the OUBC during the summer of 1928. He had been at Shrewsbury and Oxford with

Tim Shaw as a young man

Alan Barber as a young man

his great friend, Alan Barber, and was then in the process of persuading him to join the staff of Ludgrove too. Alan eventually did so two years later in the Michaelmas term of 1930.

The friendship between Tim and Alan was to develop into a professional partnership that would take Ludgrove to new heights of fame and reputation in the four decades from 1930 to 1970. With their appointments to Ludgrove's staff we leave the 'Roaring Twenties' behind, and enter new and altogether more challenging times.

Chapter V

HARDER TIMES
1930–37

"Possunt quia posse videntur." Virgil
(They can, because it is seen that they can)

What was the tone of the school in those opening years of the 1930s? The late Duke of Devonshire who, as Lord Andrew Cavendish, was at Ludgrove from 1929 to 1932, summed it up in affectionate terms:

Tower Bridge, March 1931

> When I hear the word 'Ludgrove' today, the first thing that comes to mind is Happiness! I was wholly happy there, and they were very kind to me. It is not unfair to say that they were rather games-oriented, and I was no good at games at all – but I never suffered from that. I can remember them all – Mr. Oakley, Mr. Henley who was convivial and a very good singer, Mr Blore, Mr. Stanbrough, the younger masters of course – Alan Barber and Tim Shaw, Sergeant-Major Goldie and a charming Matron. I can see their faces as if it was yesterday.
>
> The tone of the school could be called 'discipline with a light touch'. I really don't remember any bullying, and there was no beating either as I recall (unlike Eton). If you were an offender you were kept in. Of course the school was very closely oriented to Eton, and I remember that Mr Oakley and Mr Henley very much wanted Eton to win the Eton and Harrow match; they used to take the boys every year to see the match at Lord's, Mr Oakley wearing a black top hat and Mr Henley a grey one. We were very well

The late Duke of Devonshire

taught - indeed almost too well, since I took Upper IV at Eton when it would probably have been more suitable for me to have got Lower IV! There were high standards, and among the things we were taught was to develop good manners, which I have always thought terribly important.

Among my most vivid memories is frequently seeing the R101 airship flying over the school to and from its base at Cardington in Bedforshire, and in fact we got up early to see it go over a few hours before it crashed near Beauvais in France, on its way to India in October 1930. That did make a tremendous impression on everyone.

The R101 leaving Cardington   *Remains of the R101 after crashing near Beauvais*

Another memory is of Mr Oakley going round the dormitories at night after the lights were turned out to make sure that no one was talking, and wearing rubber-soled shoes so that we wouldn't hear him coming,

It was such a beautiful location. I can see those playing fields now, the cricket ground with its pavilion stretching up to that lovely garden next door – Philip Sassoon's house, Trent Park – and below that the football ground. I went back there recently and it was all completely recognisable, I was surprised how much came back to me. All in all, the Ludgrove I recall was strong on teaching and strong on games, and while I wasn't much good at either I recall my days there as a time of great happiness.

The Duke spoke a trifle modestly about his achievements at Ludgrove – he came top of his form in numerous subjects, won a mathematics prize in 1931 and was in the School 2nd XIs for cricket and football. Nevertheless it is a remarkable testimony to the Ludgrove ethos of that time that, for a boy who was not a sporting "star" of the sort which private schools in those days sought and promoted, he nevertheless recalls his days at Ludgrove with such affection.

It is a sentiment shared by the Earl of Harewood (1932–36), who as Lord George Lascelles was there in the early 1930s:

The Earl of Harewood as Managing Director of English National Opera, in the 1980s

I enjoyed my time there very much. It was not a harsh environment – although I do recall the cold of the classrooms, and I dreaded lunch on Mondays when we would invariably have tinned fruit salad and rice pudding – which I have hated ever since – and while it was a well-disciplined school, the discipline was enforced naturally rather than through sanctions. Nor do I recall any bullying. In those days there was much more conformity to life in general – there were no wars then (apart from Abyssinia and the Spanish Civil War of which no one spoke too much), and the word "protest" had not yet been invented – so I think we were all quite easy to deal with, and the masters were all agreeable, and inspired us with their enthusiasm. I have a strong affection for Ludgrove; it is one of the things in my life on which I look back with great warmth.

Cricket – four years of supremacy

Ludgrove's pre-eminence in cricket infused all parts of school life. Lord Harewood recalls that one of the proudest moments of his schooldays was to receive the prize for History one year at Supper Night with his form master's accolade: "This prize goes to Lascelles Major, who I have to say knows his history books as well as he knows his Wisden".

On the field of play itself, after the disappointment of all the cancelled fixtures of 1930, the Ludgrove Cricket XI embarked on four years of unchallenged supremacy. In 1931, under C.D. Clark, they set a new school record by winning every match they played. Not a match was lost in 1932 either, and R.O. Stanley was the best Ludgrovian batsmen of the 1930s, scoring 317 runs in school matches for an average of 63.

The 1933 season was unaffected by illness, "the sun shining from beginning to end of the season". In 1934 too the side was undefeated, with two centurions – R.A. Henley

Ludgrove cricketers of the 1930s: R.O. Stanley, J.R. Warrender and R.A. Henley

(a nephew of FAHH) making 129 against Stanmore Park and J.R. Warrender 117 against South Lodge – and Henley himself made 408 runs in school matches with an average of 102, the second highest in the school's history.

Stump cricket

The record of the winter term 1934 includes the first mention of Ludgrove's unique game of 'Stump' cricket:

> Winter practice at 'Stump', when played properly, improves bowling and batting beyond recognition. Those who have done best in the Elevens have been ardent 'Stump' players.

'Stump', played during break in all weathers

'Stump' goes back to the days of Arthur Dunn. It is played by everyone in the school in all weathers the full year round, in the school yard during morning break. Played with a narrow, shaved down bat, a tennis ball, and a solid wicket, 'Stump' provides boys with noisy fun, exercise, and good fellowship, being a game in which everyone – no matter what his cricketing skills might be – can participate and enjoy. It is a tradition which Ludgrovians of every generation remember, and it continues to be played today with undiminished enthusiasm.

The Sets

A major innovation in Ludgrove's life took place in the Spring term of 1933 with the introduction of the Sets:

> With a view to encouraging team spirit, the whole School was divided up into Sets, to which were given names of distinguished Englishmen of the past. Marks were awarded for success in work and play, behaviour etc. in such a way that every boy in the school had a chance of helping his side – or the reverse.

The "distinguished Englishmen" were Drake, Haig, Jellicoe, Kitchener, Nelson and Wellington. There is no record of how these great men were chosen. Were they summarily decided by Oakley and Henley alone? Were the masters asked to chip in their ideas too? There is a logic in the formula of three Generals and three Admirals, with three from history and three modern. Within these, Drake, Nelson and Wellington were probably self-selecting. But what about the remainder: why was Marlborough omitted in favour of Kitchener? How did Jellicoe get past Collingwood? And how did the controversial Haig – whose strategy in the Great War had been responsible for so many casualties with so little result – come to be included in the list? The record is silent.

Drake   Nelson   Wellington   Kitchener   Haig   Jellicoe

The new Sets quickly became the structure around which the whole life of the School revolved, and their names and role remain unchanged to this day. Fierce loyalties and rivalries are generated, and competition between them comes to a peak each year with the unique game of Inter-Sets Football, played with up to 30 players on each side, with three referees and three footballs. It is still a highlight of the Michaelmas Term at Ludgrove in the 21st century.

THE OLD ORDER CHANGETH

Walter Stanbrough

The end of the summer term of 1934 also marked the end of an era. First Walter Stanbrough retired. He had been a Cambridge classicist and an international footballer when he joined Ludgrove in 1900, and had taught the four main subjects – Classics, Mathematics, French and History – for 34 years. On his departure, a parent wrote to Bill Oakley as warm and generous a tribute to this stalwart Ludgrovian as it is possible to read of a schoolmaster:

> How often have we heard "Mr Stanbrough told us or showed us", and then something about a bird, insect or flower; or in later years:
> "I must write to Mr Stanbrough". Of all their kind friends, the remembrance of him will be one of the most vivid in the happy memories of Ludgrove boys during the last 34 years.
> And why? Will it be because of his love of nature and understanding of boyish

Oakley's last term: Front row (l. to r.) Walter Stanbrough, Frank Henley, Bill Oakley, Willie Blore. Back row (l. to.r.) W.A. Drury, Tim Shaw, Alan Barber

hobbies, his quiet ways and gentle manner, his friendly reproof or encouragement given with a smile as impossible to forget as to describe? All those delightful characteristics are his – but there is more.

In the dawn of life it is easy to see into an older person's heart, and in his heart every Ludgrove boy has seen something extra good. They and also many Ludgrove parents would gladly begin school days again if they knew Mr Stanbrough would be there; and – as that is impossible – let us hope that we shall often meet him, happy and well, in years to come.

Bill Oakley's retirement...

The same term Bill Oakley retired. He was 61. He had joined Ludgrove in 1895 as a young Oxford graduate with international honours in both football and athletics, and had been an assistant master for seven years before taking the helm with G.O. Smith following Arthur Dunn's untimely death in 1902. For 32 years he had guided the School to become one of the most famous prep schools in the land, and formed outstanding partnerships both with Smith and Frank Henley, two men of very different personalities. He was the rock on which Ludgrove's name had been built up in all these years. In addition to his teaching, his coaching of all sports, his singing at all the concerts and his frequent lectures on science and nature, Bill Oakley had always handled the external side of the school, in particular communications with parents and the selection of staff, and his large, re-assuring presence was known and respected by generations of Ludgrove boys and parents alike as the essence of Ludgrove.

Unlike G.O., who stayed at Ludgrove throughout the holidays, Bill Oakley knew how to relax. He would routinely write all his reports over three concentrated days and nights at the end of each term, often working non-stop through the night to complete them. Then he would ride his motorbike and sidecar up the old A5, back to his family home in Shropshire to recover there for a few days from the exertions of the term, before travelling over to Brancaster in Norfolk to play golf with good friends. His niece, Dorothy Barber, recalls these thrice-yearly visits to the family home:

> We always looked forward so much to welcoming him back, he was a really super uncle, calm, re-assuring, so gentle for all his physical size and sporting achievements, an upholder of all the old-fashioned virtues and values. He was the kindest of men, and for all his talents he never blew his own trumpet. He was the ideal partner for G.O. whom he would pacify whenever he got into a flap. He was always marvellous to me, and of course I adored him.

The same parent who had written about Walter Stanbrough wrote of all that Bill Oakley had done for Ludgrove during his long stewardship of the school :

> It is very hard to imagine Ludgrove without one who has been the best of leaders and the kindest of friends to boys and parents for 38 years. [...] May the best of health and happiness be with our old friend for many years, with the sound of our heartfelt "Thank You" ever ringing in his ears.

...and untimely death

No one could have guessed how tragically short his retirement was to be. He had retired in July. In August, while driving back to Shropshire on his way from shooting and fishing in Scotland with two Ludgrove parents, he had a car-crash near Carlisle, and died in Carlisle Infirmary the following day. He had not even enjoyed one full month of retirement.

The whole Ludgrove community was stricken with grief, and St. Mary's Church, Shrewsbury, where his memorial service was held, was full to overflowing. His friend and partner G.O. Smith wrote these moving words to his memory:

> *"And Glory is the least of the things that followed this man home"*
> Ever since the news came to me of the tragic death of W.J. Oakley, these lines have been ringing in my ears. They seem to me peculiarly applicable to him, for though he was an athlete of large achievement, and won great renown in many branches of sport, it is not for his skill at games that he will be chiefly remembered by his intimate friends, but for his other sterling qualities.
> I knew him probably better than anyone else: we were freshmen at Oxford

together, went to Ludgrove together, and worked there for many years in the closest association, and the impression of him that remains is one of quiet strength and real solid worth. In all our long comradeship, I never remember him being ruffled: I can recall no angry word, no unselfish act. There was no parade about him – indeed words did not come easily to him – but one knew and felt that in any time of difficulty he was always there – a loyal friend on whom one could rely with perfect confidence.

It can in truth be said of him that he shouldered the burdens of many another, and bore them without complaint. I need scarcely add that he threw himself wholeheartedly into his work at Ludgrove, and won the respect and affection of the boys whose welfare and best interests were seldom far from his thoughts. It is inexpressibly sad that a life such as his should have come to so sudden a close. But though he has passed to the Great Beyond, I am certain that his influence will long abide and be an inspiration to all those who were privileged to have been under his care. They can pay no better tribute to his memory than by determining to follow the example of their friend and master in becoming the upright Christian gentlemen that he was himself.

Two years later, in 1936, a permanent memorial to this great Ludgrovian was established on the cricket ground, with the following inscription :

This score-board continued to operate at Ludgrove until it was replaced at the new site in Wokingham in 1980.

The passing of 'Bunco'

Later in 1934, after 11 years of retirement, the death was announced of Arthur Neville ('Bunco') Brown, who had retired in 1923. His friend and colleague Willie Blore wrote a full appreciation of his work as a schoolmaster and astronomer-extraordinary, and his name lives on in the annals of the British Astronomical Association as one of the leading amateur British astronomers during the first half of the 20th century.

Willie Blore, 1935

The spring of 1935 saw the retirement of Mr Blore (known universally as 'Bluff') to become Librarian at Canterbury Cathedral – he of the kindly spirit and calligraphic credentials so admired by Roland Pym. Blore had joined the staff in 1900, the same year as Walter Stanbrough, obedient to Arthur Dunn's injunction "to be punctual for early school and breakfast on Sundays" and was the last survivor of the original quintet of Smith, Oakley, Brown, Stanbrough and Blore who had been recruited by Arthur Dunn and who each served the school continuously for 30 years or more. Frank Henley wrote:

> For 35 years Mr Blore has been such a part of Ludgrove that somehow we cannot realise that we shall not find him with us next term. To use the word "find" seems hardly appropriate, for Mr Blore has never had to be found. We have always known exactly where he would be, and what he would be doing at any hour of the day, even when he was not in school – whether walking in the yard before breakfast, giving out library books during tea, playing the hymns at evening prayers, or presiding at the organ in Church on Sundays. For all these years he has never failed to carry out his duties in obedience to the strictest demands of conscience, while the many examples of his illuminated lists placed about the school bear ample testimony to his devotion to Ludgrove and her sons.
>
> We wish our old friend every happiness in his new home in Canterbury. We shall sadly miss the Peddars' Way which he has trodden by the side of the football ground, but we shall like to picture him treading the pilgrims' path in his own city, beneath the shadow of the cathedral that he loves so well.

THE HENLEY YEARS – 1934 TO 1937 – A TIME OF CHANGE

With Oakley's departure, Frank Henley now took over sole command as Headmaster of Ludgrove. The flavour of the school in those days is well captured by Bruce Spicer who went there two years later:-

I was told by my parents that I would be going to school at Ludgrove for the summer term. There was no entrance examination or interview, and the only qualification was a visit to the school tailor – Messrs, Stimpson in Hanover Square – to be fitted for a tweed knickerbockers 3-piece suit, which was the normal daily wear at Ludgrove in 1936, and a smart blue suit with long trousers for Sundays. No longer would I don the grey flannel shorts worn in 1936 by most 9-year olds.

Recollections of my first term were

PETER ROBINSON

BOYS' COMPLETE
SCHOOL OUTFITS

Catalogue of Youths' and Boys' Clothes sent on request
PETER ROBINSON, LTD.   Oxford Street and Regent Street, W.1.

The old carpentry shop

mostly connected with dormitories! Firstly, being nightly taken down a peg by the older boys, and then spending several weeks in bed with measles, chicken pox and German measles in quick succession.

For me, the most important person in the school at Cockfosters was a retired torpedo-man from the Royal Navy who ran the carpenter's shop. The first task by anyone taking carpentry as an extra was to make a wooden tuck box 24" x 17" x 11". He must have been a good instructor, because my box still survives! The carpenter's shop was also home for a large number of spiders, much to the horror of a member of the Royal Family who was terrified of them.

On Sundays we walked to the local church in a long crocodile. It wasn't until later in life that I appreciated how exceptionally well Frank Henley could read a lesson. If it was fine we would walk back for lunch via the grounds of Trent Park, Sir Philip Sassoon's residence resplendent with all the daffodils out in the spring. No games were allowed on Sundays. The afternoon was spent writing the weekly letter home, and Mrs Henley read to us in the evenings.

"…a smart blue suit wth long trousers for Sundays."

Out of work, 1931

The clouds gather

But darker days now beset the school and threatened its future. The early years of the 1930s had been the time of the Great Depression: after the Great Crash on Wall Street on 29th October 1929, fortunes were lost, the world markets for British goods dwindled, the economy contracted, unemployment in England soared to over 3 million and there were many ready to believe that the traditional economic order had broken down. At the same time the birth rate in England and Wales was declining dramatically: between 1915 and 1935 the number of births fell by over a quarter, from 815,000 per annum to just under 600,000, with the inevitable impact on the forward order-books of all schools.

At the same time the uncertainties of the international situation were growing: as early as May 1932 Winston Churchill gave his first formal warning to the House of Commons of approaching war in what he called "the darkening scene".

Confidence was the biggest victim, and people everywhere began to pull in their horns. The Preparatory Schools Year Book for 1934 noted glumly:

> Many prep schools are now lower in numbers than they have been for many years, and some – whose position a few years ago seemed impregnable – have closed down altogether.

In fact, between 1930 and 1940 no fewer than 185 preparatory schools throughout the UK either went out of business or amalgamated, succumbing to the same pressures that were bearing down on Ludgrove. The casualties included several schools in North London which Ludgrove had played against for many years, such as Bengeo, the Grange at Cockfosters and South Lodge at Enfield Chase.

As far as Ludgrove itself was concerned, another adverse factor had arisen to add to these wider difficulties: the rural setting of the school – probably its greatest single asset – was threatened by the arrival of the Piccadilly Line in July 1933, which terminated at Cockfosters.

Cockfosters station, northern terminus of the Picadilly Line, 1933

The school was now no longer a haven of peace within 20 miles of London: it had become part of the metropolis. People were now spilling out from the new station into Games Road and Hadley Wood, surrounding the school with urban bustle and changing for ever the rustic beauty and tranquillity of the original setting. Parents now wanted to send their sons to boarding school in the country (there was a great increase at this time in the number of prep schools located near the sea), and away from Greater London, whose spread had turned Ludgrove into a suburban establishment.

Ludgrove's appeal was now noticeably waning. Although few boys were withdrawn, the forward 'order-book' began to shorten, and its numbers contracted dramatically. In the summer of 1929. The number of boys in the school had peaked at 67; the following year there were 64; in the Michaelmas term of 1932 they were down to 58; 1933 saw a further fall to 52; and in 1934 there were no more than 47. Within five short years, Ludgrove had lost nearly a third of its pupil roll.

At the same time three of the five most respected and longest-serving members of staff – Oakley, Brown and Blore – on whose foundations the whole reputation of Ludgrove had been nurtured for a third of a century, had all gone in the space of a year. Stanbrough and Bowmar-Porter, (the drawing master) were to follow shortly; while the retirement of Frank Henley himself was only two years away.

One of history's timeless lessons is that survival is not mandatory. There was nothing pre-ordained about the survival of Ludgrove in the early 1930s. In the summer of 1934, as Bill Oakley passed the mantle to Frank Henley, Ludgrove stood at the crossroads of change and oblivion.

It is the highest tribute to those at the helm during this testing time that Ludgrove did not follow so many of its contemporaries into the pages of history. It is at such times as these that the strength of leaders is tested, and true character asserts itself. Ludgrove's leaders determined on change, the most radical since the foundation, evoking the spirit of the Aeneid, which the shade of Arthur Dunn would unquestionably have endorsed :

Hos successus alit: possunt, quia posse videntur
(These men are nourished by success: they can, because it is seen that they can) – Virgil

THE TAKEOVER

The change they now planned was the most far-reaching since the foundation. Frank Henley was to retire in 1937. It was agreed that Alan Barber and Tim Shaw would jointly succeed him; and that Ludgrove must move away from Barnet, with its now crowded woods encircled by bustling suburban life, and depart elsewhere to recapture the rural

Wixenford school, circa 1930

character of the original foundation while remaining within easy reach of London, which had always been its main constituency. In the choice of her leaders, in the timing of the succession and through the new location they found, Ludgrove's future was secured.

The search for a suitable site continued for over three years. During that time Alan and Tim looked at many possible partners and numerous alternative sites. They were not short of options: as we have seen, many preparatory schools were succumbing to the same pressures that assailed Ludgrove at that time. In due course Alan and Tim heard on the grapevine that Wixenford, a prep school in Wokingham, Berkshire, was looking for an amalgamation. Wixenford had been founded by Robert Arnold in 1889. It had been purpose-built as a school, and was equipped with fives and squash courts, an indoor swimming pool, a chapel, magnificent gardens, and playing-fields which included a 9-hole golf course. Indeed around the turn of the century none other than the great W.G.Grace himself had visited Wixenford to play a round of golf on the school course. Its location in

W.G.— the golfer

Even the great W.G.Grace played golf at Wixenford

the Berkshire countryside within easy road and rail distance of London was ideal; and it was leased from the estate of Lord Downshire, which meant that no capital outlay would be involved in taking it over.

Wixenford seems to have had sterner origins than Ludgrove. A letter from one of its old boys, Sir Harry Verney, written to the Headmaster of Ludgrove in 1955, hints at a world of fear and misery in its early days:

> I was at Wixenford from 1890 to 1895…..I am sorry not to have sent my sons –
> 5 of them – to Wixenford; but my terror of the then Headmaster, which still
> survives though I am over 70, made it difficult…"

N.E.F. Dalrymple-Hamilton as a Commander RN in 1958

In the past Wixenford had had a strong reputation. Among its famous Old Boys were Kenneth Clark (later Lord Clark of 'Civilisation'); Willie Whitelaw (later Lord Whitelaw, Deputy Prime Minister under Margaret Thatcher); and Michael Palliser (later Sir Michael, Head of the Diplomatic Service in the 1980s). Its list of Old Boys abounds with names familiar to future generations of Ludgrovians: Benton-Jones, Bonham-Carter, Cayzer, Clive, Dunkels, Gurney, Heber-Percy, Herbert, Moore, Lambton, Stopford and many others. But by the early 1930's the school had fallen into decline. It was beset by the same pressures as Ludgrove, only more so. In the summer of 1931 there were 65 boys, the normal number for a private school in those days. But the numbers began to dwindle rapidly: twelve boys left that July and only three new boys came in September. By 1934 the numbers were down to 26 and the school was hard pressed even to raise sides for school matches, let alone win any. One of its old boys, Capt. North Dalrymple-Hamilton, R.N., reflected on its deterioration during his time there:

H.T.Wallis, joint headmaster of Wixenford

> I have often wondered what caused Wixenford to go into
> terminal decline, and I conclude that – in addition to
> not reducing its fees in the early 1930's like most other
> prep schools of the time (at that time they were about
> £80 a term) – it must mainly have been due to bad and
> old fashioned management. The school was owned by
> three partners, Mansfield, Garnet and Wallis. Garnet was
> an elderly, shadowy figure who made no impression on
> the boys. Wallis took some part in school activities, but
> the only things I remember about him was that he had

The Rev. Charles Mansfield as Mayor of Wokingham

an old and smelly terrier called Spot which was not averse to taking a nip at boys' legs; and that he used to do the Times crossword while umpiring at cricket, thereby producing some strange and unjust decisions.

The Rev. Charles Mansfield himself was a formidable figure, usually dressed in a dog-collar and dark suit. He had a pronounced beak-like nose and was known as "Punch" by the boys. He ran the school on very autocratic lines and was over-keen on corporal punishment. This he administered with seeming relish with a fives bat, a short-handled wooden weapon which was used in the old days to play fives at Rugby. This was kept on top of the book-case in his study, and I well remember the sinking feeling when he reached up to get it down while ordering me to bend over a chair. When applied to the backside it made a formidable crack and had a considerable sting though, unlike the cane at Eton, it made no interesting stripes to display to one's favoured friends afterwards. Although we had a certain respect for Mansfield he did not inspire affection, unlike his second in command Captain Reed…. I suspect that it was largely due to Reed that the sinking ship was kept afloat for as long as it was.

Mansfield had also been Mayor of Wokingham, and probably paid rather more attention to his civic duties than to running his school. In 1934 he retired and his place was taken by a Mr. Greig, in partnership with Wallis and Reed. But by 1935 its numbers had fallen to below 20, and the writing was on the wall.

Alan and Tim made their first approach in 1935 through an intermediary, Alfred Peard, whom they had both known as a boy at Shrewsbury, and who was, by this time, a respected solicitor. He was asked to contact the Headmaster of Wixenford as the representative of "a possible purchaser". Wixenford's response was cautious: whoever was expressing an interest, they wanted an amalgamation, a merger between equals – the last thing that Alan and Tim had in mind. Wixenford also asked for payment of a considerable sum to represent 'goodwill', though with only a score of boys in a school of that size the would-be purchasers could see no reason for paying any consideration at all for goodwill. However, Alan and Tim were prepared to bide their time to get the right deal, and negotiations were 'parked' for a year, while Wixenford's numbers declined still further to a mere dozen. A second approach was made in 1936, and after lengthy discussions the deal was done. Wixenford would close, one master only – C.G. Reed – would be taken on from the former school staff, and four Wixenford boys – Peter Walmsley, John Reed (a nephew of CGR) and two Houston brothers – would be accepted at the new Ludgrove. The lease was re-negotiated with the Marquess of Downshire's estate at £700 per annum; and the move was planned during the summer holidays of 1937.

Last days at Barnet

While these negotiations were under way, school life at Barnet continued unaffected. The records of triumphs and disasters in the School Notes revealed a different style of writing; new hands were at work There is little doubt that the same determination with which Alan Barber had led Yorkshire C.C. in 1930 was behind the following strictures to the Ludgrove Cricket XI in 1935:

> It must be remembered that Cricket is a difficult game to play well, and if Trouble or Thought are in the least neglected the penalty has to be paid…

The staff was also being re-shaped into a new nucleus of masters who became dedicated and long-serving servants of the school. Two new masters joined in the summer term of 1935: Alan ('Bungy') Ellis, educated at Shrewsbury, where he had been Head of School and a member of the cricket and football XIs, and later a

Alan "Bungy" Ellis   *F.V. Selfe*

scholar of Keble College, Oxford; and F.V. Selfe, a former scholar of Magdalene College, Cambridge, who had himself been headmaster of another prep school, Sandroyd. These two, with a year or two's break in the case of Mr Selfe, were to be on the Ludgrove staff for almost 20 years.

Marriage: ATB and Dorothy Shaw

In the Spring of 1937, just before the move, there took place an event which was to have huge consequences for the whole future history of Ludgrove – the marriage of Alan Barber and Dorothy Shaw. Dorothy was Tim Shaw's sister and Bill Oakley's niece, and she and Alan had first met in the 1920s during Oxford days, when Alan was 'a dry bob' and Dorothy a supporter of 'wet bob' Tim, then President of Boats. Their friendship developed later on the

Tim Shaw (far left) with his brothers and sisters in 1915. Dorothy is second from the right. The others are Mary, John (centre) and Robert.

127

Alan proposed to Dorothy in this Singer tourer

tennis court near Dorothy's house in Shropshire, where Alan went during the holidays while he was tutoring the son of a nearby family, and they had also played together in a two-club golf competition in Shropshire. Subsequently Dorothy was a frequent visitor to Ludgrove to see her uncle, brother and Alan.

They were married on 6th April 1937 in Christ Church, Cockfosters, which Ludgrove boys had attended for over 40 years. The School Notes record Ludgrove's "good wishes for every possible happiness and success". How amply were these sentiments fulfilled down the years! The story of Ludgrove was to be principally determined for the next 70 years and beyond by the happiness of their marriage, their influence on the school's character, and the legacy of

Alan and Dorothy Barber's wedding in April 1937

their family. The partnership of Tim, Alan and Dorothy was to shape Ludgrove's fame and fortune for the middle decades of the 20th century in as lasting a way as the legacies of Arthur Dunn, G.O. Smith, Bill Oakley and Frank Henley.

Retirement of Frank Henley, 1937

Frank and Margaret Henley retired as planned, just before the move, in the Spring term of 1937. Frank had come to Ludgrove in 1905, and had been at the School for 32 years, for 11 of them as Joint Headmaster, and three as sole Headmaster. His had been a towering contribution to the School and among his many achievements, none was more important than securing Ludgrove's future by ensuring that his succession was in the most capable hands possible. Willie Blore wrote this appreciation of all that he had done, capturing so well the 'atmosphere' which through all the school's long history has always been one of its most important if least definable assets:

Frank Henley and his wife Margaret, 1935

> Few schoolmasters can have been so fortunate as to have worked at Ludgrove for 35 years, and to have served under four headmasters like Arthur Dunn, G.O. Smith, William Oakley and Frank Henley. To be on the staff of Ludgrove was to be a member of a true 'Band of Brothers', and to enjoy a wonderful comradeship with masters and boys alike. [...]With the retirement of Frank Henley from Ludgrove, there goes the last of the old band, and Ludgrove will, in a sense, be beginning a new epoch in its history.
>
> Of Frank Henley, one can say that he fully proved himself a worthy successor of his three predecessors; and this was, I think, largely due to the fact that he was imbued with a deep devotion to Ludgrove, an intense pride in its achievements in the past, and a determination to leave nothing undone to maintain its reputation.

The Move

The last term at Cockfosters was an emotional one. Everything was being done there "for the last time". The School Notes recall that

> the Summer term of 1937 will naturally be remembered as our last season at Cockfosters, and it is with very great regret that we bid farewell to our beautiful ground and its perfect wicket.

The batting averages of that last season were led by A.R.D. Pilkington and the bowling by A.K.R. Stroyan. And at the end of the record appears this note:

> It is sad indeed to be leaving the old Ludgrove. But let us think rather of the beautiful spot to which we are going, and remember that it is the buildings only which will be different. We intend to preserve all that has been for years so precious to Ludgrove and her sons – the name, the customs, the traditions, and even the atmosphere.
>
> The move will be no light task, but we expect everything to be ready and in place by September 22nd.

The move was indeed no light task. It took place during the summer holidays, in a dozen huge pantechnicons. But it was not a task in which Alan himself took any part.

He had been invited by the Countess of Harewood (the Princess Royal) to go to Harewood House in the summer holidays, to tutor the young George and Gerald Lascelles during a visit by Queen Mary (the Countess' mother) to Harewood – and Dorothy recalls that "He didn't say no! I was so angry!"

On delivery, the Ludgrove furniture was piled high alongside the Wixenford furniture they had inherited. The Headmasters sorted it all out, the gardens were spruced up, the lawns mown, and before the beginning of the autumn term, in a still empty drawing-room, Alan, Dorothy and Tim gave their first cocktail party to the staff and parents to inaugurate the new era. It was the first example of the legendary hospitality at the new site – a feature which subsequent Ludgrovians have always considered to be so integral to the family atmosphere in that happy house and school.

Alan arrived just in time to supervise the unloading at Wixenford!

What else was happening in 1937?

Above: Sir Oswald Mosley's fascists caused riots in Bermondsey.

Left: May 1937 saw the coronation of George VI. He succeeded his brother Edward, who had abdicated in order to marry Mrs Wallis Simpson.

Prime Minister Baldwin resigned in favour of Neville Chamberlain; but the appeaser was soon being savaged by Churchill, Boothby and other opponents of Nazism.

Billy Butlin opened his first holiday-camp.

Walt Disney's Snow White and the Seven Dwarfs was released in the US. It was not immediately shown in Britain because the Censor considered the 'apple of death' too horrific.

Nuclear fission was a hot topic, but science would not be taught at Ludgrove for another 28 years.

"I'm not sure, Sir, but I **believe** I've split the atom."

Chapter VI

A NEW BEGINNING
1937–1950

"We haven't got enough Barbers, Mrs Hymnbooks!"

Tommy Pilkington

The new site to which Ludgrove moved in 1937, set deep in the heart of the Berkshire countryside, has a calm and beauty all its own. The visitor approaches the school from Wokingham down half a mile of a narrow lane on the outskirts of the town. After the railway bridge, the low outline of almshouses appears with its familiar small roof tower and weather vane: this is the Lucas Hospital, Wokingham's only Grade 1 listed building.

This beautiful building dates from 1665. One Henry Lucas (1580–1663) left a legacy of £7000 to acquire 30 acres of land and build a home for 16 "brethren of limited

The Lucas Hospital, built in 1665 for 'brethren of limited means"

"…a magnificent expanse of lawn…" Ludgrove, Wokingham, in the 1930s

means" and "of good conversation" (ie. behaviour). Although called a 'hospital', it has always been a place of 'hospitality' rather than of medicine. It is considered to be one of England's finest examples of almshouse design, and to have set the pattern for almshouse development, which was to spread throughout the country in the 17th and 18th centuries. Today the building has been converted into a private house.

As you pass it, the games fields of Ludgrove now become visible in the distance; a turn off the lane and a sweep of gravelled drive bring you to the school, facing a magnificent expanse of lawn encircled by trees.

The late Victorian building is clad with wisteria and ivy and its russet-bricked and half-timbered façade, triple gables and high, pointed doorway giving it more the feeling of a country house than a school. On entering, you are greeted in the hall by the bark of spaniels – one of Ludgrove's most recognisable sounds, heard there since the first day of the school's new occupants – and you walk through into the fine, large, welcoming drawing-room.

Through its picture-window you see the garden stretching away across lawns, flower beds, borders and rockeries, to the wide, dense

"…you are greeted by the bark of spaniels…"

Painting of the rock-garden created by ATB

ring of pines, firs and spruces which encloses it all. It is a peaceful, secluded scene of rural beauty.

The facilities inherited from Wixenford by the new incumbents were among the most complete of any preparatory school in England. Unlike most of these, Wixenford had been purpose-built as a school. The main building, housing classrooms, dormitories and dining-hall, was set in the middle of 130 acres of grounds, containing three cricket fields, a nine-hole golf-course, a grass tennis-court, several football-pitches, a chapel, two of the best Eton fives-courts in the country, a wooden-walled squash-court, upper and lower yards for 'stump' cricket and six-a-side football, and an indoor heated swimming-pool, all laid out and built to the original design of the school in the late 19th century. Wixenford also owned a small farm, run in conjunction with the school, and supplying much of its meat, milk and vegetables for many years.

The Chapel is a feature of particular importance to Ludgrove. It is a simple all-wooden building at the back of the school, between the fives-courts and playing-fields. Originally thatched, it now has a shingled roof, and a little path leads up to the porch flanked by neatly-mown lawns and beds of roses and wallflowers.

As one enters the west door here are reproductions on each side of four famous paintings. The one by Sir Frank Dicksee, dominating the entrance entitled *The Two*

The thatch-roofed chapel in the 1930s

The chapel's interior has changed little since it was built

Crowns, shows a medieval king in golden crown and armour on a white charger returning home in triumph to the cheers of the people, and looking up towards the Crucifix where another crown, one of thorns, sits upon Christ's head – a famous Victorian allegory of sacred and temporal glory.

In all, the Chapel contains fifteen well-known reproductions, including a large one of Da Vinci's *Last Supper*. Throughout the building, the Wixenford origins have been carefully preserved, and the memorials of the two schools are everywhere to be seen side by side. The fine east window, containing six scenes from the Old and New Testaments painted on the glass by Leonard Pownall in 1904, is a testament to a Wixenford tragedy with its inscription:

To the Glory of God and in loving memory of Sheldon Douglas Wardrop Smithson,
born April 1893, died June 1905 –
This window was dedicated by his sorrowing parents

Above: *The East Window, by Leonard Pownall, 1904.*
Right: *The Two Crowns, by Sir Frank Dicksee R.A. The original hangs in the Tate Gallery.*

The chapel organ, replaced in 1986, was given to Wixenford in memory of her old boys killed in the First World War. Three Rolls of Honour hang on the south wall:
- Wixenford 1914–18, with 64 names, including two masters
- Ludgrove 1914–18, with 65 names in Walter Stanbrough's impeccable calligraphy and underneath the inscription *"Scribantur haec in generatione altera et populus qui creabitur laudabit dominum"* (*"Let these things be written for the next generation and the people who will be created will praise the Lord"*)
- Ludgrove 1939–45, with 48 names (see Appendix 6).

On the south wall behind the Headmaster's chair is a brass plaque commemorating Arthur Dunn, G.O. Smith and W.J. Oakley, and another for F.A.H. Henley. Behind the fine carved wooden eagle lectern bearing a Bible donated by Timothy and James Ward in 1964, another plaque commemorates A.T. Barber and T.W. Shaw. On the north wall a bronze tablet reads:

> *Robert Francis Villiers Wheeler, for 34 years assistant master at Wixenford.*
> *Born 1859, died 1924. The Altar in this Chapel was given by his sister.*

Next to it is another Wixenford tablet further commemorating the same boy to whom the East Window is dedicated:

> *Douglas Smithson, Born 1893 Died 1905. This tablet is erected by his schoolfellows.*

The pews give a possible clue to the date of the building itself, since each one bears the carved initials of its donor, with dates from 1925 to 1932. The front two were donated by the Princes Richard of Hesse (1930) and Valdemar of Hesse (1932), great grandsons of Queen Victoria through her second daughter Princess Alice, who had married Grand-Duke Louis of Hesse-Darmstadt.

The Chapel is the physical and spiritual heart of the school. For Old Ludgrovians it is remembered as a place of calm and peace. To enter it again is to conjure up long-forgotten associations: of hymns and psalms sung to the sound of the organ (hand-pumped until the 1960s by a boy ensconced in a cubby-hole behind it), of Alan's intonation as he led the prayers, of Dorothy leading the singing, and even one or two vaguely remembered sermons. One of the most eloquent of all Ludgrove's preachers in modern times was the Rev. John Eddison, who preached in Chapel over 90 times, telling his unforgettable parables about "Heart Castle" with its gallery of characters such as the determined Will Power, the ever-complaining Ivor Grudge and the dreaded Annie Mosity. And where

Ludgrove's visiting preacher, the Rev. John Eddison

today but in the Ludgrove Chapel can one still hear the magnificent General Thanksgiving, or John Eddison's Prayer for Cheerfulness?

> O Lord, inspire us to be cheerful, and to look whenever possible on the bright side of life…Drive from us every sullen and gloomy mood, give us grateful and uncomplaining hearts, and lead us ever forward in the sunshine of your presence.

The New Leadership

One of the keys to Ludgrove's success is that it has largely been run by men who have grown up with it and have committed their entire working lives to its cause. Four men had governed Ludgrove in the 45 years between its foundation in 1892 and the move to Wokingham in 1937. Now taking Ludgrove into its new era, Tim Shaw and Alan Barber were to direct its fortunes as joint Headmasters for the next 30 years. Together, they consolidated the move, recovered the momentum of former years, saw the school once more through the turbulence and trauma of war and built up its numbers and reputation to new heights.

Tim Shaw (TWS)

Tim Shaw was born near Shrewsbury on 27th April 1905 and educated at Dunchurch Hall, Rugby (where his uncle Charles Oakley was Second Master), and Shrewsbury. There he was Captain of Boats, and in 1924 rowed in one of the greatest Shrewsbury VIIIs of all time, winning the Ladies' Plate at Henley. The press wrote in ecstatic terms:

> Shrewsbury had the finest school crew seen at Henley for years. They were the first school other than Eton to have won the Ladies' Plate, and would undoubtedly have won the Grand Challenge Cup had they entered it…

Tim Shaw, Joint Headmaster 1937–68

and at Shrewsbury the great victory was celebrated in verse:

> *When to Henley we go,*
> *Where the rowing you know*
> *Of superlative premier grade is,*
> *It is hard to keep cool*
> *When a school's matched with school,*
> *That's the one race that counts as the Ladies'.*
> *What a crowd on the crafts,*
> *Punts, canoes, barges, rafts,*
> *And the launch you could not get a seat on;*

Whilst I'm told that the cheer
Reached from Henley to here,
For the winners – the winners weren't Eton!

Roars! Roars! Of stentorian applause,
Raise in honour of Shrewsbury's crews;
Unexampled the speed
Of the Chatterton breed,
Leaving Eton all wrapped in their Blues!
From 'A Song of Shrewsbury', 1926, by F.T. Prior, a master at the school

From Shrewsbury Tim went to Christ Church, Oxford, where he won rowing Blues in three of his four years. A newspaper report of the 1926 Boat Race described him as "the best man in the crew", and went on to say: "No-one rowed his stroke so well as T.W. Shaw at 2". In 1928 he was elected President of the OUBC, where his enthusiasm and leadership gained him much affection and respect. A light-hearted article about the 1928 Oxford Crew said:

> Tim Shaw is a man of ready laughter and a vast repertory of stories: little wonder that he is so popular at the House [i.e. Christ Church]. When he feels thoughtful, he goes fishing, and his brawny arms are well suited to illustrate the size of his catch. When he does not feel thoughtful he goes to watch horses running races. As the saying is, he is not above an occasional flutter – only, 'occasional' with Tim means fairly frequent!

and another, slightly racier reporter wrote:

> Girl undergraduates at Oxford have voted this year's Oxford Crew the best looking since the War, and the towpath is thronged with female admirers. Their first favourite is the President, Tim Shaw, who was once invited to 'star' in a film about undergraduate life.

Shrewsbury too celebrated the fact that in this year the Oxford and Cambridge Presidents of Boats were both Old Salopians:

Blues! Blues! Of the duplicate hues,
All the stars of the various Clubs
Bow at Oxford to Shaw, and at Cambridge adore
The Salopian President Tubbs.

While Tim was at Oxford his other schoolmaster uncle, Bill Oakley, suggested he come to teach at Ludgrove after Oxford, with a view to succeeding him within a few years; and Tim

"…the towpath thronged with female admirers…"

joined the staff of Ludgrove in 1928 where for many years he took form 6A for most subjects, and also ran the athletics and swimming. Having invited Alan Barber to join him on the staff there, they became Joint Assistant Headmasters of Ludgrove in 1934 and, after Frank Henley's retirement in 1937, they ran the school together until Tim's retirement in 1968.

In 1941 Tim volunteered to join the Royal Artillery, and after various home postings he served as a Captain in India and Ceylon for the last two years of the war before returning in 1945 to resume his duties at Ludgrove.

Tim was known universally as 'Sammy' to the boys, who recall his large, friendly figure in the classroom, or clad in wellingtons around the swimming pool and down on the farm, or striding down the corridor accompanied by his Yorkshire terrier 'Smudge', jangling his keys with the familiar cry, "Anybody want my Cupboard?" – a veritable 'wheelbarrow full of surprises' in which he stored and sold every sort of stationery item a schoolboy might require.

Like his uncle Bill Oakley, Tim was a powerfully-built, handsome man of about 6 foot 2 inches, as befits a world-class oarsman. One boy, recalling a discussion of his own schooling, said that his grandfather had advised: "Send the boy to Tim Shaw, you couldn't do better. He will be well taught, and he may even be steered towards the Boat Club at Eton!"

"No-one rowed his stroke as well as T.W. Shaw at 2." The Oxford crew in 1926.

Among his many talents, he was especially good with the very young: kind, re-assuring, always cheerful. Normile Baxter (who was to become one of the first Governors of Ludgrove) gives a marvellous testimony to this quality in recalling this great servant of Ludgrove:

> I was instinctively drawn to Tim Shaw from the moment I arrived. He was such a
> big man, not only physically big but mentally big too, and he always had time to

listen to you. He was very approachable, and would look at you or ask you something, which gave you confidence that he cared. When Tim Shaw spoke to me I don't think I ever left without thinking that I had tucked away something useful; and even if the full meaning hadn't been borne in on me because I was too young, it would dawn on me later that day, or as I grew older, how important what he said had been. He was always helpful and encouraging, never, ever destructive, and I thought the world of him. He was a fine looking man – I remember that my mother delighted in his presence, and I'm sure most other mothers did too. He was altogether a very attractive person, and I shall always remember him with admiration and great affection.

The words written of his uncle Bill Oakley were as true of Tim Shaw: "There was no parade about him …but one knew and felt that in any time of difficulty he was always there – a loyal friend on whom one could rely with perfect confidence…and he won the respect and affection of the boys whose welfare and best interests were seldom far from his thoughts."

Alan Barber (ATB)

Alan Theodore Barber was born on 17th June 1905, the second son of Harold and Winifred Barber of Todwick House near Sheffield, where his father was a chartered accountant in the firm of Jarvis Barber & Sons. Alan had a sunny, gregarious nature, combined with a stubborn competitiveness – even obstinacy – of character, and from his earliest days he showed a remarkable ability at games. He excelled at cricket, soccer, golf,

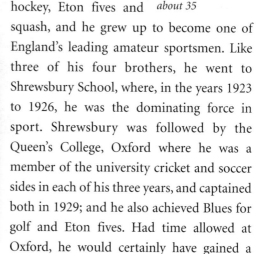

Alan Barber, aged about 35

hockey, Eton fives and squash, and he grew up to become one of England's leading amateur sportsmen. Like three of his four brothers, he went to Shrewsbury School, where, in the years 1923 to 1926, he was the dominating force in sport. Shrewsbury was followed by the Queen's College, Oxford where he was a member of the university cricket and soccer sides in each of his three years, and captained both in 1929; and he also achieved Blues for golf and Eton fives. Had time allowed at Oxford, he would certainly have gained a Blue for hockey as well.

Alan with his parents, when captaining Oxford's XI

As with Tim Shaw's Presidency of the OUBC, Shrewsbury too celebrated Alan's prowess – this time at football, where he played for Oxford alongside his great Salopian friend Philip Snow, who was to become the housemaster both of Alan's son Gerald and Nichol Marston at Eton 30 years later.

Mark! Mark! All the Blues light and dark,
And full well the Oxonians know
Their defence at the back can resist all attack
When they're guarded by Barber and Snow.

Subsequently Alan was a regular member of the great Corinthian soccer sides of the 1930s, whom he represented in the FA Cup, and he was selected as a reserve for England's amateur soccer side in 1933. At Eton Fives he became national champion, winning the sport's premier pairs trophy, the Kinnaird Cup, in 1934 and 1936, and – as one of the longest-serving Presidents of the Eton Fives Association – he donated its leading inter-club trophy, the Alan Barber Cup, in 1973. As a golfer he played for years in the annual President's Putter competition of the Oxford & Cambridge Golfing Societies at Rye off a handicap of 4. He and Frank Henley used to drive down to this event together.

He also played in many a victorious Salopian team in the Halford Hewitt (golf) and Arthur Dunn (football) Cups. He was President of the Arthur Dunn Cup for 20 years from 1963, and President, too, of the Oxford Harlequins Cricket Club. It was said that on the Ludgrove squash court he was unbeatable, and on its lawn-tennis court unplayable.

But it was at cricket that he achieved his greatest sporting fame. In 1929, his last year at Oxford, he was approached by Yorkshire County Cricket Club and invited to join the team as soon as he left university. He was then chosen to succeed Sir William Worsley (who had been at Ludgrove in 1900) as Yorkshire captain for the rest of the 1929 season, and for 1930.

In those days, most county cricket sides were captained by amateurs. Since the days of Lord Hawke, twenty years earlier, Yorkshire's captains of the 1920s were said – in a delightful euphemism of the time –

In 1930 A.T. Barber made 792 runs for Yorkshire

Alan captained Yorkshire when he was only 24

to have been "more well-intentioned than dominant"; and as a result the senior professionals had been allowed to assume control of the side. The Yorkshire XI at the time read almost like a Test side, since no fewer than nine of them had played for England: Herbert Sutcliffe and Percy Holmes opened the batting, followed by Maurice Leyland, Arthur Mitchell, George Macaulay, Emmott Robinson, Hedley Verity, Bill Bowes, Arthur Wood – and the senior professional, one of the world's greatest all-round cricketers, then in his last year as a player, Wilfred Rhodes. They were all veterans with immense knowledge and experience, men of typically Yorkshire character who had become used to having their own way.

Into this team of titans came Alan, fresh from university, aged 24, small of stature and armed only with his own cricketing talent, a relentless determination to win and – the first quality of a captain – the gift of natural authority.

That authority was soon put to the test: in his first Yorkshire match against Essex at Leytonstone, when Alan decided to bat on after lunch, one of the other Yorkshire players said "But, Skipper, Mr Rhodes has declared". Mr Rhodes found his 'decision' quickly reversed. In the second match, Rhodes challenged a change of bowler by the new captain: Alan replied "Wilfred, I know you were playing cricket for England before I was born – but *I* am the captain." After the game he sent Rhodes home, and telegraphed to the Yorkshire Secretary to send a replacement bowler from the ground staff at Headingley to play in the next match against Leicestershire at Hull. Rhodes never forgot it: he would refer to Alan Barber in later life as "'im who sent me 'ome". But the effect was electric. It was now clear to the Yorkshire side who was captain. Alan had gained the players' respect and established a rapport with them.

An example of Yorkshire's new, more competitive style under Alan occurred in the match against Derbyshire at Chesterfield, when the Yorkshire innings ended just before 6.15 pm on the first day. There was at that time an unwritten agreement amongst county captains that if an innings closed within 20 minutes of official close of play at 6.30 p.m., the captains would "call it a day" and draw stumps. As he came off the field, Guy Jackson of Derbyshire, one of the senior county captains of the day, said that he would see the

Alan opening for Yorkshire with Percy Holmes

Yorkshire team shortly in the bar; Alan replied that, with a 10 minute interval, 5 minutes' playing time remained from 6.25 pm, and that he would see the Derbyshire opening batsmen at the crease. Guy Jackson was not pleased – but Derbyshire's openers did duly appear, making 7 without loss. The new style manifested a new resolve to win. Yorkshire were third in the County Championship in 1929, and in 1930. That year the title was won by Lancashire, who were captained by Peter Eckersley. Later, Eckersley's sons Peter and Roger would follow distinguished careers both as pupils and governors of Ludgrove.

Alan's performance as captain and cricketer in that 1930 season aroused continuous praise from the press. At the crease he made 792 runs – more than any other Yorkshire captain for over a quarter of a century. He was also one of the most successful Yorkshire captains as a close fielder, taking 30 catches in the season and electrifying the crowd with his agility and courage. On one occasion he brilliantly caught the Australian captain, Woodfull, at close short-leg in the Bramall Lane match against that year's tourists.

Another time he was almost killed in the in-field by the Surrey captain, P.G.H. Fender, who struck a half-volley with full force into Alan's face from five or six yards. He probably owed his life to the fact that the ball struck the peak of his cap.

But it was for his captaincy that the plaudits really flowed. No captain in Yorkshire's history has so often declared the innings for victory. In the first eleven games of the season, he declared no less than nine times, and The *Yorkshire Post* wrote:

> He is one of the very few Yorkshire captains to realise that the very essence of true
> sport must be the hazard in it. He is prepared, through daring declarations, to risk
> defeat to win. And in his will-to-win spirit, he is always thinking of victory rather

than of first innings points. That attitude in a captain is what Yorkshire has not seen for many years.

Later in the season they were to write:

> Not many captains can have worked such a change in the teams under them in so short a time. A.T. Barber has led the side magnificently throughout the season, showing a keen insight into the technicalities of the game, a wise and far-seeing knowledge of tactics, a happy blend of disciplinarian and being a real friend to the professionals under him, and both the inclination and ability to take risks to win.

Towards the end of the 1930 season the England selectors approached Alan to ask if he would captain the MCC side due to tour the West Indies that winter. He would have dearly loved to accept the invitation: he told Bill Oakley that it was the chance of a lifetime. But by then his appointment at Ludgrove had been confirmed. Oakley could see that this was a cross-roads for Alan, and replied firmly that the time had now come to choose between a teaching career and cricket: he had already agreed to wait one term, but if Alan did not come in September 1930, then a replacement would have to be found. So with huge reluctance Alan chose his career. He declined Yorkshire's appeal to him to stay on as captain, turned down the MCC's invitation, and left forever the world of first-class cricket on which he made such a mark in so short a time.

On his departure, the Yorkshire team, in a unique display of affection, presented him with a silver salver inscribed with all their signatures; and George Macaulay said of him: "It is an irreparable loss to our side that our skipper cannot lead us for the next five years". Herbert Sutcliffe, one of the greatest of Yorkshire and England batsmen, later wrote the definitive judgment on Alan's captaincy of Yorkshire in his autobiography :

Herbert Sutcliffe with Alan

> A.T. Barber was a young man with a natural ability for leadership…I shall always have the keenest admiration for the manner in which he tackled his job when he joined Yorkshire in 1929. When he was compelled to leave county cricket at the end of the 1930 season, he was sorry; but his regret was no greater than that of the members of the Yorkshire side, for they knew they had lost a first-class captain. Indeed they felt that they had lost the lead of a man who, had he been able to devote himself to county cricket, would have qualified…for the captaincy of England. Barber…earned the respect

and comradeship of every member of the side. A great captain was A.T. Barber – one of those rare men with the power of inspiring confidence.

ATB and his cricket boys

ATB as Headmaster

Alan was about 5 foot 9 inches, a man of unsparing energy, a fierce determination, a boundless talent for making friends and (as he used to say) "keeping his friendships in good repair". And he had a mischievous sense of humour, crowned by a gift for laughter never forgotten by any who heard it.

The Fur Coat

ATB's sense of humour sometimes caught him out. Late one evening he was celebrating with colleagues in Piccadilly after an Arthur Dunn Cup final, and wearing a voluminous fur coat, bequeathed to him by an outsize uncle. It was patently a misfit, and as it happened, there had been a spate of fur coat thefts at the time. A police constable emerged from the shadows, stopped him and asked where he had obtained his coat. Alan, rather the worse for wear, replied "As a matter of fact, Officer, I've just pinched it from the Ritz!" The PC tried to arrest him, and a legend grew up about what happened next: Alan tripped over the vast garment in which he had become enmeshed; and the PC, surrounded by Alan's colleagues and fearing an attack, blew his whistle to summon aid, whereupon a muffled voice from within the furry mass on the ground was heard to call out "Was that half-time or a free kick?" The upshot was a night in the cooler for ATB, from which he was only with difficulty extracted by his friends early the next morning – fortunately before any scandal broke.

He had a rare talent for recounting a story and was the most generous dispenser of courtesy and hospitality to all. It was always fun to be with Alan – yet in his determination and will to win he was unrivalled.

At Ludgrove he was joint Headmaster with Tim Shaw for 30 years and sole Headmaster for five years after that. Inevitably known to the boys as 'Ali Babar', he was the principal figure of authority throughout this time. He ran Ludgrove very much as a reflection of his own personality, and promoted above all else the success of the School, for which every boy was brought up to be a standard-bearer. Generations of Ludgrove boys will remember his energetic and ubiquitous presence around the school; his immaculate appearance, always "on parade", surmounted by a succession of colourful and prominent club ties; his unmistakeable laugh punctuating his deliberate, easily-imitable speech, in sharp contrast to the energetic pace at which he ceaselessly walked around the school, encouraging, advising, "chivvying" boys with whom he came into contact. Then there was his copperplate handwriting, which filled the notice boards with teams, orders and awards; his passion for winning; the encouragement he would give especially the youngest boys, who so often surrounded him; and the importance he placed on good manners, a strong sense of duty and on everything that was straight, truthful and upright.

He was physically tough – he took a cold bath every day until very late in his life – and was intolerant of anything in the young that fell short of physical courage and endurance. He was not receptive to change, believing sincerely in the merit of tradition and of "how things have always been done"; he accepted but did nothing to encourage the artistic and musical life of the school; he enforced discipline by a not infrequent use of the cane; and he gave rather more emphasis to success on the games field than in the classroom – as long as he was satisfied that every boy was giving of his best in both.

In many of his qualities there are close parallels between A.T. Barber and A.T.B. Dunn, in addition to their uncanny similarity of initials. ATB probably had a tougher inner core than ATBD, and ATBD certainly had a much stronger cultural sense than ATB. But both were magnetic personalities with marvellous gifts for friendship, both capable of inspiring people, both small in stature but larger than life in heart, both sportsmen at the highest levels in the land, both leaders from the front, and both enjoyed the happiest of family lives. They shared an identical set of simple Christian values which they spared no effort to impart to the boys in their charge; and they both taught and upheld in their own lives standards of personal behaviour which, in the recollection of their pupils, were their abiding legacy to generations of Ludgrove boys.

A surviving note from Alan – addressed to one of his children – gives an insight into some of the simple truths he held:

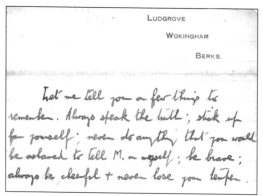

ATB's exhortation to his children

It is a real measure of the man that no one who knew him well would ever have known Alan himself depart from those simple precepts.

Dorothy Barber

Niece of Bill Oakley and sister of Tim Shaw, Dorothy had married Alan in 1937. Almost single-handedly she planned and managed the move to Wokingham. It was mainly during her visits with Matron to the sick bay that Dorothy came into the boys' lives, and of course in her readings to the whole school on Sunday evenings in the drawing-room. But to parents, staff and Old Ludgrovians she embodied all that they loved about the school, through her open and inclusive personality, the warmth of her welcome to every visitor, her instant recall of names, faces and interests, her encouragement to young and old alike, her unending interest in the doings of others, especially Old Boys, her ceaseless supply of laughter, and her constant communication with them about their sons' health and progress – all within the framework of the happy home and family which she made for Alan and their three children at Ludgrove.

On taking over with Alan in the last days at Cockfosters, somewhat fearful of the task ahead, she recalls a visit by Helen Dunn who told her: "Dorothy, there's just one thing I must tell you: always remember that the parents are your customers. Always treat them properly; you must forgive a lot".

It was advice that she valued at the time, and was never to forget.

To the Headmaster's wife falls the crucial responsibility for the domestic side of the school, the menus, the cleaning, the supplies, the staff and the health of the whole

Dorothy, Alan and their children Gerald, Joanna and Theodora

school. An insight into the way Dorothy handled this central role was given by a friend, Fiona Laws, whom Dorothy asked to run the dining-hall at Ludgrove during the war:

Dorothy was fondly known as 'the Duchess'.

> To work for Alan and Dorothy was a marvellous experience. They were both always the same, never perturbed by anything however alarming or irritating, and both so incredibly hard-working. In all the five years I worked for them I cannot recall a cross word. So much too was due to the marvellous Matron, Jane Ramsay, who ran her side of the show superbly, being a wonderful cook, first class at flower decoration, and also so good with her staff. We never stopped working from 6.30 a.m. to midnight. After the first three weeks I was so exhausted I thought I would die – but I stayed for five years and enjoyed every minute of it.

After the war the problem of finding domestic staff did not ease, and Dorothy turned to Spain and Portugal. Devoted and hard-working domestic staff were recruited there – and in one instance love blossomed when Bazyl, the Polish cleaner, married Paquita; today they live happily in Spain after a combined service of over 200 terms at Ludgrove, much of it under Dorothy's caring and committed guidance.

Dorothy was fondly known as 'the Duchess', and boys will remember her particularly for her famous readings on Sunday evenings; for the splendid lead she gave to the singing in Chapel; and for her accompaniment of the hymn-singing before prayers at night. She herself recalls Tommy Pilkington hastily putting out the hymn-books as the school filed into the Dining Room for prayers, and rushing up to her to blurt out: "We haven't got enough Barbers, Mrs Hymnbooks". The laughter with which she responded can surely still be heard by those who care to listen! She was a magnetic personality at the heart of Ludgrove, and loved by all with whom she came into contact over the years. One Old Ludgrovian speaks for all in describing Dorothy as "a serene and gentle lady", and her marvellous partnership with Alan guided Ludgrove for 36 years of total dedication until they retired in 1973 to the Garden Cottage by the Chapel Ground.

THE NEW START IN WOKINGHAM

As the school assembled for its first term on the new site in September of 1937, there were 64 boys in the school – 55 boys from Cockfosters, four from Wixenford and five new boys. From the boys' point of view the move was just another facet of school life. Bruce Spicer recalls that "the move from Cockfosters to Wokingham did not involve the boys at all. We just turned up at the new buildings formerly occupied by Wixenford School."

Gordon Reed, who joined from the Wixenford staff.

One master only, Gordon Reed, joined from the Wixenford staff. He had been one of its partners, and came to Cockfosters the term before the move. His memory still lives in the affections of boys who remember his gruff yet kindly guidance. He had been through the Great War, in which he had been severely deafened, and his complexion was florid because, it was rumoured, he had been gassed after handing his gas-mask to someone else and covering his face with his hands. To the boys, he was universally known as 'Cabbage' Reed, allegedly because his ears were 'fitted' flat against his head as opposed to the cauliflower variety. North Dalrymple-Hamilton recalls him at Wixenford with great affection:

> He was a bachelor, a dedicated schoolmaster and a charming man whose whole life was bound up in Wixenford. He knew exactly how to handle small boys and we would have done anything for him…

and Alexander Thynne (OL 1941–45, now the Marquess of Bath) speaks for many in writing:

> It always depended upon who was teaching me for me to obtain the best results: I felt an undoubted rapport with 'Cabbage' Reed, and always did well under his tuition.

The old generation of masters was now giving way to the new. Robin Milford, who was in charge of music, left Ludgrove in the Spring of 1938, "in order to devote more time to composing". Frank Henley wrote kindly of him:

> His was a retiring nature. He never asserted himself, and this was often reflected in his work, which had something very tender and human about it, though it could be forcible as well. It had moreover a distinctly individual character, his turn of phrase being like no one else's, and it often reached something very perfect.

As we have seen, his life after Ludgrove was to follow a progressively difficult and ultimately tragic course. He was succeeded by Mr E.R. Thompson.

Nurse Pattinson retired at the end of the Michaelmas term, after 15 years of strenuous work. She had looked after several generations of boys during their time at Ludgrove with unfailing care and kindness.

Nurse Pattinson looked after generations of Ludgrove boys.

INTO WAR ONCE AGAIN

War against Germany was declared on 3rd September 1939, which meant that the new team under Tim and Alan had had only two short years in which to settle into their new surroundings. Once again, as with the death of Wilfred Bird in the Great War, Ludgrove's staff was soon to suffer its first loss, Basil Beale, who was killed in an accident at the beginning of July 1940. He had joined Ludgrove in 1934 to teach Classics, English and French, and had said farewell only at the end of June to take a commission in the Royal Artillery. Sudden death is utterly remote from the world of the preparatory school, and the sense of shock was poignantly expressed in the words Tim Shaw wrote about him:

Basil Beale, Ludgrove's first casualty of the war

> During the six years that Basil was with us, he endeared himself with a very real affection to masters and boys alike. His kind and cheerful personality, combined with a strict sense of what was fair and for the good of Ludgrove, commanded a feeling of love and confidence among the boys he looked after and taught, and his keenness in helping with the games will always be remembered. We have lost a great friend, but our memory of him will live for all time.

Alan 'Bungy' Ellis joined the Navy in 1940

As the country plunged into war, the team which had been so carefully selected and built up began to disband in response to the higher call of King and Country. In 1940 Alan Ellis joined the Royal Navy, and the same year Miss Glover, the Matron, went off to nurse soldiers.

In the summer of 1941 Tim Shaw joined the Royal Artillery, and was later posted to India to face the Japanese threat; Mr. Head joined the Admiralty; and John Rickards, who had arrived from Eton and Oxford in 1939, left in the summer of 1940 to join the Coldstream Guards. Others were soon appointed to fill the gaps: John Rickards' place was taken by Lieut. Peter Hammond-Chambers-Borgnis R.N., who had been invalided out of the Navy with only one lung in 1938 after contracting tuberculosis. He was followed in the winter term of 1943 by K.B. Morrison, who was placed in charge of the top form for Classics. Miss Glover was succeeded as Matron in March 1943 by Miss Ramsay.

Tim Shaw served in the Royal Artillery

The most pressing issue was whether the school could remain in occupation of its premises. During the phoney war from September 1939 to June 1940, some three million children were evacuated to the country from London and other major cities, and some prep schools were requisitioned at short notice by the military authorities.

Some neighbours evacuate

Elstree's Headmaster, Ian Sanderson, was told that 160 officers and men of the Royal Horse Artillery were to be billeted on the school indefinitely: in just over two weeks the entire school had moved from Hertfordshire to its present location in Berkshire.

Heatherdown too was evacuated, to Downton Hall in Shropshire (now owned by the Wiggin family).

Ludgrove itself was within an ace of moving to McGill University in Canada, with whom all the arrangements had been set up, but the scheme was abandoned at the last minute because of problems of finance and transport. So Ludgrove would see the war through where it was. Like a number of other schools in the area, such as Woodcote House in Windlesham, Sunningdale, and St. George's at Windsor, Ludgrove stayed put. An air-raid shelter was dug below the yard where the present sports-hall is. It was an expensive undertaking, for which Alan had to raise the money through the school fees.

Dear

Owing to the menace of war, we have built a concrete air-raid shelter, which will house safely all our boys in an emergency. Although Ludgrove is admittedly in a comparatively safe area, we feel sure that parents will approve of this precautionary measure, + be willing to subscribe towards the large expenditure by paying one pound per term for one year. With your approval, I propose to add this to your account.

yrs sincerely

Alan's circular to parents, to raise funds for the air-raid shelter

As in the First World War, school life was relatively untouched by the conflict, apart, that is, from the shortage of masters, reduced heating, a restricted menu, the occasional sound of doodlebugs on their way to Reading – and the ubiquitous presence of Alan himself, wearing, at times when danger threatened, a helmet slightly too small for him and his uncle's famous fur coat, several times too large. On more than one occasion the Germans dropped incendiary-bombs, aiming unsuccessfully at the ammunition huts situated along the drive to the school. It should be noted that Ludgrove made several official representations to have these dangerous huts removed, hoping that the presence at the school of Nicholas Eden, son of the Foreign Secretary, Anthony Eden, would help. Surprisingly, it did not.

In the event, the air-raid shelter was only used twice in the whole war – once at the very beginning, shortly after Neville Chamberlain had made his fateful speech to the nation; and once when a Luftwaffe pilot unloaded his unused bombs on his way back from a raid on the Midlands.

A bomb falls on Wellington College

On the latter occasion Ludgrove was unscathed, but Wellington College took a direct hit, and the sole distressing casualty was the Headmaster, Robert Longdon. Ironically, he had just been round the school to see that everyone was in their shelters when a bomb fell on his house and he was killed.

Bruce Spicer (1939–43) captured the atmosphere at Ludgrove during the hot summer of 1940, as the Battle of Britain reached its climax in one of the most decisive moments of the War:

> The Battle of Britain stayed east of Berkshire, and no bombs were dropped on the playing fields. ATB was to be found most summer afternoons sitting on his shooting stick, complete with Free Foresters tie, umpiring one of several cricket matches in progress all over the playing fields.

The first reference to the war in Ludgrove's annals was the report of a handicraft exhibition in 1940 which, amidst the fretwork and model-making, mentioned (uniquely) "Knitting Prize: T.T.S. Gray, which included many squares which were joined together to make blankets for soldiers". This reveals a little-known fact: that in those days knitting was something everyone did. Normile Baxter remembers it well:

> It might make you laugh, but we knitted then for the war effort. My mother was Danish and she taught my sister and me to cook, to do housework, to sew and to knit, and many other useful things. So I learnt to knit the continental way, which is pretty fast. Anyway, we made scarves, squares and balaclavas, and you'd see boys wandering around the school knitting for the Forces. Because I went fast, my own scarf got longer and longer, and one day Alan Barber came up to me and said 'Baxter, what's that great bundle you're carrying under your arm?' I replied 'It's my scarf, Sir', and I proudly laid it out for him; it must have been about two yards

long. And he said 'Well, you've got to cast off' and I said 'Well, I don't know how to', and ATB said 'Oh, it's quite simple', whereupon he seized a pair of scissors and cut it in two!

What appears to be another mysterious reference to the war comes in the middle of 1942 when we read in the School Notes of "infection in enemy camps", raising the possibility that the German forces had been struck by an epidemic. But in fact it is only a reference to rival prep schools, always referred to in Ludgrove parlance as "the enemy".

Once again, as in the Great War, the sombre lists of Ludgrove's dead and wounded began to accumulate. Between April and July 1940 alone, no fewer than nine Old Ludgrovians perished in the carnage of Northern France. In all 48 Old Ludgrovians were to die in the Second World War, significantly fewer than in the Great War, in spite of the inauspicious start. However, just as the Great War had brought the deaths of the three Barrington-Kennetts, three brothers from one family, the Hamilton-Russells (cousins of the Earl of Harewood), were killed in World War Two. So too was Arthur Dunn's grandson John Boldero, tragically mirroring the death of his uncle Johnny 25 years earlier.

Arthur Dunn's grandson, John Boldero, was killed in the war

A scroll containing the names of Ludgrove's fallen was dedicated by the Dean of Windsor in the Ludgrove Chapel in 1948, when the lesson was read by Brigadier-General T.R. Pelly, "Ludgrovian Number One" from 1892 .

Ludgrovians served in all the theatres of the war. Lord Harewood, who as George Lascelles had left Ludgrove in 1936, recalls being taken prisoner and confined in Colditz where he was astonished to find himself in the company of no fewer than half a dozen fellow Old Ludgrovians, including Ken Sutherland and Archie Orr-Ewing. Again,

Colditz Castle, near Leipzig, and George Lascelles' PoW identity-card

stories of Ludgrovian heroism abound in the letters written to the school by bereaved parents and by the boys themselves, and they provide the drama behind the award to Old Ludgrovians throughout the war of fourteen DSO's, twenty-four MC's, three DFC's and three DSC's. One story alone will suffice; it comes from a letter written in November 1941 to Frank Henley:

Dear Henley,

In reply to your kind enquiry, I think I can claim that my three have lived up to the finest Ludgrove traditions.

Charles, in September of last year, was the hero of the epic adventure set out in the enclosed cutting…(See below). His adventures are rivalled by Michael's, who sailed in January 1940 to Palestine, was turned into an armoured unit and put on coastal defence in Crete. When our Army capitulated there on June 1st, Michael was made a prisoner, but after two days escaped with a brother officer, an Australian, a New Zealander and a Greek officer. After two months of hair-raising adventures, the Germans often searching the villages in which they were hiding, they secured a boat and reached the Greek islands and finally Turkey, and are now back in Jerusalem, though Michael is in hospital with a broken arm and a

damaged right eye and ear. He has been promoted Captain, and sends the most cheerful cables…

Godfrey is a Sub-Lieutenant in the R.N.V.R. in the Fleet Air Arm, and now flying in Orkney near Scapa Flow…

Yours very sincerely

A.W. Parish

Charles Parish at Ludgrove

The story in the cutting concerned his son, Charles Woodbine Parish.

He was born in 1915 and educated at Ludgrove and Eton. He was a fine swimmer; with his brother Michael he had swum across the Sound of Mull in 1932, a feat which legend said had last been done by a clansman in The Young Pretender's uprising in 1745. Being an outstanding swimmer was to save Parish's life in 1940 when he was among the crew who had to bale out of a Wellington bomber, when two were simultaneously shot down over the North Sea. Parish swam seven miles in five hours to reach the Suffolk coast, only to discover that he was the sole survivor of the two crews. In 1940 and 1941 he made 29 raids over Germany, and was invalided out after getting frost-bite in the foot over Bremen. However, after 18 months he became 'operational' again at his own request and, as captain of a Stirling bomber, joined Bomber Command's elite Pathfinder Force. He made 25 further sorties over Germany and Italy, but after his 54th raid he was limping home with one engine disabled when he was shot down by an enemy night-fighter and killed. His surviving Canadian engineer, who had been with him on 19 of those missions, wrote to his father:

> Words cannot express my praise for your son. He was a first class pilot, and a real skipper.

Stirling bomber, of the type flown by Charles Parish

Charles Parish was posthumously awarded the DFC in 1943. His citation states:

> Flight Lieut. Parish has attacked many targets in Germany and Italy. An exceptional pilot, he has always shown a calm precision in the face of heavy opposition. This officer, by his personal example, has contributed much to the high efficiency obtained by his crew.

Pathfinders

To Flight Lieut. C.W. Parish DFC, reported missing in April 1943, now presumed killed in action, and his crew

> Through the dark nights they flew, the flares they sowed,
> Lit up the targets for the rest to find.
> They are lost; but shall we falter with our load,
> Searching our targets? Though the night be blind
> Still their bright memory lights us on the road.
>
> Arundell Esdaile*

* Sometime Secretary of the British Museum and President of the Library Association

In Memoriam: Katherine Smith and G.O. Smith

The spring of 1941 saw the death of G.O.'s sister, Katherine. She had been the principal female influence at Ludgrove from the time of Arthur Dunn's death until 1922, and was always remembered by "her" boys with huge affection. Frank Henley wrote of her:

> All those Ludgrove boys who were privileged to have been under her care will have read of the passing of Miss K.E. Smith with a very real sorrow mingled with a sincere affection for one who devoted herself untiringly to them. She came to Ludgrove in 1902, when her brother G.O. Smith, together with W.J. Oakley and A.N. Brown, succeeded A.T.B. Dunn. For 20 years she made the welfare of Ludgrove her chief aim in life, never sparing herself in her thoughts for the

happiness and comfort of those around her. Her nature was always kind and sympathetic, and her unselfish character will ever remain imprinted in the minds of all who knew her.

Her beloved brother G.O. died two years later, in December 1943. After paying tribute to his famous century for Oxford against Cambridge in 1895, and to his matchless skill as one of the greatest of all English centre forwards, Frank Henley wrote:

> G.O. never sought popularity, but to every boy in his care he was a hero. He was modest in everything he did, scrupulously fair and a staunch friend at all times. He imbued everyone under him with the spirit of Ludgrove, which means so much to all of us who are or have been in any way connected with it....All of us who bear the proud name of Ludgrovian owe him a debt of gratitude which we shall never forget.

THE CHARACTER OF THE SCHOOL

The Barber-Shaw Partnership

Alan and Tim were very different in personality – Alan always visible, on the move, leading from the front; Tim calmer in temperament, wise in advice, working more behind the scenes. Neither was a born academic, though both had gallons of common sense and good judgment; they were both strong traditionalists, were extremely approachable, and they both had an easy manner when dealing with people. Although Tim was the 'senior partner', having brought Alan into an essentially family concern when his uncle Bill Oakley was Headmaster, it was decided that since Alan and Dorothy were already married when the move took place, they should live from the outset in the main school. Tim, as a bachelor, lived in the school until he married Peggy Aylwen in 1939 and moved to the East Lodge. After the war he lived in Wokingham, later moving to nearby Binfield.

As joint Headmasters, Alan and Tim agreed on a clear division of labour: Alan would run the daily life of the school, Tim would oversee the administrative and

The Ludgrove 'troika'!

financial side of things, and also manage the farm. While Tim was involved with the parents, especially at week-ends, it was sensible that the main responsibility for external relations would fall to Alan and Dorothy who lived "over the shop" and were therefore in a natural position of contact with all Ludgrove's main constituencies of parents, staff and suppliers. Alan and Tim both had desks in the Headmasters' study. They developed their roles in a way that was open and complementary, and both

Tim Shaw married Peggy in 1939

taught a variety of subjects: Alan taking Latin and Old & New Testament History, Tim teaching Mathematics and Swimming, and running the Library.

Paul Foot (1948–52) who was to become a well-known journalist, and founding editor of "Private Eye", recalled that Alan was the first person who told him that he could write well. "He taught us Old Testament History, and I remember writing an essay for him about Jonah and the Whale. He said 'I've had all your essays in and I'm going to read one of them out to you' and he read my essay out to the whole class. I remember thinking 'Why has he read this out?' But he had particularly liked some of the phrases I'd used like 'Jonah, not wanting to go,…', a participle that just came naturally to me, and when he'd finished he said 'If only some of you could write like that I'd be better pleased…' Even now, aged 66, I've never understood why I can write better than others. But Alan Barber was the first person who really suggested to me that I could".

Given the division of labour on which they decided, it is inevitable that the picture of Ludgrove under their leadership will be painted more from Alan's perspective than from Tim's, since to Alan fell the duties of day-to-day direction, discipline and development, including the Headmaster's report on each boy at the end of term. But this story should also be seen very much as Tim's too, with his guidance, commitment and administrative focus providing an invaluable counter-balance and foundation to the success that together they achieved at Ludgrove for over a third of a century.

"Out of the Mouths…"
Alan once included the following question in an Old Testament exam:
"Write down what you know about Lot."
A boy wrote in answer:
"Lot had many sheep. His wife was also a pillar of salt by day, and a ball of fire by night."

Unchanging routines

Throughout the time that Alan and Tim were Headmasters of Ludgrove the structure and state of the buildings was largely unchanged – very little capital investment was made throughout their reign – and in the same way the daily routines of school life also changed little. The pattern of a boy's progress through the school in 1940 would have been immediately recognisable to a boy of 1970. The focus on games of all sorts was emphatic throughout the period; other activities such as boxing, swimming, carpentry, the cultivation of boys' gardens and the Dramatic Society all featured for most boys in their weekly round. The arts, music and singing were secondary in the overall scheme of things; and while Common Entrance was always a key target, scholarships were not at a premium.

Work versus Games

The rather uneven balance between the classroom and the games field at Ludgrove is perfectly captured in the Headmaster's summer 1947 report on Christopher Bathurst, who won one of Ludgrove's rare scholarships to Eton that year, but in the same term

Classroom activities were often overshadowed…

narrowly failed to get into the cricket 1st XI. Alan's report began: "Christopher has had a disappointing term…"

It was an age when it seemed to be part of the natural order of things that boys would pass their Common Entrance into the school of their choice; so the emphasis on the games field, for the good of the boy and the reputation of Ludgrove, played to all the strengths in the school's armoury, with its delightful grounds, its athletic pedigree and the personality of the Headmaster *in situ* as one of England's most famous amateur sportsmen of the day.

But this bias did not always bring out the best in the boy who did not shine at games. Nothwithstanding some outstanding teachers like Ken Morrison, John Rickards and Peter Borgnis, the winning of scholarships was never one of Ludgrove's central aims during the Barber-Shaw years. On occasions Ludgrove's academic standards aroused more than merely

…by Ludgrove's athletic pedigree.

adverse comment: there was a time in the early 1950s when it was suspected that some Eton housemasters excluded Ludgrove from their preferred list of feeder prep-schools, since they felt that the Ludgrove boy was less than adequately prepared for life at Eton, especially in the classroom. But this was never an official proscription, and was only a temporary setback for a school from which over half of all leavers have always continued to go on to Eton.

Culture

There is no doubt that cultural studies were peripheral to Ludgrove's core curriculum. Alexander Thynne (now Marquess of Bath) is a highly talented musician and artist, but he wrote of Ludgrove's endeavours to address those skills:

> Tuition in both Music and Art was uninspired, and my ability in each of those fields stagnated [while I was there].

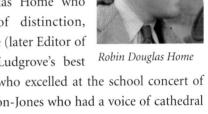

Robin Douglas Home

Artistic talent seldom gave a boy much advantage in his progress through the school, and it was rare indeed to come across a Ludgrovian singer, violinist or painter of note, notwithstanding the talent many boys had in these areas, such as Robin Douglas Home who became a painter of distinction, Charles Douglas Home (later Editor of *The Times*), one of Ludgrove's best pianists of the 1940s, who excelled at the school concert of 1949, and Simon Benton-Jones who had a voice of cathedral chorister quality and made a number or recordings.

Charles Douglas Home, former editor of The Times

After the last concert of the music master, E.R. Thompson, Alan wrote a farewell notice that unwittingly summed up the lack of credibility commanded by music at Ludgrove:

> It requires very special qualities to teach Music and Singing to boys…and to maintain over a period of years the understanding and goodwill of masters who naturally tend to disapprove of the 'would-be' musicians leaving the classroom to attend practice.

Thompson was succeeded by Michael Howard, another talented musician who was to make his name in the wider world of music after Ludgrove. But his blunt, even savage, approach to teaching music at Ludgrove was very much of the rigorous school, and as a teacher he enforced his view – sometimes painfully- that mistakes are offences which contribute little to learning. Accordingly he did little in his time at Ludgrove to enhance

Michael Howard, a music teacher of the rigorous school

boys' appreciation of a subject which, in any case, the culture of the school did not generally encourage. He subsequently became the Organist at Ely Cathedral, followed by many distinguished church music appointments, and it was written of him:

> When the definitive history of the British early music movement comes to be written, a survey of the immediate post-Second War decades would be seriously incomplete without a proper assessment of the work of conductor, organist, composer and teacher Michael Howard. (*The Musical Times*, 2002)

But his legacy at Ludgrove is not one that lent distinction to his name.

More popular than the concerts were the lectures and especially the films of that era. These provided magic moments of escape. Old Ludgrovians remember talks by the blind naval officer, Esmond Knight (later a film actor); and another by a diver dressed in full deep-sea kit complete with helmet, who talked about exploring the ocean depths. At one point he juggled a stick of gelignite from hand to hand and riveted the boys to their seats with the startling words: "I use this to blow my way into sunken ships – if I let it fall it will blow up everything from here to Wokingham". And many have said that the films shown then were among the most enjoyable they have ever seen: *We Dive at Dawn, In the Wake of the Red Witch, Henry the Fifth, The Black Arrow, Under the Red Robe, The Cardboard Cavalier, Bambi, Tom Brown's Schooldays, Goodbye Mr. Chips*, and many others. Richard Gooch (1950–55) still recalls his despair at being forbidden to attend a number of films because he was confined to Detention for having a bad Order Card.

Discipline

The Duke of Devonshire had described the tone of Ludgrove in the early 1930's as "discipline with a light touch". This would have been too lenient a phrase to describe the school during the Barber-Shaw years. While the Headmasters expected that everyone should know where the boundaries were fixed between right and wrong, Alan's cane was never far from sight, and a latent awareness of its presence was woven into the atmosphere of the School in those days. In fact, a number of old boys today believe that Alan overdid its use, though one OL said that "it was never the full wrist action", and many have also acknowledged that they probably "deserved it". It was undoubtedly a robust regime, and few boys came through their Ludgrove days during his reign without at least one memory of an evening visit to the study for summary chastisement.

Here again it must be emphasised that corporal punishment was very much 'of its time' then, both in prep schools and public schools, and there was a very real sense in which boys were expected to 'join the club' by receiving the dread summons while at Ludgrove, so that in tearful bravado they could show off their stripes afterwards. There was always a sound reason; boys always knew what it was for, and immediately afterwards the matter was forgotten – unless you were a persistent offender.

The Cascara Pills

One event, which would have incurred certain retribution if discovered, is recounted by Normile Baxter:

"Nicky Beaumont and I played a dreadful trick on Mr. Head. There were some laxatives we'd been given called Cascara pills – one was enough to send you to the loo – and we ground up about a dozen of these and put them in his stew at lunchtime, Nicky and I sitting either side of him. It was powder by then of course, the way we'd ground them up, so he didn't seem to notice – but in fact it didn't have the slightest visible effect on him at all......!"

Indeed discipline was not invariably enforced by the cane. Peter Ainsworth (son of Mike Ainsworth) who was at Ludgrove from 1964 to 1970 and is now MP for Surrey East, recalls an incident in the early 1960's:

> I once threw a piece of liver at a boy during lunch and this was spotted and found to be reprehensible. So I had to go and see ATB, who made me write out 40 times
> *'The Winchester motto is Manners Makyth Man. This was chosen for no small reason'.*
> I can still hear him saying those words!

Peter Ainsworth as Captain of School, 1970

Another way in which discipline was enforced was 'the Drill', in which small boys had to run around the gym doing exercises with a Lee Enfield rifle – minus its bolt – held above the head. After a few circuits this became agonisingly painful. In 1940 a boy collapsed under the strain and was thought (wrongly, as it turned out) to have done himself serious harm. Robin Warrender recalls the aftermath of this event:

> As a result, a group of us decided to stage a protest revolution. Manifestos were circulated and surreptitious meetings held outside the school. The symbolic storming of the Bastille was to throw into the pond the Drill Book, which for many years had recorded the names of miscreants and the offences they had committed. It was soon noticed that the Drill Book was missing, and the hue and

cry began. Its whereabouts were discovered through the grapevine, and – to our great satisfaction – Alan Barber was seen up to his waist in mud, dredging the sludge and eventually salvaging the book.

The school had been put under an interdict until we had confessed, and we waited for the inevitable retribution. As things turned out, he lectured us on the foolishness of what we had done, characteristically emphasising the famous

ATB salvages the Drill Book from the pond

names recorded in the book which we had tried to destroy, and then gave us all a perfunctory caning. I have often wondered in retrospect whether he may have had some sympathy for the revolt.

The Drill continued to be part of the disciplinary scene until the mid-1950s with the retirement of the last of the Sergeant-Majors, Arnold Hartmoor, with his half-chanted war cry bellowed at full volume during "Strict P.E" –

One two three four
What do you think I'm talking for?
Five six seven eight
Come on boy you're doing it late
Knees up, arms out – nine ten
BLOODY LOUSY DO IT AGAIN!

Alexander Thynne, Marqess of Bath, recalls one of the more memorable disciplinary events that took place a few years later. A pipe leading to the cistern of one of the lavatories was discovered to have had a hole bored through it, so that the water came cascading down onto the head of the next boy who pulled the chain. Damaging school property was a most serious breach of discipline. Alan summoned the whole school into the Big Fifth form room, but when he demanded that the culprit declare

The Marquess of Bath himself, not a boy spoke up. Consequently the next half-holiday was denied to the whole school, until the Duke of Kent was persuaded (probably by the monitors) to own up on the grounds that ATB would never dream of "swishing" so august a personage. But a phone-call was made to his home, permission given and punishment administered. Not until a year or two later did it emerge that the real culprit had in fact been Robin Douglas Home!

The issue of bullying is more complex. There is undoubtedly a measure of physical and mental bullying in all closed institutions; but recollections of its severity at Ludgrove differ. It was considered a heinous crime for a younger boy to be "cheeky", and various sanctions were undoubtedly enforced. A number of boys recall this or that savage dormitory monitor, a flailing scout belt, an enforced trip to the squash courts after hours, incarceration in the "priest's hole" underneath the boards of one of the form rooms, and the persecution meted out – sometimes persistently – by particular individuals on those younger or weaker than themselves.

The Marquess of Bath again recalls one such event :

> [J] was a boy with a reputation for bullying those younger than himself, and had been terrorising the new kids by imprisoning them for spells of half an hour or so in a drawer intended for rackets inside the changing-room of the squash court. With the spirit of letting the punishment fit the crime, we decided to give [J] a taste of his own medicine. He was ambushed, dragged into the First Division where a trap door, which gave access to a shallow, dusty space beneath the floor, had been opened up in readiness for his imprisonment. He climbed in without demur, but then displayed sufficient ingenuity to escape, so that the whole process had to be repeated – with greater attention this time to the placement of something heavy on top of the trap door. On this occasion the sentence was completed, and we congratulated ourselves upon what we regarded as the successful enforcement of law and order – by ourselves as the self-appointed vigilantes.
>
> From his Autobiography, Vol. I – "The Early Years"

But little seems to have been inflicted with particular severity. Bullying at a certain level was undoubtedly endemic in the 1940s and 1950s – but it was never condoned by authority, was stamped on if discovered, and does not appear to have been deeply pervasive in the school's culture.

The Sporting Scene

Throughout the war the school's sporting activities proceeded with little interruption from hostilities elsewhere – or from the major epidemics which had so disrupted sporting programmes in times past. The author of *The History of Lambrook School*, Isla Brownless, records that

> In the 1950s, headmasters rang each other before a match when there was infectious illness in the school, in case the opposition wished to cancel. As attitudes slowly changed, more schools disregarded quarantines, agreeing simply that visiting teams should not go indoors. Boys healthy enough to play in matches were thought unlikely to transmit an infection.
>
> One enlightened headmaster always replied: "Thank you for ringing me – you

know my motto, don't you?" His motto – "Never tell Matron" – was well-known among local headmasters, who thought it was just his little joke. However Philip Brownless, [the Lambrook Headmaster] watching a match at this school, once mentioned measles, and realised from the horror of the Headmaster's wife that it was not a joke. In 20 years of "not telling matron", he had not even told his wife that an 'enemy' school had an infectious illness.

That 'enlightened headmaster' was of course ATB!

Cricket: In the cricket season of 1938, inaugurating the first season after the Move, not a match was rained off and only one was lost to other schools by any of the three XIs. M.D. Hoare who captained the First XI that year, achieved the best all-round performance by a cricketer in Ludgrove's annals, by scoring 293 runs for an average of 33, and taking 31 wickets for an average of just 5 runs. Throughout the war Ludgrove's cricket improved steadily. In 1942 the cricket First XI was undefeated, and only prevented by an unlucky rainstorm from achieving victory in every match they played. Two boys in that side – W.J. Collins and A.L. Cleland – achieved respectively one of Ludgrove's best ever combinations of batting (328 runs, average 55) and

Colin Ingleby-Mackenzie, aged 8

bowling (40 wickets, average 3.1) in the same season. In 1944 Ian Lomax exceeded Collins' aggregate score with 339 runs. And, as if to celebrate the peace, 1946 saw Colin Ingleby-Mackenzie captain an unbeaten team and personally surpass all previous

achievements by scoring 455 runs in 8 innings, including two centuries, his highest score being 142 against Lockers Park. He was out only four times in eight, and ended the season with an average of 114.

This figure is unparalleled by a Ludgrove boy, and Alan Barber wrote:

Colin Ingleby-Mackenzie, as captain of Hampshire in 1961

This summer will be remembered for the partial return to peace-time conditions and for matches renewed with old foes. And in such a summer Ingleby-Mackenzie has, in eight innings against the bowling of seven different schools, scored 455 runs for an average of 114 per innings, and the experts who saw him do it consider that these figures in no way flatter his skill…I doubt if his performance has ever been equalled in the annals of Ludgrove cricket.

That same summer Colin also won eight of the twelve trophies he was eligible for, including the Athletics Cup (with a school record in the hurdles) and the Swimming Cup. In later years he went on to captain Eton at cricket, and then to lead Hampshire to the County Championship in 1961.

Alan was to name him as one of only three boys in his long reign who in his view were simply too good to play against other prep schools. We shall meet the other two later.

Football – the Oxford & Bermondsey Boys' Club: In true Arthur Dunn tradition, football was the premier winter game, played in both Michaelmas and Easter terms. In 1949 the first match was played against the Oxford & Bermondsey Club, a boys' club founded in the East End of London in 1897 by Dr John Stansfeld, a civil servant who studied and qualified as a doctor in his spare time. His aim was to provide an alternative to the streets for boys and young men in the East End of London, by offering constructive activities, sports and outings. The club was a visionary forerunner of today's modern youth projects, and happily still thrives today. Ludgrove played the Oxford & Bermondsey Club every year until 1967, but seldom won a game against opponents whose play was always so much more skilful, fast and direct than theirs.

Athletics: In 1942 P.H. Frisby won every senior event in the athletics competition – 100 yards, 200 yards, hurdles, high and long jumps, equalling a record set in 1937 by R.S. Seale. The following year, 1943, was called "Byass' year" when another outstanding all-rounder, C.W.R. Byass almost repeated Frisby's achievement in athletics by winning every event except the high jump (in which he came 2nd by one inch). He was also the school's leading squash player and crowned his last term by captaining the Cricket XI and winning the Music Prize as the school's most accomplished pianist. Only three years later, in 1945, his younger bother – then still under 12 – came within an ace of matching his elder brother in athletics, winning all the events except the hurdles, in which he narrowly came second to G.A. Shakerly.

Boxing: This was run during the war by Sergeant-Major Goldie, who had joined Ludgrove from the Royal Military Academy at Woolwich, where he had been chief instructor. Boxing had always had a place in Ludgrove's sporting curriculum from the earliest days, and the spirit which the Sergeant-Major communicated was well-summed up in 1946:

> Those who were present at the Boxing Competition this term came away well able
> to appreciate the article from the *Eton Chronicle* describing the series of contests
> in which names of Old Ludgrovians figured so prominently, for they had

witnessed the same aggressive spirit in attack, the same readiness to swap punches, the same pluck to take hard knocks, the same sporting cheerfulness (sic!) when 'Time' was called. "The Noble Art" at Ludgrove is a sturdy infant, skilfully instructed and carefully nurtured.

One of Ludgrove's best boxers of this era was Alexander Thynne, who was also Captain of the School in 1945. The year before, in an exhibition bout, he had beaten Ronald Ferguson (the late father of the present Duchess of York), who was a year senior to him. But Thynne was never able to prove his quality to the full since he was felled by measles and chicken-pox just before the finals that year, giving his opponent, Mark Jeffreys, a walk-over. Thynne was later to excel in boxing at Eton.

Alexander Thynne, later Marquess of Bath, boxing in the army, 1952

Fencing: Sergeant-Major Goldie's enthusiasm for fencing was a particular inspiration to Normile Baxter (1938-43), who was probably Ludgrove's most successful fencer ever. He went on to become Captain of Fencing at Eton in 1946, '47 and '48, and during the three years of his leadership not only was Eton unbeaten by any school, it also defeated the Army, the Navy, and Oxford and Cambridge universities, and won the Public Schools' championship in all three years. His team's only defeat was by a margin of one fight against an Olympic scratch team. Normile later presented Ludgrove with the

Tennis seems to have been the only sport at which Ludgrove did not excel

THE BRITISH CHARACTER
IMPORTANCE OF BEING ATHLETIC

Baxter Fencing Cup in recognition of the inspired coaching of Sergeant-Major Goldie during his days there.

The Scouts

The first mention of the Scouts in Ludgrove's records is in the summer of 1945, when the Patrol Cup Competition was won by the Badgers, led by Alexander Thynne, and the Troop camp was held at Stratfield Saye amidst "one of the longest and worst thunderstorms within living memory." The Scout movement, which had been founded in 1898 by the hero of Mafeking, Lord Baden-Powell, came late to prep schools. By the late 1930s only about a quarter of prep schools in England had a scout troop. Mr Selfe, when previously in charge of Sandroyd, had been one of two headmasters appointed by the Association of Preparatory Schools to be a liaison officer between them and the Boy Scout Association, in an attempt to strengthen the links between the two organisations. During the war, there were too few masters to run the Scouts, and it was not until peace had returned that the 1st Ludgrove Troop could be formed. It consisted of four Patrols: Horses, Hounds, Badgers and Otters.

The first Scoutmaster was a Mr. Moffit, said to have been a man "of inspiring leadership". Alan Ellis was Assistant Scoutmaster and took over fully a short time later. Meetings were held on Wednesday evenings and Sunday mornings, when knots were learnt and tied, first aid mastered and applied, Second Class, Tenderfoot and numerous other badges won and worn, camp fires lit and "damper" cooked and consumed. "Wide games" all over the school site were introduced (more renowned as outlets of energy rather than of scoutcraft), block and tackle was introduced for weightier tasks such as pulling trees out of the pond, and the art of concealment mastered ("there is still a tendency to betray positions through talkativeness"). Holidays were often given up to raising funds through "Bob-a-Job", covering every sort of odd job around home and in the locality; and on every Remembrance Sunday the Scouts would parade in Chapel with the Union Flag and the Colours of the 1st Ludgrove Troop proudly borne aloft.

The Dramatic Society

The "D.S.", created by Peter Borgnis (see p. 171) was probably his most enduring legacy to Ludgrove. He had the idea in 1949 after seeing 'Oliver Twist' with his family in London, and thought what a splendid thing it would be to be able to put on such a show at Ludgrove. So he posted the following notice:

Dramatic Society

If sufficient support is forthcoming, it is proposed to start a Society with the purpose of acting plays to be presented at the end of either or both the Winter terms. If you are interested in any way (there are openings for actors, electricians and other stage hands) please write your name neatly below

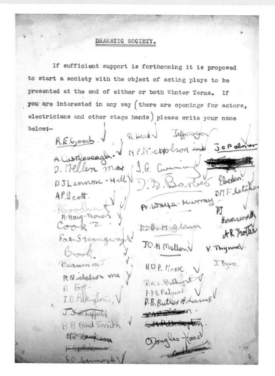

Thirty six boys signed up. The first show was *Mariposa Bung, or The Pirate's Daughter* performed in February 1950 with Paul Foot and Charlie Douglas Home in the lead roles.

No Ludgrovian in all the years that Peter was on the staff could forget the marvellous productions he staged over the next 40 years.

Stop press...

Peter had a wonderful ability to engender enthusiasm. An ecstatic Sunday letter written by a boy to his parents simply read :

"Great news! – news of the term! – Mr Borgnis has just made me 2nd reserve electrician for the D.S.!"

In one year, 1957, he put on A.A. Milne's play *Make Believe*, in which no fewer than 53 boys or just under half the school had a part. The reviews of his productions over all

C.E.B. C-P-Fane   P.J.C. Davenport   D. Webb-Carter   T.C. Pilkington
M.C. Swann   J.B. Smith   A.J. FitzGerald   N.R. Elwes

A.C Farquhar   C.T.A. Radmall   P.T. Crosthwaite   M.J.T. Clyde   K.E.S. Gooch
M.G. Griffith   N.P. Cumming   N.C.F. Barber   R.P.F. Barber   E.M.R. Davies   H.S. Dobbs
H.A.D. Cairns   C.J.R. Elton   S.N.G. Morant   F.P.W. Elton   J.J.S.L. Hardy

Drama production featuring the author, his brother and Jeremy Clyde, who made acting his career.

those years frequently praised Peter Borgnis efforts as "unsparing" and "untiring".
Gerald Barber recalls Peter's legacy:

> He had a wonderful knack of making boys feel that they were doing everything
> themselves – whether acting, creating scenery, painting vital parts for the show or
> in organising the sometimes rather dodgy lighting arrangements.
>
> He kept meticulous scripts and musical scores for all the plays, and put
> together a memorable record of his productions over the years. The stage, which
> he personally built up from scratch, was erected on the gym floor. The electrical
> box, up in a small garret near the stage, was the most lethal 'black hole'
> imaginable. The audience used to be packed like sardines on uncomfortable
> wooden chairs, with a scaffold tower near the front on which boys perched to
> operate the lighting like a searchlight. It was huge fun for everyone, and Peter's
> party for the cast and his own friends on the Saturday evening was the highlight
> of the Christmas term.

In the 1960s Peter was assisted by Micky Burton-Brown, and then by Stephen Graham
who took over fully from Peter in 1984. Today the D.S. is as enthusiastically run as ever,
a living memorial to the spirit and talent of its founder

THE STAFF IN THE 1940S AND '50S

Alan Ellis (ADE): In the Spring term of 1951 Alan Ellis (universally known as 'Bungy') left to become Headmaster of Ardingly Junior School. He had been a friend of Alan's from Shrewsbury days, and had joined Ludgrove from Lancing in 1935. He was universally popular as a teacher, games master and Scoutmaster, and on his departure Alan wrote:

> True to Ludgrove tradition, Mr Ellis has been with us for a long spell…there was
> a time when 15 years on the Ludgrove staff was considered very junior, but it is a
> large wedge out of a man's life and we must count ourselves fortunate to have had
> him for so long. A scholar and athlete himself, his influence on the work and
> games of the school was bound to be considerable, though it is perhaps as
> founder and organiser of the scouts that boys will remember him best. To say that
> he has been greatly liked and respected is a gross understatement […] We must
> wipe a tear from our eye, and wish him and Mrs Ellis good luck and much
> happiness in their new life.

Alan Ellis was succeeded by Mr H. Walden-Jones of Shrewsbury and scholar of Pembroke College, Cambridge.

During the long reign of Alan Barber and Tim Shaw, three members of the Common Room dominated Ludgrove life and determined its culture. These were John Rickards, Peter Borgnis and Ken Morrison.

John Rickards

John Rickards (AJR) had been at Eton and Christ Church, Oxford, and returned to Eton briefly to teach classics before joining Ludgrove in 1939. He was tall and elegant, invariably sporting a Leander tie, was one of the early wearers of suede shoes in those days, and he drove a green Bristol car which seemed to the boys the last word in suave sophistication. He was fiercely loyal to Eton (and on occasions would mischievously say of some non-performer: "Probably OK for Harrow!"). He was a fine teacher; one of his most successful pupils, Charles Graham, paid him this warm tribute: "John Rickards kindled in me my love of the classics and history, which has never left me".

John could be very firm, on occasions even severe, and he commanded respect among all for his intelligence, style and natural authority. Many will remember the sayings he taught his divisions to chant in unison: "*Ave Caesar! Nos morituri te salutamus*" before an exam; and (in reply to any boy who said "That's not fair, Sir!" – usually over the marks he'd received for P.R.): "Yes, my boy – Life *is* unfair – and the sooner you learn it the better". It was a philosophy that encapsulated much of the Ludgrove culture of those years.

Peter Hammond-Chambers-Borgnis, R.N. (retd.) (RPH-C-B): In 1939 Alan recruited probably the most versatile, talented and well-loved master in Ludgrove's history. Born in August 1910, Peter Borgnis went to Osborne, the naval boarding-school on the Isle of Wight, and on to the Royal Naval Training College, Dartmouth. At that time he was a scratch golfer, and played cricket for the Navy, as well as for the Combined Services. For the latter he scored 101 against the visiting New Zealand Test team at Portsmouth in 1937, and took 3 for 38 in the visitors' first innings. But with a promising naval career ahead of him, he contracted tuberculosis in 1938 and was invalided out of the Navy the following year with one lung missing. He taught for a term at Farnborough House School, Shiplake and was then destined for Heatherdown. But Alan caught him in mid-move, and persuaded him to come to Ludgrove, where he arrived in the Michaelmas term, 1940, to 'replace' John Rickards, who had joined the forces.

Peter Borgnis

In the following 45 years that he was at Ludgrove, Peter was to etch a many-faceted image in the memories and affections of all Ludgrove boys. Everything he did, he did expertly: and his astonishing range of skills – from teaching History, French and Maths to coaching cricket and golf, producing plays, singing, entertaining, gardening, baking cakes and even knitting socks and rugs – were all housed in a tall, spare, athletic frame and cloaked with a personality of charm, wit and generosity. His wonderful baritone voice and repertoire of sea-shanties were a feature of every school concert, and the great Michael Flanders himself never gave a finer rendering of his "Hippopotamus Song" than Peter.

His devotion to the annual putting competition, and his cricket coaching of the 'Rising Talent' (Under 11s) with the handkerchief target on the 'good length' mark for the bowler to aim at, the strawberries distributed in the school and at his house to those who tried hardest, his inspired leadership for 40 years of the Dramatic Society – all these still stir the affections of every Ludgrovian fortunate enough to have known him. He guided generations of boys with his wide learning, patient encouragement and quiet dignity; he never belittled a poor performer, taught courtesy and consideration virtually as a subject, and commanded respect and affection in equal measure. It is to Peter's teaching that so many owe their love of history, mathematics, French, drama, literature and music.

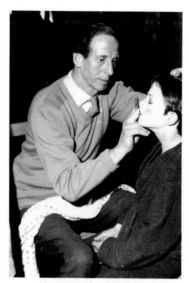

Peter Borgnis as make-up artist

His leisure time was given chiefly to gardening, in which he was an expert of professional standards, and to golf, which he played mainly for the County Cricketers G.S. He was a scratch player at 20, played off 2 when he was 60, and 8 when he finally gave up the game at the age of 84. On several occasions he was selected to play for the Great Britain & Northern Ireland Seniors' team against the USA and Canada, both of which he toured, winning a number of his matches.

No one has ever been more committed to the cause of Ludgrove than Peter. When he retired from the school in 1984 he left a legacy of one of the great preparatory schoolmasters of modern times. In 1998 he and his wife Bettine went to make a new home in the south of France, and it was there that he died in 2002, just before his 91st birthday, mourned by all who had known and loved him.

Ken Morrison (KBM) was probably the best classical scholar in Ludgrove's history. He had been at Harrow from 1907 to 1911, and in his last year opened the bowling at Lord's, when he took 4 Eton wickets in their first innings. He won a demy-ship to Magdalen College, Oxford, but family misfortune made university impossible. The Great War then took him to Egypt, which he hated. Thereafter he taught at a number of schools before joining Ludgrove in 1943, where he was in charge of Classics for a dozen years until retiring in 1955.

Ken Morrison

Nicknamed 'The Toad', Ken was a tall, imposing, ungainly, pipe-puffing figure, reminiscent of Dr Johnson with his vast erudition and rolling gait, a permanent halo of tobacco-smoke and a general air of dilapidation. He taught Classics brilliantly to the able; at best tolerated the less gifted; and entertained strong prejudices – especially against philistines, laziness, the 'new' pronunciation of Latin, and 'hybrid' words of mixed Greek and Latin roots (such as 'television', always to be referred to as 'teleopsis'). Other objects of his odium were actors (he dismissed the Dramatic Society as "theatricals"), and untidy desks (he called them "whited sepulchres": neat in aspect when closed, full of mess and corruption when opened). He and his great friend, 'Cabbage' Reed, were to be seen most evenings wending their way after school to the White Horse pub at the top of the lane by the East Lodge.

To the ordinary boy, Ken could be a remote and forbidding figure. But to the academic ones he was an inspiration. Vivid recollections of this idiosyncratic and brilliant teacher are given by some of his former scholars.

Paul Foot, who sadly died in July 2004 aged 67, recalls KBM's teaching:

Paul Foot

> I remember with startling clarity how he inspired us. He taught us an understanding of Latin verses, the glory of the hexameter and the elegiac couplet, and the rhythm of it all, and instilled in us at the age of 12 or 13 a real delight in the majesty of that verse. He taught us almost to think in elegiac couplets, and he inspired me with real affection for these verses and also for the Greek dramatists, especially Aeschylus and Euripides. With some other masters you hoped that the clock would quickly come round to the three-quarters of an hour mark; but Ken's 'Kings and Queens' was completely different: two periods of an hour and a half and all the boredom lifted away for ever. Three of us were picked out by Morrison for his early morning lesson before breakfast, and it was wonderful. We had to be downstairs with him by 7 a.m., terrifically early for us. In the winter getting out of bed was a horrible moment, but Matron came to shake you, and when you realised it was one of Morrison's lessons you were up like a flash, dressed and downstairs with a great pot of tea specially made for us and some biscuits, and there he was writing Greek letters on the blackboard. And then he would teach us Euripides or inspire us with some of the Iliad or some Latin verses. When I took the scholarship exam for Shrewsbury, I had finished the Latin Verse paper in about 20 minutes. When the results came through, I'd got 96% and the next highest was about 30%. It was then that you realised that what you'd been taught by Morrison was on a completely different scale from what anyone else had been taught.

Sir Thomas 'Tommy' Stockdale Q.C.

Sir Thomas Stockdale (later Q.C. and a current Governor of Ludgrove) said of Morrison:

> One of the principal features of Ludgrove for me was being taught by Mr Morrison. I still used things he'd taught me when I was at University, particularly about the Peloponnesian War. He made the Ancient World come completely alive; for example, he used to divide his Division into Spartans and Athenians – I was an Athenian – and the fact that I managed to obtain a scholarship to Eton was entirely due to him. He was

pretty intimidating, a disciplinarian in his teaching, but he was so obviously fascinated by ancient history himself that he just inspired you to be as fascinated as he was.

Nicholas Barber (today Chairman of the Ashmolean Museum in Oxford) said that four teachers in his life had been in a different league to all others, and two of these were at Ludgrove: Ken Morrison and Peter Borgnis. He agreed that Ken was not a master who inspired the average boy; but he would make the brightest feel they could do anything.

Nicholas Barber

He would introduce you to idioms and intricacies, and things beyond the call of the syllabus, in a way that made you feel that you were on the inside of a conspiracy – especially when you were chosen to have Greek lessons before breakfast which made you feel privileged and special. He taught us how much more subtle a language Greek is than Latin, and to write Latin elegiacs that were almost elegant. For example he would spot a woodpecker outside the window and put up some lines about it which could have come straight from Ovid – he made it such fun. Of course he could be completely arbitrary in whether he liked you or not – but if you were a classics scholar or a cricketer (or going on to Harrow) you were in with a chance!

Ken retired from Ludgrove in 1955, was succeeded briefly by a Mr Burn-Hill, and then by another outstanding teacher, Micky Burton-Brown, who oversaw the teaching of classics until the late 1960s. During that period Ken would come back from retirement to invigilate and to coach for Common Entrance. It was during one of these visits, in 1964, that he died in his sleep in the Bungalow. The remarkable thing was that during the night of his passing there was an incomparably loud clap of thunder over the school – a salute from Zeus, no doubt.

Peter Borgnis wrote this valediction:

With the death of KBM has come the end of an era for Ludgrove. He was born into a different world, a world peaceful and spacious, a world of classics and cricket, and at both he excelled…For 21 years Ludgrove was his life: the holidays merely gave him the time to write Latin verses of great felicity on a Test match, the deeds of some boy in his Division, or the life and death of Guzzle the woodpecker, which fed daily outside his schoolroom window…Who can ever forget his kindly wisdom? Who can forget his justifiable rage when suspected of bias as an umpire? Who can forget "Kings and Queens"? Will anyone of those lucky enough to have known him ever forget him?"

Chapter VII

A "FASHIONABLE"
SCHOOL: 1950–1973

*"We don't know who you are or where you dwell, but
we know you come from Ludgrove."*

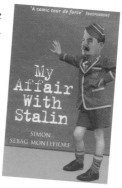

A vivid picture of the start of a new school year at Ludgrove is given by Simon Sebag-Montefiore in his novel *My Affair with Stalin*:

> Whenever I hear the crunch of majestic cars on golden gravel, I can see Coverdale School at eight o'clock on a Sunday evening. It is suffocatingly dark as my parents' Volvo motor car trundles along the pot-holed drive towards the school, parting the gravel like an ice-breaker…I can no longer speak because I do not want to cry.

> The drive is crowded with cars. Their headlights are blazing. It is an army decamping. Everyone is unpacking and carrying bundles like wealthy refugees in a time of turmoil. The cars are parked carelessly on grass or gravel with their doors open. You cannot see too much: just glimpses of small boys in grey trousers, tweed jackets and v-necked sweaters – their pale cheeks glow like masks. They are sometimes accompanied by Englishmen in pin-striped suits – their fathers – or women in elegant winter coats of camel hair or cashmere. A hundred differently luscious perfumes and acrid Colognes rise from the fine wrists of mothers and the rough jaws of fathers to mingle into a single cloud of drowsy but intriguing luxury. A couple of boys are led by chauffeurs in uniforms who step out of Rolls-Royces and are probably kinder than their parents could ever be. [1]

The image of Ludgrove as 'a fashionable school' had taken root from its earliest days in the 1890s as its reputation grew by word of mouth, and many titled families did indeed send their sons both to Barnet and to Wokingham. It was not alone among prep schools in this: Ludgrove's predecessor school, Wixenford, had educated such a profusion of boys from the aristocracy in its heyday that it was jocularly known as "The House of Lords".

One of Wixenford's pupils, Richard Heaton, recalls his acute experience of this in 1929:

> My best friend at Wixenford was Prince Richard of Hesse. I was asked to stay with him at the family Château de Marlioz in France.....but the Headmaster told me very tactfully that [his parents] had found out that my family was in Industry, and in those days people in Industry were not supposed to mix with the very high social class from which his family came in Europe, so I was not allowed to go.

Ludgrove was cast in a similar mould. To illustrate this, of the first fourteen Old Ludgrovians reported killed, wounded, missing or taken prisoner in the early months of the Second World War, half were peers or baronets: Major the Earl of Erne, Lieut. Lord Frederick Cambridge, Lieut. The Earl of Coventry, Lieut. the Hon. G.L. Hamilton-Russell, Lieut. Sir E. Bradford, Viscount Brackley and the Earl of Hopetoun. In a quite different context, the Fathers' XI of 1949 consisted of four peers (Lords Adare, Cadogan, Londonderry and Mountgarret), a general, a brigadier, three colonels and two humble civilian commoners.

While Ludgrove has never refused entry to any boy who could hold his own with his colleagues, and whose parents could pay their way, there is no doubt that an aura of wealth and privilege surrounded Ludgrove during the middle decades of the 20th century. Alan Barber made it clear in all sorts of ways, to parents, masters and boys alike, that it was a privilege to be at Ludgrove – and numerous sons of the Establishment gave credence to this. There was a profusion of boys with triple-barrelled names, such as Montagu-Douglas-Scott, Clive-Ponsonby-Fane, Anstruther-Gough-Calthorpe…

Charles Clive-Ponsonby-Fane

Colin Ingleby-Mackenzie, whose family owned a rather battered old Wolseley, remembers appealing to his father not to drive it up to the front door of Ludgrove in case it should be compared with the cars of other boys; Admiral Ingleby-Mackenzie replied robustly that not only would he drive his car up to the front door but through it too if he wanted to!

The different backgrounds from which Ludgrove boys came was clearly demonstrated when Dorothy Barber was going round the sick-bay during an epidemic in the 1950s. She asked one boy, the son of an Irish peer, how his mother was. He replied: "Well, the hunting season has just ended and the shooting season hasn't quite begun, so she's a bit bored actually", and the voice of a little North Country boy in the next-door bed piped up: "Hasn't she got any housework to do?"

But such culture-clashes were rare. A sense of privilege surrounded the school, and Ludgrove's elite reputation attracted people to a setting in which they felt their sons

"We know you come from Ludgrove"

Ludgrovians in 'Pop' at Eton, c.1956: Adrian Hohler, Patrick Boyle (now the Earl of Glasgow), Robin Higham, Richard Burrows, Peter Smith and Jeremy Palmer

A symbol of Ludgrove was a photograph prominently displayed in the drawing-room – next to a signed 1937 photograph of Lord and Lady Harewood and their family in their Coronation robes – of six Old Ludgrovian members of Pop at Eton in full regalia. Underneath was the legend:

"We don't know who you are or where you dwell, but we know you come from Ludgrove."

would be at home with their own kind. In keeping with this, Ludgrove under Alan Barber and Tim Shaw always stood for things which they considered indispensable attributes of any position of responsibility – strong values, good manners and high standards of behaviour.

The daily round

Everything at Ludgrove was ordered by the ringing of a hand-bell. Its first peals broke the peace at 7.30 a.m., when boys rose, washed and presented themselves for breakfast, over which ATB would preside. This was followed by "Morning Parade" when the boys formed up in long queues for the lavatories, collected the precise and requisite length of paper from the master on duty, and emerged after due process to report in formal tones on his success or failure with the words "Correct, Sir" or "Incorrect, Sir". The answers were solemnly recorded and presented to Matron, who would then prescribe the

Jane Ramsey, Matron, and her team

necessary antidotes to constipation, mainly in the form of Syrup of Figs, the nostrum of those days for such an affliction.

This ceremony was then followed by half an hour's 'stump' cricket in the yard, already described in Chapter 5, which everyone played throughout the year. Morning lessons came next, punctuated by a break for drinks and fruit, when running in the corridors to "Mr Shaw's cupboard" was strictly forbidden.

And so to the Dining Hall for lunch, where the saying of grace would trigger the indescribable noise of 100 boys all talking at the tops of their voices. On occasions the cacophony would become too great, and there would be a solemn request for silence. Lunch on some weekdays saw the ceremony of masters carving individual joints of beef or mutton on every table, usually accompanied by parsnips and potatoes; and then came the puddings for which prep schools are so renowned – 'spotted dog', 'squashed flies and custard', 'toenail pudding', stewed prunes and custard, rice pudding and apricots, treacle tart made of cornflakes (often burnt) and many other concoctions, which conjure up indelible memories whenever they are encountered in later life. Sometimes lunch would be followed by an

Oxford sinking soon after the start of the 1951 Boat Race

announcement – and who present will ever forget Boat Race day in 1951 when Alan rose slowly to his feet after lunch, as the expectant hubbub of boys died away, to make the imperishable announcement:

"Oxford…have sunk!"

After lunch, games for all, accompanied in winter by the cry "Is it sweaters, Sir?" (to which Peter Borgnis once retorted: "Parse-that-sentence!"). The sports available included football, cricket, squash, fives and golf; and for the non-athletic boys a variety of hobbies such as the cultivation of their own private garden plot.

With this embarrassment of choice no boy had any excuse to loiter: I myself, as boy at Ludgrove, once came out of the school and paused momentarily on the steps facing the

Gardening is still popular in 2004

Chapel to decide which of these multiple options I should select. I was immediately pounced on by Ken Morrison, who summarily decreed: "Barber – Minus mark". In astonishment I stammered "W-Why Sir?" to which Ken just replied "Two!" and walked off!

The author at Ludgrove

On half-holiday afternoons, everyone went to support the school teams. In the summer, at school cricket matches, the whole school sat around the boundary, every boy with a score-book on his knees, all to be subsequently collected and marked by the Headmaster. This ceremony does appear a little absurd today, though some have said that it nevertheless gave the opportunity for longer and more relaxed conversations with masters than the normal routines permitted – as it did also for the playing of 'Splodge' cricket with friends, and the composition of fanciful Test sides from antiquity who would have been the match for any modern Australian touring side. One such team remembered by David Gay (1929–1934) was:

1.	HOPHNI	8.	ACHITOPEL
2.	PHINEAS	9.	ABSALOM
3.	SHADRACH	10.	JEHOSHAPHAT
4.	MESHACH	11.	JEHU
5.	ABEDNIGO	12th Man:	ETHELRED THE UNDREADY
6.	TILGATH-PILEZER Capt.	Umpire:	SOLOMON
7.	AHASUERAS	Scorer:	JEZEBEL

For older boys, visits were made in the summer term to the Test Match at Lord's, and in the winter to Highbury to see "the Arsenal" (as ATB used to call it). An Old Ludgrovian, Denis Hill-Wood, was chairman of the club for many years, being succeeded there by his son Peter (sometime Governor of Ludgrove).

Once a term there were merit half-holidays for the first 70 boys in the school whose net balance of Plus and Minus marks justified their selection.

Dennis Hill-Wood and his son Peter with the F.A. Cup, won by Arsenal in 1971.

A Late Merit Half

Donald Shaw (Tim's nephew), who went to Ludgrove in 1949, was awarded no Merit Halves at all during his time at the School, and he recalls :

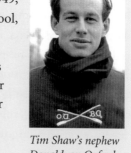

> Tony Haig-Thomas (OL, 1949-53) and I went into business partnership together in '72. One day we were discussing our time at Ludgrove and discovered that neither of us had ever been awarded a Merit Half. So in 1978 we decided to make

Tim Shaw's nephew Donald, an Oxford rowing Blue in 1959

> a special award of a Merit Half to TWS and ATB themselves, since we knew that they had never had one either!
>
> Their reward was to come to lunch in our office together with two others who also had never had one, Anthony Scott and George Jeffreys. It was a memorable day, you can imagine the fun we had – and certainly no work that afternoon.

Tony Haig-Thomas, RAF pilot in the 1950s

Like his uncle Tim, Donald gained a rowing Blue at Oxford. He went on to row for Great Britain in the Rome Olympics of 1960.

Tea was followed by free time for reading, often from the literary residue of Empire piled high around "the Big Fifth" in the form of the *Sphere*, the *Illustrated London News* and the bound volumes of the *Boys' Own Paper* with their tales of imperial derring-do. But from the 1950s, the *Eagle* (sent on subscription) overtook them in popularity.

This was also the time for playing board-games like "L'Attaque" or "Dover Patrol", and of course ping-pong or billiards.

Prep (known as P.R. or 'Pupil Room') then lasted an hour from 6.30 p.m. until Evening Prayers in the dining-hall. On Wednesdays hymns were sung, accompanied by Dorothy on the piano, and followed by announcements, cocoa, prayers and bed. On special occasions the proceedings would be interrupted with the award of School Colours – the school captain would burst into the room festooned with the Ludgrove shirt (for soccer) or blazer (for cricket), and shout "First XI colours have been awarded to – Robinson!" Then up would go Robinson, amid the cheers of the whole school, to collect the coveted garment, in one of the proudest moments of his young life. These proceedings were rounded off with a plastic beaker of cocoa, usually so repellent that I still recall the physical effort needed to drink it. And if I hesitated too long before the first sip, there was ATB at my elbow, with the characteristic words "Come on, R.P.F. – Sink it like a man!"

And finally everyone would kneel as Alan intoned the prayers in his measured way, always finishing with the marvellous prayer attributed to Cardinal Newman, which few contemporaries can hear today without recalling Alan's voice:

> *O Lord, support us all the day long of this troublesome life, until the shades*
> *lengthen and the evening comes and the busy world is hushed, the fever*
> *of life is over and our work done. Then Lord, in Thy mercy, grant us safe lodging,*
> *a holy rest and peace at the last –*
> *Through Jesus Christ our Lord. Amen.*

… and so to bed.

Mrs. Barber's Reading

The usual Sunday routines of chapel, writing letters home or going out with parents concluded with a tradition which had begun with the foundation of the school: the reading to the whole school by the Headmaster's wife. It had begun with Helen Dunn. She handed on the tradition to Katherine Smith, whose reading was so vividly portrayed by Roland Pym. Margaret Henley took it on from Miss Smith, and Dorothy Barber followed her. "Mrs Barber's Reading" is one of the experiences that Old Ludgrovians of that era best remember. Paul Foot, of *Private Eye*, had the clearest recollections of it:

> She was absolutely brilliant, I remember being transfixed. She was a very good
> reader and she picked very good adventure stories, really exciting. The whole

The Reading outside

school filed into the drawing-room, a hundred boys or so; they all listened intently and were very silent. Each time we quickly remembered the previous episode and she read exactly the right amount. It was very, very good, and she was really most impressive.

The readings were held most of the year in the spacious drawing-room and, on warm evenings in summer, underneath the lovely chestnut tree on the lawn in front of the house.

Dorothy herself recalls it:

> At Cockfosters we had about 60 boys sitting round with their rugs – but by the end of our time at Ludgrove there were over 125 boys, which was a large number to get in. I used to go down to W.H.Smith in the holidays and browse through all the possible books. Some boys would sit very close to me, and read over my shoulder, they could see when I changed a word – for example I used to modify the language, "a bloody nuisance" would become "a bothering nuisance", but of course they always knew!
>
> My reading gave a focus to Sundays. It would make everyone get back on time when they'd been out with their parents. It helped a lot of tears, and it was so much better to hold it in the drawing-room than in the school, because it helped boys settle back into school life again. It was a good tradition, and I always enjoyed it.

The other all-important female figure at Ludgrove throughout this period was, of course, Matron.

Jane Ramsey was Matron for 22 years, from 1943 until 1966, when she left Ludgrove with enormous regret – she described it as "the most difficult decision of my life" – to go back to her home in Monmouth to look after her elderly father.

Jane Ramsey revisiting Ludgrove for the Centenary in 1992

Jane (her real name was Phyllis, and she was nicknamed 'Squashball') ruled the upstairs world of dormitories, bathrooms, medicines, clothes and under-matrons, and Old Boys' memories of her are unfailingly warm, with respect for her authority – which one never breached – admiration for her nursing skill in any emergency, and love for her caring and ample heart.

She ran her small team of under-matrons with unfailing courtesy – Bridget Holmes, Jane Evans, Peggy Ware, Bridget Clarke (who married Micky Burton-Brown) and many others over the years – and they returned her care in full measure with their loyalty. Her room was always full of flowers picked from the School gardens, which perfumed the air as she dispensed from her cupboard doses of malt extract, Syrup of Figs, Milk of Magnesia, and other time-honoured nostrums. Richard Gooch (1950-55) recalls an alarming incident from the sick bay in the 1950s:

> In my second year I was very ill as 'flu went to pneumonia, and was on fearsome injections from Matron. One night Matron woke me when Dr. Rose was there and I heard him say that I must drink – "Give him anything he wants", he said. I suppose I was dehydrating, and must have been near delirium because I weakly asked for beer. Even at that age I liked it! Next thing there was dear Matron with a medical mug full of bitter. At this stage I began to realise that things were serious. Mrs Barber too was up all night, beer seemed to appear at regular intervals, and the next day I went by ambulance to Great Ormond Street Hospital where I had a whale of a time. I think I could probably claim to be their youngest patient ever to arrive with a hangover.

In recalling her years at the school, Jane said: "I spent the happiest years I have known at Ludgrove"; and just before her reluctant departure in 1966 she came back for the first two weeks only of the new term "to help Dorothy settle the boys in before I went. But I didn't tell any of them I was leaving, for if I had done so I knew that my heart would have broken".

Her influence has never been forgotten. In 2003, George Pope (1951-56) organised a dinner for those who had entered Ludgrove with him in 1951, and they sent Jane the flowers and a signed menu from their dinner table: "With love and many memories – Ludgrove educated us to the real values in life, last night was a real compliment to all,

The menu, signed by all OLs who had entered the school in 1951, in honour of Jane Ramsey

and to yourself in particular."

New teaching staff who came to prominence in the first post-war decades included Gertrude Paul, Alan Cattley and Roddy Carr-Gomm.

Gertrude Paul, ('Paula') was Swiss-German from Basel, and had been governess to the Strang-Steel family before joining Ludgrove in 1942 where she taught the junior form, Division 6, for 26 years. She is fondly remembered for her sing-song accent (the boys would imitate her "*So-so*" – which became her nickname), her weather-beaten face with never a trace of make-up, and a firm manner which could sometimes prove formidable to an 8-year-old.

Her great passions were gardening, cats (by whom she was always surrounded in her flat above the yard), cooking

'Paula', Gertrude Paul

(with the ever-present whiff of garlic) and the Wokingham Girl Guides, whom she led for many years. She died of cancer while still in harness at Ludgrove in 1968. The curtains hanging on either side of the altar in the Chapel were given in her memory.

Alan Cave went to Rugby and Trinity College, Oxford. He joined Ludgrove in 1948, teaching most subjects in Middle School. A softly-spoken man of great charm, he was also a fine games-player. He played cricket for Berkshire, helped ATB coach the cricket First XI at Ludgrove and was also President of the Oxford and Cambridge Golf Society. In 1971 he was Captain of the Royal and Ancient. He left Ludgrove in 1958 to teach at Home Grange.

Alan Cave

Alan Cattley was a fine scholar of French, which he taught for 20 years from 1952 to 1972. He had been a keen athlete in his Oxford days, where he had run with Roger Bannister. He was of unpredictable temperament but he imbued generations of boys with a love of French, which many cherish to this day.

One of his former pupils, Peter Ainsworth MP, recalls him well:

> Mr. Cattley was an extraordinary man: when the sun came out he was the first to take us outside and sit us down on rugs, he even played an old wind-up gramophone with music from Imperial Russia on some old '78s because he was of course a White Russian by

Alan Cattley

origin. One always felt with Cattley was that there was a much wider cultural hinterland to his teaching, which I think was unusual, and for me very valuable.

Roddy Carr-Gomm had been at Oriel College, Oxford, and taught Division 2 for 19 years from 1954 to 1973. He also ran the squash for many years. (He himself still recalls that on the Ludgrove court ATB could beat him left-handed!). Discipline in Roddy's classes was erratic, and there would be occasional stentorian outbursts and showers of missiles to put the ship back on course. But his boys remember him with great affection, a man of generous spirit, with a heart of gold and famed for regularly giving the funniest speeches at Supper Night each term, when he had his audience in fits of laughter that echo to this day.

Roddy Carr-Gomm

SOME EMINENT OLD BOYS

By now a number of Old Ludgrovians from the early days of the School had made their names in very different spheres. Four of the most distinguished careers were those of Robert McCormick (1892–1895), Victor Hope (Lord Linlithgow) (1895–1900), Oliver Leese (1903–1907) and Dennis Mahon (1919–1924).

Robert McCormick : Newspaper proprietor and editor

In 1949 Ludgrove received a visit from Robert McCormick, proprietor and editor of the *Chicago Tribune*, whom we met briefly in Chapter 2 as the third boy to enter the School on its foundation in 1892. This time he was shown round by ATB, whose photograph appeared in a two-page spread on Ludgrove in the *Tribune* a few days later.

McCormick was the son of an American diplomat who had been appointed to the U.S. Embassy in London in 1889 ("My parents were splendid diplomats because they had no inferiority complex."). Initially he went to another English prep school where "the brutality of one of the masters was so great that I have remembered it for sixty years", but in 1892 he and his brother Medill were moved to Ludgrove where he recalled that "the Headmaster's wife was a lovely and kindly woman and the Headmaster was a splendid and kindly man." McCormick went on to become Chairman of the Chicago Tribune Company in 1911, to serve with distinction in the U.S. Army during the Great War, and then in 1925 to be the sole Editor of the *Chicago Tribune*, which he ruled with a rod of iron and an eccentric whim for 30 years.

Known as 'The Colonel', he was one of the great American newspapermen of the

20th century (The hero of Orson Welles' film *Citizen Kane* was modelled in part on him, though principally on William Randolph Hearst). He was a wayward genius, being at various times soldier, city administrator, inventor, historian and, of course, publisher. He was one of the fiercest opponents of Prohibition, waged a ceaseless battle with President Roosevelt in opposing the New Deal, considered that British imperialism was indistinguishable from Nazi aggression, was the fiercest critic of the pomp of British royalty and aristocracy, and was an ardent opponent of the founding principles of the United Nations, as being a threat to constitutional government.

Through contact with Sir Shane Leslie about a contribution to Mrs Dunn's 80th birthday present, there sprang up a remarkable correspondence lasting two years, from 1947 to 1949, between McCormick and the elderly Mrs Dunn herself. She clearly touched a chord in the heart of this complex man, and it was with pride that he recorded in his autobiography: "I corresponded with Mr. Dunn's widow as long as she lived." There is a hint of his robust personality at the end of one of his letters to her:

> I do not know why I have survived all of my contemporaries, because I have done everything I can to get killed, including two years in the old Wild West, a year in exploring the Arctic, polo, fox-hunting, mountain climbing and two wars. I guess I was born to be hanged.

These remarkable letters, taken from the McCormick Archive in Ohio with permission of the *Chicago Tribune*, are published here for the first time. They are shown in Appendix 7 of this book.

Lord Linlithgow, Viceroy of India

Victor Alexander John Hope, the 2nd Marquess of Linlithgow, was Viceroy of India from 1936 to 1943. His father, the Earl of Hopetoun and 1st Marquess of Linlithgow, had been Governor General of Australia (1900–1902).

Lord Linlithgow was born in 1887 and went to Ludgrove in 1898. One of numerous Ludgrovians to serve on the Western Front in the Great War, by 1924 he was Deputy Chairman of the Conservative & Unionist Party. He was introduced to the problems of India first as Chairman of the Royal Commission on Agriculture in India in 1924 and then in 1933 as Chairman of the Select Committee for Indian Constitutional Reform. He helped to formulate the Government of India Act of 1935, and was appointed Viceroy in 1936 in succession to Lord Willingdon.

Initially he succeeded in gaining the confidence of the Congress Party in the granting of provincial autonomy, but he offended them when in 1939, without consulting them, he declared that India was at war with Germany. Congress Party members refused to join his Executive Council, and in 1942, at the same time as Japanese military forces were threatening to usurp British control of India, Congress organised a massive campaign of civil disobedience against British rule. Lord Linlithgow's response was to intern the Congress leaders and to suppress resistance to government. However, it was under his subsequent direction that the Indian contingent of over 2 million men was raised to join the Allied military effort in the Second World War, and fight in North Africa, Europe and South-East Asia.

He returned home from India in 1943 after eight years, the longest serving Viceroy in India's history. He was succeeded by Lord Wavell.

Lieutenant-General Sir Oliver Leese Bt KCB DSO, army commander in the Second World War

Oliver Leese, who inherited a baronetcy, was born in 1894 and was at Ludgrove from 1903 to 1907. He left Eton in 1914, and immediately joined his many contemporaries on the Western Front, where he was wounded three times. His bravery at the Battle of the Somme won him a DSO.

Having chosen to make the army his career, he commanded the Coldstream Guards from 1936 to 1938. At the outbreak of war he was Deputy Chief-of-Staff to Lord Gort in France, and played a major role in the evacuation of Dunkirk in June 1940. He

Lt-General Sir Oliver Leese (left) with Winston Churchill on his visit to the Italian front in August 1944

fought in North Africa under Montgomery, to whom he was a loyal friend, admirer and subordinate. In October 1942, shortly before El Alamein, Monty gave him the command of 30 Corps, which was to play an important part in the 8th Army's crucial victory over Rommel and the pursuit of the *Afrika Korps* out of North Africa.

In July 1943 Leese was still commanding 30 Corps in the Allied landings in Sicily and southern Italy. In December that year Montgomery returned to Britain to start planning for D-Day, and Leese took over from him as G.O.C. 8th Army. The British and US forces under Field-Marshal Alexander and General Mark Clark were now fighting their way up through central Italy, but the Americans, on the western side, were blocked in midwinter by strong German defences around Monte Cassino. In May 1944 Leese led his troops undetected across the Appenines from the east and, with the help of the Polish corps, who admired his leadership, captured the key German stronghold on 17

May, opening the way for the liberation of Rome. Later he re-crossed the Appenines, once more taking the Germans by surprise, and broke through a second defensive line. For this, Leese was knighted in July by King George VI, during the monarch's incognito visit to the battle area. He also received a high Polish decoration, in addition to his French *Croix de Guerre.*

In September 1944 Leese, who had always been championed by Winston Churchill, was appointed Commander-in-Chief of Allied Land Forces in South-East Asia, reporting to the Supreme Allied Commander, Admiral Lord Louis Mountbatten. General Slim's 14th Army, under Leese's overall command, succeeded in driving the Japanese out of Burma. But Leese was temperamentally unsuited to the rarified atmosphere of high strategy. He clashed both with Slim and Mountbatten and his posting was terminated prematurely. He retired from the army in 1946 having earned a reputation as a brave and popular leader of his troops in the field, though quick-tempered, rather traditional in outlook and impatient with paper-work. He always shunned publicity.

In peacetime Leese was President of the Royal British Legion (1962-70) and greatly increased its membership. He was also sometime Chairman of the Old Etonian Association, and President of Warwickshire C.C. for 16 years. He was President of the MCC in 1965, being succeeded by fellow Old Ludgrovian Sir Alec Douglas Home. He died in 1978, aged 84.

Sir Denis Mahon C.H. – Art scholar and collector

Denis Mahon was born in 1910 and was at Ludgrove from 1919 to 1924.

A scion of the family which founded the merchant bankers, Guinness Mahon, he studied art history under Sir Kenneth Clark at Oxford, and Nikolaus Pevsner at the Courtauld Institute. It was largely due to the inspiration of these two mentors that he embarked on what has been described as "one of the most extraordinary careers in British – or indeed world – art history." Today Sir Denis Mahon is the world's leading authority on Italian art of the late 16th and 17th centuries, particularly known for his work on Caravaggio and Guercino; and – through the purchase over many years 79 paintings and numerous drawings – is the owner of a collection of priceless masterpieces of the *seicento,* which is unique in the world.

Through his immense prestige, Sir Denis was the main influence behind two landmark decisions in British art history. He persuaded the Treasury many years ago to accept the donation of works of art in lieu of inheritance tax; and in 2001 to allow museums to recover VAT in return for not charging an entrance fee.

He has now left his priceless paintings to the National Arts Collection Fund, which will place them on permanent loan to a number of galleries in Britain, Ireland and Italy – imposing the condition on British galleries that, should any of them decide to charge an admission fee or to dispose of any part of their permanent collections, it will immediately forfeit all the works loaned from the Mahon collection!

Sir Denis Mahon has received Honorary Doctorates from the Universities of Oxford, Newcastle, Rome and Bologna, and in 2002 was made a Companion of Honour. He is a Ludgrovian whose influence on the knowledge and appreciation of art extends throughout the world.

LUDGROVE IN PARLIAMENT

In the 1950 General Election, when the Conservatives came within a few seats of ousting Labour, Ludgrove was well represented in the House of Commons, with no fewer than eight MP's.

The Hon E. Carson – Isle of Thanet

Brig. A. Head – Carshalton

Col. D. Heathcoat Amory – Tiverton

Lord Dunglass – Lanark

Lord John Hope – Edinburgh Pentland

Col. W. Kingsmill – Yeovil

Hon. P. Remnant – Wokingham

Hon. R.O. Stanley – North Fylde

In due course Derick Heathcoat Amory (later 1st Viscount Amory) was to become Chancellor of the Exchequer under Harold Macmillan, 1958–1960; Lord John Hope (later Baron Glendevon) was Minister of Works in the same Government, 1959–62; Anthony Head (later Viscount Head) Secretary of State for War and then Minister of Defence, 1951–57), and Lord Dunglass (later Sir Alec Douglas Home) Foreign Secretary, 1960-63 and Prime Minister 1963–64.

In 1951, Winston Churchill, grandson of the wartime premier, arrived as a new boy at Ludgrove, and later became an MP himself.

THE DEATH OF HELEN DUNN

In July 1947 Sir Shane Leslie, one of the earliest pupils at Ludgrove, organised an 80th birthday party for Helen Dunn, widow of the founder, at which a presentation was made by Lord Linlithgow.

It was seconded by Lord Strathmore, the brother of the Queen. In July 1949, two years later almost to the day, Helen Dunn died.

Alan Barber wrote:

> Ever since her husband's death and her retirement, she has
> taken an intense interest in Ludgrove and her Old Boys. During
> her visit here only a few weeks before her death, she spent over
> an hour studying the name boards in the Dining Hall, and
> refreshing her memory of the boys who had been under her
> care. We who were born later owe more to her than we shall
> ever know, and her passing severs one of the last remaining
> links with Ludgrove's earliest years.

Helen Dunn in old age

The correspondence with Robert McCormick already referred to,
which Helen Dunn maintained for the last two years of her life, gives a vivid insight into
the personality of this much-loved figure.

THE WIND OF CHANGE

Gordon 'Cabbage' Reed was succeeded in 1952 by Tony Dunkerley; and the music
master Michael Howard left to be succeeded by Jetta Robertson, who
had trained professionally as a singer and had given solo concerts
in London. Her comments on one of the early concerts she put
on underlined the magnitude of the task facing anyone in
charge of Ludgrove's music at that time:

> The chorus singing struck me as lifeless and lacking in
> resonance…since none of the boys seemed to know their
> words with any certainty…Selbie has rather a weak voice,
> and found Purcell's song too much for him, where his
> intonation was at fault, possibly due to nerves.…I have heard
> Meynell play better in practice; in this concert his performance
> was musically incoherent…and two of the songs proved too much
> for the choir, with two who were guilty of failing to listen properly and count
> their beats able to lead astray the remainder of the choir.

Jetta Robertson

Jetta in fact revived the tradition of putting on concerts by local musicians to enhance
the School's appreciation of music, a practice that had not been seen at Ludgrove since
the times of Arthur Dunn; and notable musicians of the period whom she remembers
include Jeremy Clyde, Nigel Cumming, Nigel Downes and Jeremy Goulding. But in
spite of the support of such members of staff as Peter Borgnis, Gertrude Paul and even
Ken Morrison, Ludgrove's massive disinterest towards musical endeavour, combined
with the appalling state of the school pianos which stood in dusty corners and corridors
and were seldom maintained, meant that little cultural progress was made during the

Jetta's choir of 1955; the author is top right.

Barber-Shaw years. It was little surprise that Jetta left after a few years to continue her career as a professional singer.

Scholastic achievement

Ludgrove has never required an entrance exam to be taken by its pupils, and could never have been considered an academic forcing-house like some of its contemporaries. In the 36 years of Barber-Shaw and Barber *seul*, from 1937 to 1973 when Alan retired, the school achieved just 25 scholarships, which was probably low by the standards of any leading prep schools of the time.

However, in the early 1950s there was a significant increase in scholarships won: in 1950 Charles Douglas Home won a scholarship to Eton; in 1951 Paul Foot won one to Shrewsbury; and in 1953 Nicholas Barber and Tommy Stockdale won scholarships to Shrewsbury and Eton respectively. For each of these awards the school was granted a half-holiday in celebration. Nicholas stayed on one extra term – his award gave him entry to Shrewsbury in the Spring Term 1954 – and at the end of the Michaelmas Term 1953 he carried off the form prizes for every single subject in Division I (a feat never previously achieved) and also won the senior Essay Prize. He was in the 1st XI for cricket and football, and took the leading part in the school play.

As Prince Giglio in Thackeray's *The Rose and the Ring*, he played opposite his brother, the author, as the Countess Gruffanuff, in a scene together that was described

N. Barber (second from right) and R. Barber (second from left) in 'The Rose and the Ring'

as "full of understanding"! Reviewing this production, Alan Cattley called it "without doubt the most enjoyable play that your scribe has ever seen at a preparatory school".

Three teachers from the Class of '58

In recruiting staff ATB's approach was to rely strongly on a combination of the views of the candidate expressed by others, and his own innate sense of who would and would not fit in. In setting their salaries, his only two questions were "Have you got any means of your own?" (a number of the Ludgrove masters did have private means – and needed them), and "What is your current salary?" That was usually the last time money would be discussed.

In 1958 he recruited three new members of staff, who gave distinguished and loyal service to the School: Micky Burton-Brown, Margaret Maldwyn-Davies and Mike Ainsworth.

Micky Burton-Brown's recruitment in 1958 to run Classics was a good example of ATB's selection technique. Micky had been brought up at Bradfield, where his father was a house-master, and he himself was a scholar of Charterhouse and Pembroke College, Oxford (where he had also been University captain of Eton Fives). He was an outstanding teacher, a natural enthusiast and a fine player of all ball games. He was about to leave his teaching post at Rugby for Marlborough when Alan persuaded him to come to Ludgrove on the understanding that Micky would succeed him and Tim Shaw as Headmaster "in due course".

Micky recalls:

> I didn't really have an interview as such. I went there for supper with Alan and Dorothy one evening, after which we adjourned

Micky Burton-Brown

to the drawing-room, when I thought I would at last be asked some searching questions. But the questions never came. By about 10 o'clock I thought perhaps I'd better ask some questions myself. So I can remember asking two questions: if I came to Ludgrove, what would you ask me to teach? And what are you going to pay me? Alan said he'd like me to teach Latin, Greek and English to the top form; and as far as pay was concerned he said "Well, what are you being paid now?" At the time I was being paid £500 a year by Rugby, so Alan said he'd pay me the same which was pretty good in those days…although not quite so good 10 years later when it was still about £500! And that is how I came to be offered the job.

In those days masters were paid one third of their salary three times a year, on the last day of each term. Micky stresses what a challenge this was, especially to have no income between the cheque at the end of the summer term in July and the next one just before Christmas. Nor was there a pension scheme in place, unlike most other preparatory schools. There is no doubt that Alan and Tim considered that people were "jolly lucky to be here at all", and that this was in itself an important part of a master's compensation! So money, like succession, was little discussed. As Micky explains:

> There was of course no contract of employment – so no formal commitment to my succeeding him either – just an understanding between us that this would happen "in due course". In fact it never did. After 10 years, in 1969, I knew that I had to advance my own career elsewhere, and so I left to become Headmaster of Edgeborough in Surrey.

Yet, for all their reticence about money matters, Alan and Tim recruited a remarkable group of people to the team, many of them born teachers who committed their whole careers to the Ludgrove ideal, who thrived on the atmosphere the Headmasters created, and were fiercely loyal to the leadership they gave. Micky Burton-Brown himself said later:

> What hit me first was the atmosphere of the place – both in the school and in the masters' Common Room. I'd never been in a school that was so obviously happy. There was always a huge amount of noise going on, and in later life when I became a Headmaster myself, I used to recall Alan's words "Noise is healthy!" because boys really can't be unhappy when they're making a noise. I always used to try to cultivate a similar atmosphere in my school to the one I had known at Ludgrove.

In his ten years at Ludgrove Micky had played a pivotal role in many domains of school life – in the classroom, on the games field (he ran the 1st XI football) and in the extra-curricular activities such as the Dramatic Society. His departure left a gap that was keenly felt by all.

Margaret Maldwyn-Davies ran the music at Ludgrove from 1958 until 1985. One of Ludgrove's 'characters', she was primarily a pianist and 'cellist, and a music teacher very much of 'the old school', stressing the beat with an occasional rap over the performer's knuckles and bringing to her instruction a vigorous approach and a strong personality, which her pupils still recall with a mixture of apprehension and affection. She produced a number of pianists of real distinction, and coached her choirs to high levels of achievement, culminating in the carol services in the Chapel and (informally) in the old gym, where Peter Borgnis would regularly sing the part of Good King Wenceslas, and the whole school would join in "The Twelve Days of Christmas". For many years she looked after the two dormitories adjoining her flat, sometimes complaining that ATB always sent her "the villains". But she brought her own style of efficiency and humour to the role, and many a boy enjoyed his terms there under her supervision. She retired to Wokingham in 1985 where she entertained in great style until her death in 1997. She was a loyal servant of Ludgrove, and a notable member of the local community.

Margaret Maldwyn-Davies

Mike Ainsworth (MLYA) was born in 1922. At Shrewsbury (1935–41) he was one of the outstanding cricketers of his generation. On leaving school he joined the Royal Navy, serving in the Mediterranean, where he was twice sunk before gaining his commission. After the war, while taking the naval staff-course at Greenwich, he played cricket for Worcestershire in 1949 and 1950. He captained the Combined Services XI for seven years (1953–59), and – like Peter Borgnis before him – played for them against the visiting Australian and Pakistan Test sides at Portsmouth (in 1953 and 1954 respectively). Mike was also an Eton fives player of real distinction, reaching the final of the Kinnaird Cup in 1960.

From the Navy he joined Ludgrove in 1958, where he taught geography, ran the cricket, rugger and fives, and sang in the choir until his premature death at the age of 56 while playing cricket for the Incogniti at Chenies, near Amersham, in 1978.

Mike Ainsworth

No one who knew Mike ever saw him other than cheerful, positive and approachable, from his cheery greeting in the morning to his departure the end of the day. Known affectionately to all as 'the Commander', he had that quality of constancy on which everyone could rely. He made people around him glad to be in his company, and with his happy disposition and imposing presence (especially on the fives court) he was one of Ludgrove's most recognisable figures for the 20 years that he taught there. He was truly a man for all seasons.

On his death, as a mark of their affection for him, the Free Foresters Cricket Club instituted 'the M.L.Y. Ainsworth Scholarship' to provide three days coaching at Lord's for one boy a year from (in rotating order) Ludgrove, Shrewsbury and Bradfield (where his son Peter had been at school). It is an award that is highly-prized to this day, honouring in perpetuity the name of this distinguished and devoted servant of Ludgrove.

In Mike's memory, his wife Patricia presented the School with a cup for the best all-round sportsman of the year. The Ainsworth Cup is the most coveted sporting trophy to be won at Ludgrove today.

FEATS OF THE FIFTIES

Cricket

The 1952 cricket season garnered a severe critique from ATB, which included the comment "on average three catches were dropped in the first six overs of every match, and few of them could have been termed difficult". However that season is especially memorable in the mind of the author, then in his second year, for the defeat of Lockers Park, whose side contained the Nawab of Pataudi, later to captain Oxford, Sussex and India.

'Tiger' Pataudi, batting for Sussex.

He had made centuries against other schools with great regularity all season. But against Ludgrove that year he scored a paltry 14 before being clean bowled by a boy called Browne. One week later, Browne was mysteriously renamed Lord Altamont (presumably on the death of his father). But not being familiar with the rules of aristocratic succession, it was clear to my youthful eye that Browne's bowling of the

The young Lord Altamont; enobled for clean bowling Pataudi?

great Nawab was considered by Alan to have been so stupendous an achievement that it went beyond the mere awarding of 1st XI colours. Only elevation to the peerage itself could be adequate recognition!

It was a long time before I was persuaded otherwise. Browne's triumph was savagely revenged the following year when the Nawab made 104, took 3 wickets, and held two catches "which no other member of his side could have touched".

Many feats of arms were recorded in the years of the 1950s – the analysis of that wily leg-spinner Richard Gooch against Elstree in 1955 is of particular note:

Overs	Maidens	Runs	Wickets	Average
5	5	0	5	0

But nothing can compare with the sustained assault upon enemy sides, which was delivered in the years of the mid-1950s by Mike Griffith. Mike was the third boy (together with Colin Ingleby-Mackenzie and the Nawab of Pataudi) whom Alan Barber said in later years he considered too good to play against other prep schools.

Mike Griffith was the son of S.C. "Billy" Griffith who had kept wicket for Sussex and England, and was at that time Secretary of the MCC. He came to Ludgrove in the winter term of 1951. By the time he left in 1957 he had been in the Cricket 1st XI for four years, and had surpassed Colin Ingleby-Mackenzie's record score in a single season in each of his last 3 years – scoring 532, 554 and 679 runs in school matches between 1955 and 1957. This performance has never

Mike Griffith keeping wicket for Sussex

been beaten at Ludgrove. In addition to his batting supremacy he was probably the best wicket-keeper Ludgrove has ever produced, achieving a record number of stumpings in one season (nine – including a hat-trick of them against Lambrook off the bowling of Charles Cordle).

ATB commented:

> 1956 should be known as 'Griffith's year'…on no occasion was his behaviour other than that of a born cricketer who had acquired by association and upbringing the habits of a mature player.

While at Ludgrove, Griffith also won the cups for cricket, football, fives and squash. He went on to Marlborough where he kept wicket for the 1st XI in each of his five years there. He captained the Southern Schools at Lord's and subsequently played for Cambridge University and Sussex. In later life he played hockey for England and Great Britain.

A mischievous line was added in the commentary on that 1957 season about another member of the side, Julian Holloway, son of the great comic actor Stanley Holloway, and now an actor himself:

Julian Holloway today

It was suggested to Holloway that he should act the part of some brilliant fielder like Neil Harvey or Tony Lock – but unfortunately this proved beyond even his considerable powers, and he remained a very conspicuous passenger.

In the same year, James Beard, opening the bowling, took a record number of wickets, 60 in 13 matches for an average of 2.95. Sadly, James died of cancer several years later. His sister's unsuccessful attempt to save his life by donating her bone-marrow was the subject of a television programme; it was one of the first attempts to combat the illness in this way.

James Beard in 1957

In contrast to these Herculean feats, this single line of an analysis in 1955, when Ludgrove played the Horris Hill eleven including one G. Barber, has for ever remained in the memories of the bowler and fielder – but not, one suspects, of the batsman:

G.W.P. Barber – c. R.E.S. Gooch b. R.P.F. Barber   2

Gerald Barber (on the left, in pads) in the Horris Hill 1st Eleven

It should be added that Ludgrove were soundly defeated on that occasion by 64 runs!

Golf

Ludgrove's 9-hole golf course is acknowledged as one of the finest preparatory school courses in the country. Many Ludgrovians have swung a golf club for the first time on this course and quite a number made their mark while at the school. The highlight of the golfing year was the annual match against ATB's team, in which Alan assembled a random group of scratch club players, parents, staff and on occasions Dorothy and himself, to challenge the boys over 9 holes, giving them a handicap of a stroke a hole.

This invariably proved too much for the adults, who in some years scored scarcely a point. Gradually this handicap was reduced, and some extremely close matches took place. Probably the best golfers during the 1950s and 1960s were Garth Milne, (subsequently Captain of Sunningdale, and of Eton's Halford Hewitt Cup side) and Andy Swanston, who played for Cambridge and won the President's Putter at Rye.

Squash

Garth Milne was also the outstanding squash player of the 1950s, beating Mike Griffith narrowly in the Ludgrove final of 1955. This provided a foretaste of things to come, for Garth turned his early skill at squash to outstanding success on the rackets court at Eton. He became the only person up to that time to win the H.K.Foster (Public Schools) Cup in successive years (1960 and 1961); in the latter he beat his old adversary, Mike Griffith of Marlborough in the final. The match was so close that over the five games the loser actually scored one point more than the winner. Milne came back from 8–14 down in the fifth to win it 17–16, and an extract from the record of this extraordinary match between these two Old Ludgrovians is worth quoting:

Garth Milne (right) after narrowly beating Mike Griffith for the H.K.Foster Cup in the Public Schools Rackets Championship, 1961

> It is no extravagant claim to suggest that this was one of the finest matches on record at this level, not only in the high standard of play…but in the thrill and tension of its vacillating score; for this at least the match can seldom have been exceeded.

George Pope in action at Eton

Athletics

The achievements of Ludgrove's two Olympians, Gerard Anderson before the First World War and Lord Burghley in the 1930s, set them apart as Ludgrove's two greatest athletes. But many excellent athletes competed during the 1960s, such as Anthony Farquhar, Mike Griffith and Simon Hanbury. Outstanding among these was George Pope (1951–55). In his last year at Ludgrove he won the 220 yards, Hurdles and High Jump. Later at Eton he twice won the school Steeplechase and Mile, and in the London School Mile race at the White City in 1960 he set a new Eton school record, which still stands.

The School in the Sixties

The 1960s brought a number of significant events for the school:

Old Ludgrovian Society founded

Charles Wiggin in the Cricket 1st XI, 1898

In the spring of 1960 the first meeting took place at the Hyde Park Hotel of the Old Ludgrovian Society, organised by its Secretary, Hilary Warr. Thirty-eight old boys attended it, and an Old Ludgrovian tie (designed by Normile Baxter) was displayed for the first time. Alan Barber and Tim Shaw presided. Alan spoke about the history of the school from its earliest days, before introducing Sir Charles Wiggin, who recounted scenes from his life at the school at the end of the 19th century.

Frank Henley dies

Frank Henley died in 1963. He had joined the Ludgrove staff in 1905, and retired in 1937 after 33 years, 15 of them as Headmaster. William Douglas Home wrote:

> I can see him now, as if it were yesterday, sitting on his shooting stick in an IZ blazer umpiring a cricket match – or teaching Divinity on the blackboard with a host of different coloured chalks: always friendly, always comforting, always somehow avuncular and ageless, with his friendly smile…when he came to my wedding, twenty five years after I had last seen him singing a sea-shanty on my last Supper Night, I was struck by the fact that in appearance, friendliness and charm he had not changed at all…a normal, happy man with a great sense of humour and an unfailing understanding of and kindness towards the small boys in his charge.

School numbers climb

At the time of the move, Ludgrove had recovered its numbers rapidly from 47 in 1934 to 59 boys in 1937 – though still fewer than the 62 boys at the time of Arthur Dunn's death in 1902. But numbers shot up during the war, from 67 in 1940, to 102 by 1945. Throughout the 1950s the size of the school stabilised at around 90, but during the 1960s they rose again, reaching 112 by 1969.

The winter of 1962–3

In 1963 the pond froze for weeks and most of the term's exercise was taken on ice. Ice-hockey was played every day for weeks on end, and the match against Heatherdown – who had no pond of their own – was won 13–0!

Music – a master adjudicator

D.C ("Ceddie") Hammond-Chambers-Borgnis, Peter's brother, was the master in charge of music at Eton at this time, and visited Ludgrove regularly throughout the 1960s and 1970s to judge the music competitions. He was a gentle and sympathetic adjudicator – on one occasion he awarded Alexander Scrymgeour (later the Earl of Dundee) 18 marks out of 15 for his outstanding playing of a Bach prelude. It was written of him that

> his comments and criticisms were a real pleasure to hear – expert, sincere and kindly. No judge ever condemned a criminal more reluctantly or acquitted him with a more helpful caution.

Science introduced to the syllabus!

It is a revealing comment on the durability of the classical tradition in English education that as late as 1959 the IAPS was recommending that science should not be a compulsory paper in Common Entrance. By 1965, however, it had recommended to prep schools that "two to three periods a week must be found for science teaching in the last three years…and it *might* (author's italics) be well to plan for the teaching of science throughout the whole of a boys' preparatory school career." That same year science was introduced at Ludgrove, taught by Tim Shaw. In 1968 Gerald Barber took it over on Tim's retirement, and by swotting the syllabus managed to stay just one lesson ahead of the brightest boy in the class! In 1975 he gratefully handed over to a new master, Simon Warner, and in the same year Science finally became a compulsory subject in Common Entrance.

Common Room changes

Peter Ainsworth vividly captures the changing culture of the Common Room in the early 1960s:

> As in so much else, Ludgrove in the 1960s was in transition from one era to another. The senior masters were people who had fought in the second world war – men in tweed jackets with leather patches on their sleeves who had had distinguished service records. One almost felt that some, like John Rickards, had fought in the First World War! My father had been in the services, as had Tim Shaw, Peter Borgnis, John Rickards himself of course, and their experience and outlook was very influential on my generation

Peter Ainsworth MP, now Chairman of the All-Party Environmental Committee

because the Second World War was not long past and with these people mentoring our lives it seemed very close indeed.

So the sort of values that they had when they themselves were growing up in the 1930s were still being inculcated into us. I remember being shown a map of the world and it was all covered red, the British Empire and all that. It left me at that early age with a certain feeling of national pride.

But this also became one of nostalgia too – because by the Sixties the world was moving on, one could feel the Winds of Change, Harold Wilson was Prime Minister and we were in his "white heat of technology", new, younger staff were now joining the School, and one could sense the pace of change beginning to quicken.

Nichol Marston

The son of a former Headmaster of Summer Fields, Oxford, where he was brought up, Nichol went to Eton and Keble College, Oxford where he played golf for the University and was awarded a Divot (the university second team). He joined Ludgrove in 1963, straight from Oxford, and has dedicated the 41 years of his career there, with indefatigable zeal, to raising and sustaining the academic reputation of the school. His particular expertise is in the teaching of Mathematics, in which, over the years, he has lifted so many boys from ordinary to excellent, and given them a love of the subject, which his pupils readily acknowledge in later years – as indeed do the public schools to which they have gone.

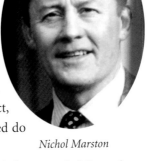

Nichol Marston

He also ran the Football in his early days, and introduced the annual skiing trip, which he continued to organise until his retirement.

As Joint Headmaster he has been the main enforcer of discipline in the school. His praise is sparing, and therefore considered by boys to be worth ten times that of other masters. He is a strong supporter of tradition and makes no secret of his suspicion of innovation (especially of the technical and computer-based variety).

"Which button do I press?" Nichol and Gerald in hi-tech mode.

Nichol has always sought to bring out the best in every boy, no matter where his talents may lie. One of his former pupils, 'Bear' Grylls, who remembers him with affection, said of him: "He has a wonderful understanding of the mind of a twelve year old". He retired in the summer of 2004.

Gerald Barber joined the Ludgrove staff two years after Nichol's arrival and exactly 36 years after his father had done so.

Gerald is the *genius loci* of Ludgrove, representing the third generation of Headmasters of Ludgrove from the same family. The son of Alan and Dorothy, Gerald was born in 1943 and went to school at Horris Hill and Eton before going to St. Edmund Hall, Oxford, where he read Geography. While there, he was Captain of the University Eton Fives Club, played for the university second teams at cricket (the Authentics) and golf (the Divots), and was a member of the Harlequins Cricket Club.

On coming down from Oxford he taught at Mowden School in *Gerald Barber*

Hove. There he met Janet Snell, daughter of the headmaster Edward Snell, himself a close friend of Alan's since their Oxford days together.

Janet Snell in 1965

Gerald joined the staff of Ludgrove in 1966, teaching history, Latin and junior mathematics, and helping Mike Ainsworth with the cricket. In 1968, on Tim Shaw's retirement, he took over the teaching of science. That same year Gerald and Janet Snell were married, and in 1969 he became Joint Assistant Headmaster with Nichol Marston. On his father's retirement in 1973 he and Nichol became Joint Headmasters.

Gerald is cast visibly in the same mould as ATB, characteristically as determined, constantly on the go around the school, devoted to the buildings, the grounds and their maintenance, and delegating little of the administration to others. As Headmaster, his main focus is on maintaining the whole character of the school, and on the relationships with all Ludgrove's external constituents, with whom his relaxed manner and ready humour have forged friendships far and wide. He has always encouraged new ideas among a team of teachers with whom he has created a strong family atmosphere and a palpable team spirit, which is one of the school's greatest and most enduring strengths.

Stephen Graham joined Ludgrove from the Black Watch in 1965 to teach English and Geography. He had a great love of words and language, and sought to impart to his

pupils a real appreciation of the sense and sound of English prose and poetry. He was known to the boys as "Hawk-Eye" for his ability to know exactly what was going on in his class even when his back was turned. He ran Ludgrove's athletics and Under-Eleven football throughout his time, and with Peter Borgnis, took the second game of cricket ('Rising Talent'), and also the Dramatic Society, which he took on alone after Peter's retirement. He fought hard to get rugby recognised as a major school sport and, with Mike Ainsworth, was in charge of this for many years. It was Stephen who introduced Sports Day to Ludgrove to replace the old Fathers' Cricket Match as the central event of the summer term. He was appointed Senior Master in 1976 in which position he managed the school timetable, and provided the crucial link between the Headmasters and the Common Room.

Stephen Graham

Stephen and his wife Mary retired to Hampshire in 1993. He will be remembered for the quality of his teaching, his meticulous attention to detail, his pastoral care for the boys and, for over twenty years, his towering support for the Headmasters "behind the headlines" in ensuring, through the huge trouble he took with everything he did, that all the moving parts of the Ludgrove machine remained in full working order throughout his time.

Duncan Beardmore-Gray

Duncan was a scholar at Eton where he was in the cricket XI, the Field, the Oppidan Wall and was Keeper of Fives. He went to Oriel College, Oxford, where he read PPE. He then farmed for ten years, qualified as a Chartered Accountant and later ran various businesses. In his early forties, he decided on a further change of career, and at ATB's invitation joined Ludgrove in 1969, where he taught English, Latin and History. He recalls that

> my education was furthered by a succession of delightful, intelligent boys who did their best to lighten my darkness in a variety of subjects.

Ducan Beardmore-Gray, "a gentle giant in a red cardigan"

He was a particular inspiration to the brightest in the school, and through his ceaseless conversations with boys always sought to bring out the best in them by encouraging new ideas, self-expression and wider knowledge. A former pupil said of him:

> I remember Duncan Beardmore-Gray as a gentle giant in a red cardigan! He was larger than life, an irrepressible enthusiast and great to be taught by, never talking

down to one. He loved his subjects, and imparted enthusiasm for them in a way I shall never forget.

For some time Duncan ran the school Fives, and also the Under-Ten cricket and football. Deeply suspicious of actors and acting, he nevertheless found himself, to his surprise, running the Middle School Play, "where I discovered" he said, "that most 11-year-old boys see themselves as budding Laurence Oliviers, with enthusiasm to match." An irrepressible enthusiast himself, Duncan retired in 1992 after 23 years' service to the school.

THE END OF AN ERA

In 1968 Tim Shaw retired. He had personally brought Alan Barber into the school; together they had nurtured its growing fame and expanded its numbers. By the time he left, Ludgrove had 115 boys, the highest number in its history. In the Michaelmas term of 1969 Gerald Barber and Nichol Marston were formally appointed Assistant Headmasters. The future of Ludgrove was slowly taking shape.

Formation of the Trust

With Tim's retirement, Alan was now in sole command. In 1970 he decided to buy Ludgrove from its landlord, the Marquess of Downshire. The purchase of the entire School complex and all its surrounding land was concluded that year for the remarkably modest sum of £31,000.

Having secured the freehold, Alan then made a further decision in 1972 to turn the whole enterprise into a charitable trust. It was a development as significant for the survival and prosperity of the School as had been its move from Barnet to Wokingham in 1937. With the advice of close friends, especially the late 6th Earl of Rosslyn, the Ludgrove Charitable Trust was formally constituted in March 1972. The first meeting of

The 6th Earl of Rosslyn

Pat Meredith-Hardy

Arthur Dunn's grandson, Ned Boldero

the Trustees took place in May 1972, chaired by Pat Meredith-Hardy, with Ned Boldero – Arthur Dunn's grandson – as Secretary, and Normile Baxter present.

The early meetings were taken up with such crucial and practical issues as acquiring the assets of the school from ATB; drawing up the first service-agreements for the Headmaster and the two Assistant Headmasters; raising the school fees and chasing late payments; checking the adequacy of the school insurance cover; evicting the tenant from the East Lodge, who had defaulted on his rent; and launching Ludgrove's first Appeal. Ludgrove's management was moving emphatically into a new, more professional mode.

For the record, the first Governors of the Ludgrove Charitable Trust, in addition to those already mentioned, were Pat Cumming, Peter Eckersley, Peter Hill-Wood, and Colin Ingleby-Mackenzie.

Finale

It has to be said the years after Tim Shaw's retirement were not easy ones for Ludgrove. Economic difficulties were compounded by Alan's infirmity. True, he bore his increasing hip pain with uncomplaining courage, and in 1972 was one of the first people in the UK to have both his hips replaced – the 'Charnley hip' – but his traditional outlook was impeding an ever more obvious need for change.

Alan and Dorothy in happy retirement

It had always been his intention to retire in 1975 when he would have been 70. However the end came in May 1973, after a stormy masters' meeting following a staff dinner. Later that evening he informed Gerald of his decision to retire at the end of that term, and that Gerald and Nichol Marston should succeed him. The following September Alan and Dorothy began their well-earned retirement in the Garden Cottage. Alan was 68.

On 10th October 1973 an Old Ludgrovian Dinner was held for 140 people at Quaglino's to mark this event. Ludgrove's most distinguished Old Boy, the former Prime Minister Sir Alec Douglas Home, was unwell, so his brother the Hon. William Douglas Home presided. Nichol Marston and Ronnie Lagden (father of Richard and Robert) spoke respectively on behalf of the School and the parents, and generous presentations were made to Alan, Dorothy, and Tim Shaw, in recognition of the magnificent legacy they had maintained for over a third of a century and were now handing on to the next generation.

THE FAREWELL DINNER AT QUAGLINOS

Dorothy Barber with Sir Martin Gilliat (left) and Pat Meredith-Hardy

Janet Barber in conversation with Pat Cumming

Two old buffers run into each other!

It was indeed the end of an era.

Chapter VIII

A THRIVING
ENTERPRISE: 1973–2004

"Famed for its TLC"
National survey of prep schools, 2002

Gerald Barber and Nichol Marston became joint Headmasters of Ludgrove at the start of the Michaelmas term 1973. It was a torrid start. With their new reign, the new school year and 20 new boys all about to start in one week, Gerald and Janet moved to their new home in the main School building on the night of 5th September. At 9 o'clock on the following morning news came through that Janet's beloved father, Edward Snell, had died suddenly of a heart-attack. He was 68. He had been the distinguished headmaster of Mowden School in Hove for over 40 years. Coming at such a time, it was a shattering blow for Janet and the whole family. At his funeral service in Hove a few days later, John Rickards and Peter Borgnis, who had known him only slightly, were both present. It was a moving sign of their deep sympathy, and an emphatic mark of their support for the new team now taking charge at Ludgrove.

Edward Snell, Janet Barber's father

That support, equally given by many other people who had played a vital part in the life of the school in ATB's closing years, such as Stephen Graham, Mike Ainsworth, Margaret Maldwyn-Davies, Duncan Beardmore-Gray and Alan's secretary, Wendy Spackman, provided an indispensable bridge from the *ancien régime* to the new. Gerald and Nichol faced the daunting task of taking over the whole enterprise at the beginning of a school year, and of introducing much-needed and far-reaching changes to the whole fabric of Ludgrove life.

Three decisions were made immediately, which were to shape the direction of the school for the next 30 years:

Wendy Spackman, secretary to Alan and Gerald Barber

- First, Gerald and Nichol, as Joint Headmasters, would operate as fully equal partners, agreeing on a clear division of labour between them, so that each would contribute his particular skills without putting the partnership at risk of confusion, overlap or disagreement.

- Second, strengthening the financial position must be their priority, since major investment programmes had to be launched to modernise and expand the buildings and curriculum, and to raise pupil intake.

- Third, this ambitious programme must be carried through in such a way as to preserve all the main values and traditions fundamental to Ludgrove's style and reputation.

Above: Gerald making white lines.
Below: Nichol serving food in the Dining Hall

The Partnership

Like G.O. Smith and Bill Oakley before them, the partnership of Gerald Barber and Nichol Marston quickly developed into a model of co-operation. They had a close personal understanding, having been contemporaries in Philip Snow's house at Eton (where Gerald had 'fagged' for Nichol) and at Oxford. In their characters they were a complementary blend of the innovator (Gerald) and the conservative (Nichol); both came from long and distinguished prep school traditions, and knew full well that the key success factor in running a prep school is total unity at the top. They would delegate to others little that they could do personally, so that everything would be carried out as they themselves wished; and at the same time they divided their responsibilities in a way that would exploit the strengths of each. Gerald handled parent and staff relations, and all administrative, bursarial and financial matters, including the sport, the management of the buildings, and maintenance of the grounds. Nichol assumed the academic and disciplinary responsibilities.

The three-way partnership was completed by Janet, who took on Dorothy Barber's role in the domestic and pastoral life of the School, investing these with her own particular brand of dedication and, over the years, enhancing the Ludgrove legend with an unsurpassed reputation for care and good communication.

Getting things shipshape

Although there were now record numbers in the school – 128 boys in the Michaelmas term of 1973 – the problems hinted at in the last chapter were becoming increasingly apparent. In the closing years of ATB's headmastership Ludgrove had become something of a drifting ship. There were symptoms of this everywhere: the decaying fabric of the buildings, with the familiar "plink-plonk" sound of raindrops falling from leaky roofs into strategically placed buckets; the antedeluvian and positively hazardous electric wiring; extensive dry-rot; primitive bathroom and washing facilities. The forward order-book was thin, with a chastening decline in the number of Old Ludgrovians putting their sons down for the school. ATB, then in his 60s, and in increasing pain from his hips, had found it physically difficult to show prospective parents round the school and was in any case rather remote from a new generation of parents half his age. The cumulative effect of all this was as serious for Ludgrove's future as the circumstances had been in the early 1930s. There were some who thought the school would not last another five years. Once again Ludgrove was waiting for new leadership in order to embrace substantial and overdue change.

In 1972, just before Alan Barber retired, Ned Boldero, as Secretary of the Ludgrove Trust, sent a memorandum on the state of the School to the Governors. It started:

> The Governors of the Ludgrove School Trust Ltd appear to have inherited a number of problems which are more serious than any of us at first thought …. Ludgrove has a fine reputation, but must face up to the present …. We face an urgent and immense task. ATB will not take kindly to some of the points that we must raise, but diplomacy with firmness is the requirement if we are to begin to accept our responsibilities as outlined in the Articles of Association: '…*to be responsible for the continuity and traditions of the school and its future development and financial stability'.*

He then highlighted four major areas of concern, around which the new Headmasters were encouraged to formulate their priorities:

- Financially, the school was in deficit, and the position was deteriorating. Analysis showed that the fees were too low compared with other schools; that too many accounts were overdue or unpaid (some parents owing more than £1,000); that control of tradesmen's bills needed tightening up; and that costs in general were rising too fast. The school finances were all the more stretched by inflation in the UK, then heading above 20%, and with the masters' pay levels and their still unpensioned terms of service falling significantly behind the market.
- The numbers in the school were inadequate. A major drive on recruiting new entrants was needed. Although there was a record number of boys in the school, the forward bookings were falling. This had to be arrested, and the intake significantly expanded.

- The fabric of the school required major surgery. Key priorities involved several unexciting but fundamental aspects of the infrastructure. This programme had to be expanded and accelerated.
- Academically, Ludgrove needed urgently to address the strident criticism from Eton and other major schools of its very modest achievements and the impact of these on its reputation.

The fabric of the school required major surgery...

A programme to address all these issues began to take shape. It was soon apparent to parents, staff and boys alike that Ludgrove had embarked upon an era of major change in almost every aspect of school life – of leadership, of management style, of academic focus, of syllabus, of renovation, modernisation and expansion. No programme of change so radical had been carried out since the move from Barnet to Wokingham over a third of a century before.

Maintaining continuity

In most institutions radical change usually goes hand in hand with major upheaval in the whole culture of the enterprise. But the new Headmasters were very aware that one of Ludgrove's most precious assets lay in the long continuity of its traditions. The values and style of the School, nurtured for so long in a close, strongly family-run atmosphere, were indispensable to its reputation. These they were determined to preserve intact in spite of all the change required. It would be a difficult balance to achieve. But symptomatic of this, in their first term they made only two changes of any note to the daily life of the school:

- they abolished the singing of *O God our help in ages past* on the first day of each term. As Nichol said, "this hymn was always guaranteed to bring tears to young eyes with its dirge-like tune and the implication for young minds of such lines as "Be Thou our Guard while troubles last...""

A new morning routine

- and they also stopped the daily 'Morning Parade' to the lavatories with the handing out of sheets of loo paper by the master on duty, and the verdicts on the state of each boy's regularity given to him afterwards – "which encourages you" says Nichol, with telling insight "to lie first thing in the morning – not a 'correct' way in which to start each day!"

Apart from those two things the daily routines of the School remained largely unchanged.

Academic performance

However the impact of new hands at the helm did quickly become apparent in the greater emphasis that the Headmasters placed on the classroom; and in their strengthening of the cultural, extra-curricular, sporting and pastoral life of the school.

Since its foundation, Ludgrove has never wavered in its policy of taking any boy who may wish to come to the school without an entrance examination, no matter what his academic ability. But Gerald and Nichol knew that, in the more competitive environment of the 1970s, a strong reputation for academic excellence outweighed sporting results. The school's centre of gravity therefore needed to be shifted from the games-field to the classroom. This was all the more urgent since Eton itself, under its Head Master Michael McCrum, was undergoing considerable academic change at that time and raising its own standards. This was being forcefully communicated to its feeder schools.

At Ludgrove, Common Entrance under Alan Barber and Tim Shaw was always an important target; but it was largely taken for granted that boys would pass into the school of their choice. Stephen Graham summed up the academic approach of those years:

> Alan would say to his masters "You've got a syllabus, you know what you've got to do, now go and do it! You should consult people who may know more about it than you do, and if you've got any questions come and ask me. But I trust you to get on with it and do it."
>
> Of course he did control who taught what, but there was no clear syllabus as such for what you had to cover. It was all very laid back. And of course there wasn't anything like the pressure then because, on the whole, boys did get into the school of their choice without any problems.

This lack of challenge had led to academic stagnation. By the late 1960s Ludgrove's reputation at Eton, by far the most important destination for its leavers, was in decline. In spite of several outstanding teachers, the content of their teaching had not changed with the syllabus, and educational standards were generally no more than adequate.

Little importance was attached to achieving scholarships; music and art were taught only as 'extras'; and science teaching was still in its infancy. A new academic rigour had to be introduced.

Nichol Marston was the main force behind this. New staff were recruited: Tony Esau, George Hughes-Games, and Tristram Yelin (returning after several years elsewhere). A new science block was created and a new science master (Simon Warner) recruited; and more was asked of the staff to raise the all-round level of teaching.

Out of the Mouths…

The study of British history has sometimes produced some intriguing insights. For example, on the Battle of Hastings:

"Half way through the battle, word goes round the Norman camp that William is dead, and morale goes down. But then William exposes himself, and morale goes back up again." – Alec Mills

Looking back on this, Nichol Marston comments:

> It would be wrong to suggest that the years 1973–2004 have been studded with conspicuous scholarship success. Ludgrove has always resisted the temptation of having an entry test. This has meant a wide range of ability, which the Headmasters have always been keen to maintain. In most years total success has been achieved at Common Entrance, with 55% to 60% of boys going to Eton and the rest to major public schools, and failures being very much the exception. This speaks highly of a very professional teaching team, and also of the personal motivation in the Common Entrance candidates themselves.
>
> At the top level the Eton Scholarship has always been the ultimate challenge for us. It's a very competitive test, with only the very best being able to achieve success. We remember James Heald's 4th position in the 1980 scholarship, and Fergus Eckersley and Raleigh Gilbert finishing 2nd and 4th respectively in 1996. All three were incidentally the sons of Old Ludgrovians. The two Graham boys, Charles and Andrew, both scored excellent awards at Wellington; and at Harrow Richard Pyman and Christopher Kaye were first scholars, while Jeremy Fowler took the top award at Radley in 1990. James Corbet Burcher won the Rosebery History Prize at Eton in 2003 – he acknowledges his debt in this to the inspired teaching of George Hughes-Games.

It is fitting that in 2004, Nichol's last year at the School, Ludgrovians gained six awards – by Freddie Tapner who won the second scholarship to Radley (and was also awarded a music exhibition), by Alexander Style also to Radley, by Harry Royds with an 'Outstanding Talent' scholarship to Harrow, and by Crispin Royle Davies and James

Garnier who came 8th and 9th respectively on the list of King's Scholars at Eton. It was Ludgrove's academic 'Annus Mirabilis'.

1986	C.C.V. KAYE	SCHOLARSHIP HARROW
	J.C.B. SMART	EXHIBITION ETON
1987	R.L. HEALD	SCHOLARSHIP ETON
1988	M.T.Y. WREFORD	SCHOLARSHIP STOWE
1989	M.A. KIMBER	SCHOLARSHIP RADLEY
1990	J.R.V. FOWLER	SCHOLARSHIP ETON
	C.H. ALLISON	SCHOLARSHIP ETON
1991	A.V. COOPER	SCHOLARSHIP ETON
1992	C.R.D. CONNELL	EXHIBITION STOWE
1994	A.G.A. MILNE	SCHOLARSHIP BRADFIELD
1996	R.H. GILLETT	MUSIC SCHOLARSHIP RADLEY
	C.H.C. GORDON	EXHIBITION HARROW
	F.J. ECKERSLEY	SCHOLARSHIP ETON
	R.M.D.W. GILBERT	SCHOLARSHIP ETON
1997	I.A. BENNETT	SCHOLARSHIP RADLEY
1998	J.M. CORBET BURCHER	SCHOLARSHIP ETON
1999	C.R.S.N. COOERBURN	EXHIBITION RADLEY
2000	B.H. CRAWLEY	SCHOLARSHIP HARROW
		SPORTS SCHOLARSHIP HARROW
200	HUGHES	EXHIBITION RADLEY
2002	J.M.D. NORTH	SCHOLARSHIP RADLEY
	D.A. DOUGLAS-PENNANT	SCHOLARSHIP ETON
2003	W.P.N. DENEHY	SCHOLARSHIP HARROW

Some evidence of Ludgrove's raised academic emphasis is provided by its scholarship record: in the 36 years of the Alan Barber/Tim Shaw regime from 1937 to 1973, Ludgrove boys won 25 scholarships to public schools; in the more competitive environment of the following 30 years of the Barber/Marston era between 1973 and 2003, 47 scholarships have been won. For a school with no entrance test, it is a fine record. A report on the school in 2003 in the *Good Schools Guide* says: "Take note: this is a competitive school with high academic standards".

Ask a silly question …

Sometimes the framing of examination questions can be ambiguous… for example this one on the Battle of Trafalgar:

Fill in the blank: Nelson was shot by a F_____ sniper.

Anonymous

A new concept: Learning Support

A major change in all schools over the years is the growth in Learning Support. There had always been remedial reading at Ludgrove, but the first person to tackle dyslexia as such was Mrs Tyrwhitt-Drake, who had been brought in to help in this area at the request of a parent. The role was strongly reinforced in the late 1970s by Mary Graham, wife of Stephen. It required great perseverance on her part to achieve recognition of the need for remedial work for children with such conditions as dyslexia, dyspraxia, Attention Deficit Disorder (ADD) and hyperactivity (ADHD), but Ludgrove owes her an enormous debt for her determination in those early days when special needs had no general credibility in the School. Today it is widely recognised that about one in ten children has reading, writing or spelling problems of some sort, and it is a tribute to Mary's pioneering work that there are now no fewer than four staff responsible for Special Learning Support at Ludgrove.

Mary Graham pioneeered special needs teaching at Ludgrove.

Why do these learning disabilities seem to be on the

increase? It is too complex an issue to cover fully here, but there seems little doubt that one important contributory factor is the pervasive power of television on the minds of those of tender years. A major survey of young children in 2003 showed that over 40% of 3-year olds today have a TV set or PC in their own bedrooms, and that the average *toddler* now spends an unbelievable five hours a day in front of a TV or PC. TV is well-known to be a mild hypnotic: studies measuring watchers' brain activity find that after only a few minutes the normal oscillation of brain-waves changes to a slower, more diffuse pattern which significantly affects the ability to concentrate. So from the age of 18 months, the average toddler has a remorseless visual diet of hypnotic, flickering images, which dilutes their concentration and affects their powers of imagination throughout their most formative years. Ludgrove, like all schools today, seeks to remedy the pernicious results of this exposure.

Beyond the curriculum

At the same time as raising the academic threshold, the Headmasters sought to expand the range of extra-curricular activity so as to encourage a much wider diversity of individual interests and talents. Stephen Graham again reflects on the nature of the change that took place:

> It will usually be true that those who are keen games players may get more out of their school days than those who are not. But where Ludgrove under Gerald and Nichol has been particularly strong is in making games enjoyable for those who are not naturally gifted. Far more consideration is now given to such boys these days – and while every boy has to play team games some of the time, many more alternative occupations have become available too.

On the sports field – where the traditional view still largely prevails, that it is educationally beneficial for children to kick and hit balls, and to play games in a team – a huge expansion was undertaken in the number of matches played at every level: today there are A, B, C and D teams right down to the under 9's, in which everyone, from his first term on, is able to play in a school match, with all the potential for team-work, participation

Jamie Holbech, a recent Pottery Cup winner

and self-fulfilment that this provides. Today three quarters of all the boys in the school represent Ludgrove against other schools in some team or another during the year.

And from the mid-1970s the range of subjects and activities available, was extended beyond the traditional art, music and carpentry to include design, computer studies and pottery; prizes were introduced for speech-making, acting and declamation; and extra-curricular activities were widened to embrace clay-pigeon shooting, judo, riding, polo and Scottish dancing. By the 1980s there was little that was not available to capture the enthusiasm or inspire the imagination of everyone in the School.

In Scottish dancing you get to meet girls!

"Out of the Mouths…"

Ludgrove boys clearly know their priorities. Discussing "The Right to Roam" in an Eton Scholarship Trial paper:

"People may put themselves in danger if they walk across a shoot. The reason others are in danger is that if they shoot and someone dies or is injured, they really are in trouble. They could lose their gun licence."

Alexander Southby

The Spirit of Ludgrove

When parents ask what particular qualities Ludgrove seeks to impart to its pupils, Gerald will say: enthusiasm for doing things well, and energy to carry them through, backed by a number of personal disciplines that determine how they are done – politeness and consideration in dealing with people, respect for others and their property, and responsibility for one's own actions and their consequences. To achieve these things, a school must above all be a happy environment, with a certain 'tone', a culture of discipline and behaviour, which encourages the qualities it seeks to impart.

Central to that atmosphere is the way in which Janet Barber manages the pastoral side of the school's life.

In 2002 a national newspaper published a survey of England's prep schools, giving the essential facts and adding a succinct comment on each of them. Of Ludgrove it said simply:

"Famed for its TLC"

Many would say that, of all its many strengths, it is "TLC" – Tender Loving Care – which chiefly distinguishes Ludgrove today. This is almost wholly due to the tireless approach

Janet took from the beginning to enhance the pastoral life of the school.

Ludgrove in the era of Alan Barber had sought to turn out boys who, as Ken Morrison might have said, were more Spartans than Athenians: stiff upper lip, 'go for it', survival of the fittest, 'no blubbing on the doorstep', 'take it like a man' – fine for those who got their school colours, but sometimes harsher for lesser mortals.

However, under Janet's influence, a different spirit began to emerge. Early signs of change were the appearance of carpets on dormitory floors, of boys' teddies on the beds

and their chosen posters on the walls. In her ceaseless communications with parents, in her encyclopaedic knowledge of every boy – their birthdays, their families, their favourite subjects, their worries – in her accessibility and care for everyone in her charge, in her partnership with the matrons and her management of the domestic staff (many of whom have been at Ludgrove for over 20 years), Janet has introduced a care of people and a devotion to boys' well-being, which are cited today as chief of all the qualities for which Ludgrove is best known.

It is hard for ordinary mortals to understand fully how Janet does it. At the start of each school year she writes by hand to every new boy's parents to tell them what to expect and how communications will be handled; she insists that parents telephone her about anything on their mind at almost any time of day or night; she always has as much time for people as they could want of her; nothing is ever too much trouble for her to undertake on behalf of the boys in her care or the staff under her management; and as numbers in the school have climbed she still manages to give the same personal care and attention to everyone, while maintaining her omniscient knowledge of the individual boys and their families. As one parent said: "Janet makes you feel that every phone call is a welcome call, and that your own boy is her favourite."

One of the most eloquent testimonies to Janet's role is in the number of mothers who have told the author how reluctant they were to see their sons sent away to school at the age of 8 – until they came down to Ludgrove, met Janet, and were at once converted on seeing the care and attention their small sons would receive, and the communication that would be maintained between school and parents.

One seasoned 8-year-old said in 2000: "I think Ludgrove is the best school I've ever been to, because it feels just like home". That perfectly sums up what Janet is trying to achieve. She herself makes light of her efforts:

It's simple really: I just love small children, and seeing them develop, grow up and come back to us. The whole thing is trust, a partnership between the parents and us. And looking after a large number of other people's children is all about being very accessible all the time. You see, we are so lucky: when you have 40-plus eight-year-olds coming into your house every September, and feel the sadness as 40-plus twelve- and thirteen-year-olds leave, you'll realise that they are truly part of our family. As I see it, parents don't "send their children away", they let them come and live with us. And when they live with us in our house for five years, it's not difficult to get to know their mums and dads, their brothers and sisters – and of course the boys themselves don't change, the same things make them laugh and cry as 100 years ago. I guess I just love the boys and their families who are at the heart of the atmosphere that we're all trying to create here.

TWO MODERN LUDGROVIANS

The flavour of the School is summarised by two well-known Ludgrovians from the 1970s and 1980s.

Simon Sebag-Montefiore (1973 – 1978), *author and historian*
When Gerald, Nichol and Janet took over in the Michaelmas term of 1973, there were 128 boys in the School. Simon was among the 20 new boys to be greeted by the new team. His number was 129: the last boy in the school. From an early stage he showed a keen interest in history and, under the inspiration of an enigmatic, unpredictable but (to many) inspiring teacher Tristram Yelin, he became fascinated by history and especially that of Russia.

Simon Sebag-Montefiore

Tristram Yelin – enigmatic, inspiring

After Harrow and Cambridge, Simon travelled widely throughout the former Soviet Union, especially to the Caucasus, Georgia and Central Asia, reporting on the bloody wars, smouldering resentments and ancient cultures of those peoples. Subsequently he worked as an investment banker, a war reporter (covering Grozny among other places), and a columnist for the Sunday Times, as well as getting two novels published. But it was through numerous articles and lectures, the presentation of several television documentaries and in particular his acclaimed history books – the biographies of Catherine the Great's lover, Prince Potemkin, and of Joseph Stalin – that Simon has become one of the foremost contemporary authorities on Russian history, and on Stalin in particular.

His second novel, *My Affair with Stalin,* appears to unite under one banner two of his lifelong inspirations: Ludgrove and Stalin! The author himself is wary of direct comparisons. "It's fictional", he says. The novel describes how a Stalinist-type regime developed in a preparatory school environment, and draws on numerous memories of the author's days at Ludgrove. He caricatures headmasters, masters (even the sadistic security boss Beria is there!) and boys; recounts tales of 'streaking' across the cricket ground, climbing onto the roof at midnight, or raiding the 'grub' cupboard undetected ("we found the key, and at the dead of night over several weeks we must have raided it for boxes and boxes of sweets that we either ate or hid behind the cowsheds").

With pitched battles in the Camps between the pupils and the local lads, and even references to Nichol's dog ('the Grunter'), the book weaves the events and atmosphere of Stalinist Russia into the characters and escapades of those formative Ludgrove years. Yet, unlike the years of the Russian Terror and the childhood traumas recounted in his novel, Simon characterises his Ludgrove years as "the happiest of times":

> I loved it; it was a place of natural tolerance and sound teaching. I was useless at games, but Gerald would think up constructive things for the non-games players to do which he called 'odd jobs', Janet was always watching out for the happiness of the boys, and I didn't therefore feel in the slightest bit left out. Nichol Marston was certainly tough but he was always fair; and John Rickards was a Roman patrician in style, exemplified by the gladiators' chorus *'Nos morituri te salutamus',* which we all chanted before he read out the exam results. I had long, fascinating conversations about Russia with Tris Yelin, the French master, himself of Armenian extraction and unpredictable temperament (he would bellow out at mealtimes: "Do start, don't eat!"). Tony Esau also had a major intellectual influence on me, and was sent to pick me up when I ran away to the station one term; and there were so many other memorable moments. Yelin, whom we called "T.Y. Russian Spy", was a genuinely international man of mystery, but with intellect and knowledge added. He seemed to belong to another age – Moscow or Istanbul in the 1920s. He would discuss Lenin, Trotsky, Ataturk, Hitler and Stalin with me when other boys were reading books or playing rugger. He could certainly be pretty brutal, but I am still grateful to him because he treated me like an adult and sowed the seeds for my later career.
>
> My Ludgrove days were happy days, like living with a family in the country with teaching thrown in. I recall it all as a sanctuary of kindness.

Edward 'Bear' Grylls (1982 – 1987), *climber and explorer*
'Bear' also has happy memories of his time at Ludgrove. He recalls the vivid impact made by George Hughes-Games's imaginary trips in class around the world in a hot-air balloon, and the School's emphasis on encouraging boys to do what they were good at,

even if (as in his case) this inclined towards climbing trees rather than frequenting the games field!

'Bear' Grylls

He has spent much of his life battling against the odds, principally in extreme environments. After leaving Eton he spent three years with the British Special Forces (21 SAS) where he specialised as a combat survival instructor and patrol medic. But he suffered a horrendous parachuting accident in southern Africa in 1995; his canopy failed to open properly. He broke his back and spent many agonising months in rehabilitation. Through determination of spirit and by holding firm to a long-held ambition to conquer Everest, he slowly recovered. In 1997 he became the youngest Briton to climb the 22,500 ft Mount Ama Dablam in the Himalayas (once described by Sir Edmund Hillary as 'unclimbable'). And then in May 1998, after experiencing extreme weather conditions, three months of limited sleep, even dangling semi-conscious on the end of a rope above a bottomless crevasse when the ice beneath him had given way, he eventually became the youngest ever British climber to reach the summit of Everest, thereby securing his place in the Guinness Book of Records. The experience was recounted in his book *Facing Up*, which was in the top ten best-seller list in 2000.

Among his many other exploits 'Bear' has rowed naked in a bathtub for 22 miles down the Thames, trained at a circus school and led the first team to jet-ski around Britain.

Today 'Bear' is able to command some of the highest fees on the international lecture circuit, where he is in constant demand for his acclaimed motivational talks to

'Bear' Grylls crossing a crevasse in the Himalayas

business audiences around the world. They are eager to hear how his experiences can be applied to achieving corporate success, especially in leadership, teamwork and the things that make the difference between winning and losing – most of all the ability to "go the extra mile" for success.

In July 2003, on behalf of the Prince's Trust, Bear Grylls made a successful crossing of the North Atlantic via the Arctic Circle in a small Rigid Inflatable Boat (RIB) accompanied by Mick Crosthwaite, a fellow-Ludgrovian (1982–87) and 'Bear's' Everest climbing partner. The journey is described in his new book *Facing the Frozen Ocean*, published in 2004.

Of his prep school days 'Bear' recalls:

> At Ludgrove I didn't fit into the conventional mode, but even so I felt that there
> was always something to aspire to, something in which to feel real pride...

and he says it was at Ludgrove that he learned one of the most important lessons upon which his subsequent career has been built – that life does not necessarily reward the brilliant, but those with the ability to keep on trying, no matter what the odds may be.

MOVING WITH THE TIMES

The tone at Ludgrove today is still set, as it was in the days of Arthur Dunn, chiefly by the spirit of the place, by the knowledge boys learn of where the boundaries lie between right and wrong, rather than by any sanctions of enforcement. To quote the Inspectors' Report of 2003 :

> The moral development of the pupils [at Ludgrove] is very good, enhanced by a
> strong school ethos, which influences all aspects of school life. Pupils have a clear
> understanding of right and wrong, and are aware that good behaviour and good
> manners are expected at all times, resulting in high standards of good behaviour.

Corporal punishment was abandoned at Ludgrove in the mid-70s, when Gerald mislaid the weapon of execution one evening. (It was allegedly hidden by Simon Sebag-Montefiore to forestall his anticipated chastisement!).

No more heads will roll...

In an article on Ludgrove anticipating the arrival there of Prince William in 1991, a national newspaper reassured its readers:
"It is now several years since Ludgrove abolished capital punishment".

However few boys relish being sent up to the Headmasters to confess to any crime or misdemeanour, or knowingly overstep the bounds of reasonable behaviour, in particular those defined by Nichol Marston, who gives the disciplinary lead to the school. Stentorian outbursts may result. One boy, Freddie Hall, said in 2001, "When Mr. Marston tells you off, you think he is going to burst". Another – a new boy – told his father: "Mr. Marston called us in and told us we were all idle. Dad, what does 'idle' mean?"

It became part of Ludgrove's philosophy that every boy in the upper school should experience some degree of responsibility before leaving, and the monitors and sub-monitors came to play an expanded role in setting this tone through their responsibilities for looking after the junior boys, whether as dormitory monitors or school prefects. Their standards are prescribed in a 'Monitors' Memo' which Gerald issues to each of them:

The Monitors' Memo
- Show respect for all members of the community
- Take pride in the school, and care for its grounds and buildings
- Look after property, both yours and other people's
- Be honest and worthy of people's trust
- Go out of your way to be polite, kind and helpful
- Take pride in your appearance
- Show determination when life gets difficult
- Tackle everything cheerfully and with enthusiasm
- Learn to work purposefully with others as part of a team
- Learn from your mistakes, and accept criticism with a good grace
- Enjoy life!

The late Duke of Devonshire's phrase about Ludgrove in the 1930s still aptly sums up the tone of the school today: "Discipline with a light touch."

Bricks and Mortar: Governors and Appeals

Scarcely a day goes by in term-time without at least one visit by prospective parents. On average about six out of every ten such visits result in a decision in favour of Ludgrove. The prime quality which Gerald seeks to demonstrate to his visitors is the essentially happy family atmosphere in the school, backed by its now magnificent facilities – the beautiful garden and grounds, the extended dining-hall, modern classrooms, new IT facilities, special rooms for music, art and crafts, the sports-hall *cum* theatre; and the new swimming-pool built in 2002.

In 1973 the new Headmasters knew that investment in bricks and mortar would be the chief means to meet the expectations of their customers and to stay ahead of the competition. In the 30 years to 2003, Ludgrove has invested about £5 million in

The new dining-hall

equipping the school with some of the most modern and comprehensive facilities of any prep school in the land. The contrast with the decaying fabric and outmoded 'plant' in the cash-strapped days of the early 1970s could not be more striking.

How has this remarkable programme been achieved? The creation by Alan Barber of the Ludgrove School Charitable Trust has made a fundamental difference, enabling Ludgrove to expand without a tax burden, to appeal to alumni for financial support, and to look to an experienced group of Governors for support and advice.

The Governing Body

Since the foundation of the Ludgrove Trust in 1972, the Governors of Ludgrove have brought their individual expertise to key issues. They have vigorously challenged the Headmasters in their plans and management, but have always given them complete freedom of action in 'sailing the ship', without attempting to tweak the helm or trim the canvas themselves. Their role has been indispensable to Ludgrove's success. Of particular value has been the continuity of leadership. In 30 years there have only been three Chairmen: Pat Meredith-Hardy from 1972 to 1982, Ned Boldero for 21 years from 1982 to 2003; and the present Chairman, Peter, 7th Earl of Rosslyn, son of one of ATB's original Trustees.

Peter, 7th Earl of Rosslyn

The Boldero Connection

Grandson of Ludgrove's founder, Arthur Dunn, Ned Boldero was at Ludgrove from 1939 to 1943. He has always been close to the School, sending his own son Jonathan there (1966-1971), who became Captain of the School. Ned was one of the founding Governors and the first Secretary to the Trustees in 1972, and was Chairman of the Governors between 1982 and 2003, throughout the most active years of Ludgrove's modern development. During these 21 years his support for the Headmasters and staff has been unwavering, and his guidance on issues great and small invaluable. His determination that Ludgrove should stay abreast of the times cannot be praised highly enough.

The continuity of the Dunn-Boldero family's involvement with Ludgrove has been further assured by Ned's grandson Freddie Tapner, who left Ludgrove in the summer of 2004 for Radley.

Ned Boldero at Eton, 1943   *Jonathan Boldero*   *Freddie Tapner*

The First Appeal, 1972

The first Appeal was launched in October 1972, the Appeal Committee consisting of ATB as Chairman together with Gerald Barber, Nichol Marston, Anthony, 6th Earl of Rosslyn and Normile Baxter. The target was set at £70,000, a sum which was raised by

What used to be the farm's dairy is now the art block.

the Spring of 1974. It was devoted to essential infrastructure: renovation of the kitchens; extension of the dining hall; a new ablutions block; and (not before time!) connection to the main sewer.

The programme of modernisation continued throughout the 1970s, embracing almost every aspect of the School. Dry-rot was cured in critical roof areas; the cow-sheds were converted into classrooms and dormitories; the conservatory was rebuilt and is now an extension to the Dining Hall. The garage block was converted into two classrooms; and a roof put over the swimming pool.

Out of the Mouths...

The boys' appreciation of the modernisation programme was summed up by a small boy in 1975 who said:

"Sir, what a relief to have the new loos working now!"

In 1982 a fine new Music Block was built next to the masters' quarters by the Chapel Ground. It includes six practice-rooms, a large orchestra-room and a room for choir-practice, while the old music rooms have been turned into a library and reading room.

"My dad would fail his Grade A piano..." Alastair Lloyd-Webber

The Great Fire of Ludgrove

However, in the summer of 1978, Ludgrove came close to losing everything in a massive conflagration. Two local lads from Wokingham broke into the farm area and climbed inside the barn, which was full of hay at the time. Around 4 p.m. they accidentally set fire to the hay, and being unable to extinguish the flames, they fled. A massive blaze then took hold, quickly enveloping the entire barn. It raged throughout the whole night. At its

height it required twelve fire engines to fight it. The walls of the main school building itself grew warm, and it was only by luck that the squash-court escaped destruction. By the morning it was put out, but not without extreme concern that 88 years of history might at any moment have gone up in smoke.

But as so often happens, good came of it. The Great Fire led to the progressive abandonment of the farmyard area, which in the end facilitated the most ambitious of all Ludgrove's expansion plans: the building of a new gymnasium or sports hall.

Judo in the sports hall

The Second Appeal

The Sports Hall was a mighty project by any standards. Gerald and Nichol considered it essential if Ludgrove were to remain in the first division of English preparatory schools. The project was approved in principle by the Trustees in October 1981, and over the next four years the plans matured to include a large sports/gym complex, two new squash courts, an extended tarmac play area and car park.

A second Appeal Committee was formed under the chairmanship of Anthony West, (father of Old Ludgrovians Robert, Tim and Charlie) and included Dorothy Barber and Peter Borgnis, in addition to the professional campaign organiser, Bernard Ashford. Its first meeting was held on 8th June 1985. Proof of Ludgrove's enormous reserves of goodwill was quickly apparent: by November the Fund stood at over £200,000; in March 1986 it exceeded £380,000; and a year later it reached £449,000 donated by over 300 people. The new complex was inaugurated in June 1987. This turned into a major celebration of Ludgrove, with a massive programme of events culminating in the formal opening ceremony performed by Dorothy Barber.

Alongside the major appeals, continuous development has never stopped. Projects have included conversion of the old squash-court into specialist classrooms; extension of the dining hall into the area occupied by the old conservatory; conversion of the old swimming-pool into four new dormitories; a common-room for senior boys with its own shower-block; and an IT centre, networking the whole school with internet access.

In addition, a major landscaping project was undertaken to improve the rather bucolic golf-course. In the past it had only been 'mowed' by the Ludgrove cows, which had to be kept off the greens by barbed wire (fatal to golfers' trousers), to say nothing of the ubiquitous hazard of cowpats on the fairways. New bunkers were generously donated by Old Ludgrovians in 1985, and today the game is more popular than ever.

The Third Appeal

In 2000, a third appeal was launched, under the chairmanship of Martin Stanley (father of Oliver and Hughie) to build a new swimming-pool, between the fives-courts and the pond. This magnificent facility was opened in 2002 by Glynis Ormsby, who had run the swimming at Ludgrove for many years, following an emotional concert in memory of Ronnie Dowson, the School's greatly loved Director of Music from 1988 to 2000 (see page 237).

"Out of the Mouths..."

Ned Boldero's grandson Freddie Tapner is clearly proud of his grandfather's achievements. In 2001 he was faced with an exam question:

"Suetonius was the Roman Governor. What is a Governor?"

To which he gave the answer:

"It's someone who raises money for new swimming-pools"

Facts and Figures

School fees: In 1972 Ludgrove's termly fees were £215. When the new Headmasters took over, they and the Governors were clear that these were both lower than other comparable schools and – when inflation in Britain was running at over 20 per cent – inadequate to cover the school's costs. The first significant increase for many years was introduced in January 1974, when the fees were raised to £255. Thereafter at Ludgrove, as in all independent schools, fees have increased inexorably, and in the summer of 2004 they stood at £5,050 per term.

School numbers

When they took over in 1973 Gerald, Nichol and Janet knew that numbers had to rise, but they could scarcely have foreseen that Ludgrove would almost double in size under their leadership. The 1970s saw a 20% jump to 132; the 1980s a 35% increase to 178; a further 8% in the 1990's to 193; and by 3% in the new millennium to 198.

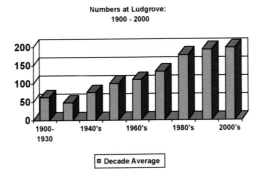

Numbers at Ludgrove:
1900 - 2000

Will Ludgrove's numbers exceed the 200 mark? The answer is probably contained in one of Gerald and Janet's golden rules: "Divorce comes after 200!" They should beware – in September 2004 Ludgrove's numbers will reach exactly 200!

But numbers alone do not tell the full story. The most striking fact is that Ludgrove remains one of only four English prep schools which has kept its 'all-boys, all-boarding' formula unchanged, still with an entry age of 8. The magnitude of this achievement becomes clearer in the context of what has been happening in the country at large. In 1982, when the Independent Schools' Council carried out its first full census of private schools, the number of boys between 7 and 13 in full-time boarding education throughout the UK was 23,000; in the census of 2003 this figure had declined to only 8,300, a reduction of over 60% in just 20 years. Today there are only four fully boarding boys' prep schools in the country. Ludgrove is one of these and its books remain fully subscribed for years to come. This suggests that there are special 'Ludgrove Factors' at work, which have enabled the school to preserve its formula so successfully.

One such factor is the almost superhuman effort made to continue to run a school of about 200 with the same degree of personal knowledge of each boy and involvement with every parent as when there were only about half that number.

The other factor – characteristic of Ludgrove since its foundation – is the remarkable quality, commitment and longevity of the teaching and other staff who today fill the places occupied a century ago by Willie Blore, 'Bunco' Brown and Walter Stanbrough. It is to the people behind the modern Ludgrove that this story will now turn.

A PORTRAIT GALLERY

Teaching Staff

In selecting his staff, Gerald looks for a number of key qualities:

> The morale of our team is crucial: as Arthur Dunn said, fitting into the
> environment here is so important. So our first criterion is personality, whether
> they will fit into our culture and common room? Number two is enthusiasm –

brightness of eye, kindness of spirit, and a passion for teaching. Three is breadth of interest – what can they give to Ludgrove outside their teaching role? Being on the staff here is much more a way of life than just a job. So someone who plays a musical instrument or collects stamps, who can coach a game or produce a play, does add vital extra dimensions to their candidacy.

Over the Barber-Marston years these guidelines have furnished Ludgrove's Common Room with individuals remarkable for their teaching skill, their range of interests, and their loyalty and long service to the school.

Tony Esau

Tony was at Magdalen College School, Oxford and a classical scholar of Worcester College, Oxford. After graduating he held a number of teaching posts, including a fellowship at Marlboro College, Vermont, before joining Ludgrove in 1972 to take Division I, teaching Latin, Greek and English. He also takes the Under 9's cricket and football.

Tony Esau

For 20 years from 1977, Tony also put on an annual open-air play on the front lawn and in the camps – usually Shakespeare, but including *Toad of Toad Hall*, *Wind in the Willows* and *Dad's Army* – all 'tailored' to run for one hour, often with a high degree of realism (as when a river to row on was created in the Camps for "The Wind in the Willows"). His 1987 production of *Romeo and Juliet* was the first to be put on in the new Sports Hall, reversing the auditorium to use the balcony for the Balcony and the store room for the Tomb.

"Wind in the Willows" on a man-made river

Through his wide range of learning, he has been a major intellectual influence on very many scholarly boys in Division I for over 30 years. His erudition has enabled him to achieve notable successes in the Times National Crossword Puzzle competition, and he has set the Ludgrove General Knowledge paper every year, a tradition which goes back to Arthur Dunn. He has played a leading role in strengthening Ludgrove's academic focus, and many an Old Ludgrovian looks back with gratitude to the lifelong influence of his teaching of Latin and Greek.

George Hughes-Games

George followed Mike Ainsworth in joining Ludgrove from the Navy in 1973, to teach History and Geography. He was in charge of history teaching at Ludgrove for 20 years, memorably enhancing his teaching with a gift for story-telling and imagery: boys particularly recall with huge enthusiasm the races in his class around the world in an imaginary airship.

He was also master in charge of squash, in which he was a coach of endless patience, spending untold hours on court with the beginners, and inspiring generations of talented players (his protégés include three Public Schools Rackets champions).

George Hughes-Games

At cricket he had played in his service days for the Navy, the Combined Services and for the Somerset 2nd XI, and like Peter Borgnis, another distinguished naval cricketer before him, George ran the Under 11 cricket for 30 years. He used to award a much-prized naval button to whoever he considered had contributed markedly to a Ludgrove victory.

George Hughes-Games with Robert Wallace (left) and Michael Briers

He produced a daily weather chart for Ludgrove, and in the artistic world was both an enthusiastic member of the choir, and a most accomplished painter, who held an exhibition of over 100 of his paintings in a Chelsea art gallery in 2003.

George is a man of many talents, and has been a devoted servant of Ludgrove for nearly a third of a century.

Simon Warner

Simon was at Repton, and then at Keble College, Oxford, from 1958 to 1962, where he read Law. Coincidentally, Nichol Marston was at Keble at the same time, but Simon's first introduction to Ludgrove came at a Cricketer Cup match in 1974 when he met the recently retired Alan Barber. Alan suggested he consider schoolmastering as a career – so persuasively in fact that the following year Simon gave up his job in London and moved with his family to Ludgrove. On the staff, he taught English and Science, and was in charge of the Science Department from 1977 to 1991.

Simon Warner

He had a particular love of biology, with a vast knowledge of flora and fauna. He was also a keen and knowledgeable ornithologist; on one occasion he introduced a pair of fledgling barn-owls to the farm buildings, reared them and released them into the wild.

For many years he also coached the 1st XI football team with infectious enthusiasm and, as an outstanding cricketer (he only just missed a Blue at Oxford), he coached the cricket 1st XI for a while.

Simon retired in 2003 to live in France. He will be long remembered at Ludgrove for his breadth of knowledge (which, to the delight of his pupils, included a love of crosswords, quizzes and conundrums), for his individualism and his strength of character.

Caroline Laws

Caroline was the daughter of Fiona Laws (see Chapter 6) who had worked with Alan and Dorothy at Ludgrove during the war, and was Dorothy's god-daughter. She taught the junior form, Division VIB, for 10 years from 1972 to 1982. No one showed more care and devotion to her boys than Caroline.

She was always on hand for any emergency and was an invaluable friend and confidante to Janet. She left to get married in 1982, but tragically died of cancer a short while later while living in

Caroline Laws America.

"Out of the Mouths ..."

Caroline was once soothing a hysterical small boy in her class, and asked him what had happened, to which he gasped:

"Sebag-Montefiore kicked me in the tentacles, Ma'am!"

Her sympathy for him only just overcame her suppressed mirth.

Suzanne Briers

Married to Nigel, Suzanne joined the staff in September 1980. For 21 years she was in charge of the first year, helping them to settle into their new life, and adapt to the rigours of boarding. No one at Ludgrove has ever done this better than Suzanne, and she particularly championed the cause of the less successful or confident boys in her class. She also ran the 1st XI hockey. In the Common Room Suzanne was a great personality, speaking her mind and cheerfully fighting her corner against any signs of male chauvinism on the staff! She left in 2001 and, now re-married, lives in the USA.

Suzanne Briers

Nigel Briers

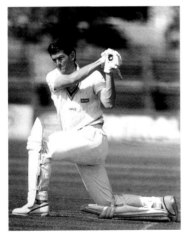

In the summer, Nigel Briers captained Leicestershire.

Nigel came to Ludgrove after the sudden death of Mike Ainsworth in 1978, and worked there for 19 years in the Michaelmas and Spring terms only, running the P.E. and Rugger, and teaching junior geography and history. In the summer he played cricket for Leicestershire, with whom he had made his debut at the age of 16 in 1975, then captaining the county from 1990 to 1995. In 1993 he was named one of Wisden's five Cricketers of the Year. Generations of Ludgrove boys remember his enthusiastic professionalism to this day.

Gordon Milne of Warwick University succeeded Tristram Yelin in charge of French in 1982. He inspired Ludgrove's annual French trips to the Loire valley, of which the boys' reports in the School magazine are written in faultless French, and his thorough method of teaching has been much respected over many years. He became Director of Studies in 1998.

Gordon Milne

Anthony Bradshaw

Anthony Bradshaw of Marlborough and Trinity College, Dublin, taught English and History from 1980 to 1996. He had a great rapport with the boys to whom he would give imaginative nicknames, and ran the Dramatic Society after Stephen Graham. He is widely considered to possess the world's fastest golf swing bar none! His wife Liz joined the staff in 1984. She was a much loved teacher whose character and kindness left an indelible mark on those lucky enough to have been taught by her.

Martin Dyson, ran the geography in conjunction with Stephen Graham, and also the 1st XI cricket from 1978 to 1985 He was an important contributor to Ludgrove's musical life, playing the piano for school plays and concerts and being a keen member of the choir.

Martin Dyson

Katharine Lewis

Katharine Lewis taught junior French for 20 years from 1982 to 2002, bringing her own unique style to the task by acting out local scenes in a French town to bring the subject alive for her young pupils. She was one of the most happy and patient of all the members of staff.

Ken Lincoln is a staff member of great expertise, who succeeded Mr Roberts in the maintenance and Carpentry department, and now also teaches Design and Technology. His wife Muriel is the daughter of Walter Butler, Ludgrove's former Head Groundsman.

Ken Lincoln

The non-teaching staff

Sue Sleight joined Ludgrove in 1983 as "the sewing lady". For 20 years she has single-handedly tackled every mending, altering and lengthening task in the school, rescuing countless boys who always knew they could go to her for emergency repairs. Her `repertoire included the creation of magnificent costumes for the Dramatic Society. She left Ludgrove in 2002.

Sue Sleight

Wendy Spackman joined Ludgrove in 1966 in succession to Ann Mellville. Her husband David had been in the TA at Oxford with Micky Burton-Brown. Wendy served for 33 years as secretary to ATB and then managed the central administration of the School before retiring in 1999. She was also Secretary to the Ludgrove Trustees. She personified diligence in everything she did, and ensured

(Left to right) Dorothy Underwood, Wendy Spackman, Sally Whittaker

Ludgrove's administrative efficiency with charm, humour and loyalty. She is a friend to all, with the happy knack of always having time for people. She was joined in 1981 by **Sally Whittaker**. One of those rare people for whom no job ever appears too arduous to undertake, Sally now runs the vital, if hidden, administrative 'engine-room' of the School.

Dorothy Underwood was Gerald's Secretary for over 18 years from 1984 to 2002. Dependable, efficient and loyal, she was a perfect exponent of that role, running the office like clockwork and unwaveringly reliable in all she did for so long.

Links with the Common Room

Links between the Headmasters and teaching staff were strengthened in 1976 by the appointment of Stephen Graham as Senior Master to liaise between the Headmasters and the Common Room. There had been few formal masters' meetings under ATB (his famous *"a word in your ear"* sufficed for most of his communications with his team) but Gerald and Nichol now hold such meetings weekly.

In their day, Alan and Dorothy used to invite to Sunday dinner only those members of staff who were resident, were teachers and were male! Gerald and Janet still hold the Sunday dinners, but these now include every member of the staff, whether teaching or domestic, male or female, resident or otherwise.

Life after Ludgrove

Throughout Ludgrove's long history many of its masters have gone on to become Headmasters and Assistant Headmasters of other prep schools. In more modern times these have included Alan Ellis, who went to become headmaster of Ardingly Junior School; Geoffrey Casson to St. Petroc's, Bude; Trafford Allen to Westbrook Hay in Hertfordshire; Gordon Perry to Querns School in Gloucestershire; and Micky Burton-

Brown to Edgborough. More recently Colin Acheson-Gray became Deputy Head of St. Anselms, Derbyshire; Philip Hoyland, Headmaster of Pinewood, near Swindon; Ben Beardmore-Gray, Deputy Head of Farleigh House; and Richard Wesley, Deputy Head of Abberley Hall.

Over the years, a number of matrimonial matches have been made between members of the staff. Following the example of Micky and Bridget Burton-Brown in 1968, there have been Ludgrove marriages between Charles and Julia Annandale, Philip and Henrietta Hoyland, Robert and Kate Lagden, Richard and Paula Wesley, Guy and Emma Barker and, on the domestic side, Basyl Paskowski and Paquita, and Andy and Vicki McBratney.

Janet's Team

As Janet puts it: "My role is that of a housekeeper in a big household, and the most important thing is the loyalty and back-up from the people I'm so fortunate to have helping me. Without them I simply couldn't do the job".

One of the most devoted of Ludgrove Matrons of these years has been **Pat Jones**, who came as a temporary appointment in 1982 and stayed until 1995. She was the epitome of cheerful enthusiasm, and her vivacity was proof against every crisis. When she retired, her colleagues wrote of her:

> Just knowing that a kindly efficient person is there to make it all better again is all that any schoolboy can possibly want. But our Matron is better than that. How many other schoolboys have a turbo-charged matron who can get down the stairs backwards in under 10 seconds; who leaves school for the doctor as if she was starting a race at Brands Hatch; or who risks life and limb on the rooftops to retrieve a lost teddy?

Pat Jones

After retirement, Pat's indefatigable energy took her cycling round Ireland at the age of 70, and at 73 she was seeking her fortune by panning for gold in Australia!

Behind the scenes

On the domestic staff, several outstanding people have been at Ludgrove for over two decades: **Charlie Marshall**, the chef, who in 1984 succeeded **Mrs Redmond** ("But boys *like* it burnt"), and has raised the standard of food at Ludgrove to new

Charlie Marshal has brought haute cuisine to Ludgrove.

234

heights, always ready to do more, and never put out by a need for extra meals; **Basyl Paskowski**, a Ludgrove institution for 45 years who always seemed to be "emptying binnies" or polishing the corridors; and the many devoted staff from Spain and Portugal, especially **Maria Carvalho**. Special mention must be made, too, of **Iris Milam** who arrived at the School from South Wales in 1948 as a girl of 16 to help in the Dining Hall, and is still helping in the School today; and of **Mrs Gray**, who was employed by Dorothy in 1967 as her 'front-of-house' helper, and who retired in July 2003 after 36 years of devoted service.

Iris Milam has been helping at Ludgrove for 56 years!

Laurie's match teas are renowned.

Outstanding amongst all these is **Laurie McGill-Smith**, who came to Ludgrove in 1977 to look after Gerald and Janet's young family. For over 25 years Laurie has been Janet's 'right arm' in all that is required to run the domestic side of the school, and her match teas are famous throughout the prep school circuit.

Without such devoted service, no preparatory school could easily survive. Ludgrove has indeed been lucky to have had such characters to help keep up high standards in every department of school life.

Maintaining the school fabric

Ludgrove has been fortunate over the years in being served 'backstage' by many loyal, devoted and talented people who have been indispensable to the smooth running of the school's daily life. **Mr Brandt** and **Mr Welsh** were inherited from Wixenford as general maintenance men; and many will remember **Mr Dally** who, in the 1950s and '60s, was the school's maintenance engineer and ran the carpentry; many are the wooden lamp-stands, egg-racks and book-shelves which boys fashioned under his guidance. **Mr. Bartlett** ran the farm for most of the 1950s; and **Fred Roberts** took over carpentry from Mr Dally and for years was the only maintenance man on the site. And no one has ever been more committed to the cause of Ludgrove than **Michael White**, who meticulously attends to every practical detail by day or night, and has now been at the school for over 40 years, first as farm manager and now as caretaker. No task is beyond him, at no moment is he off-duty. He has a heart of gold and Ludgrove is fortunate indeed to have benefited for so long from his unique sense of service.

Michael White

Another loyal colleague was **Walter Butler**, who had joined Ludgrove at the age of 12 to water the golf greens, then graduated to looking after the tomatoes and succeeded **Mr Holder** as Head Gardener and Groundsman in the 1950s. His daughter Muriel married Ken Lincoln. Today it is the **Hemmings** family, John, Richard and David, who keep the grounds in immaculate condition, sometimes preparing as many as five cricket fields at a time for the Saturday afternoon fixtures.

John Hemmings

SCHOOL LIFE: 1973 – 2004

Music

Music was at the fringes of Ludgrove's curriculum throughout the middle decades of the 20th century. Jetta Robertson was succeeded by Margaret Maldwyn-Davies, who brought a distinctive personality but little mass appeal to music-teaching compared with later years. Her successor was Val Davies. But it was the next Director of Music, Michael Hankin, a violinist, who took the first real steps in restoring to Ludgrove's music the central importance it had enjoyed in the first 40 years of the School's life. He kick-started the instrumental teaching, and his work was built on by Christopher Cole, the first person to bring in peripatetic teachers. Today one of these, Andy Smets, still teaches brass and runs the school band.

Music has regained its former position of importance.

But the inspiring personality who finally gave music at Ludgrove the verve and popularity it has today was Ronnie Dowson, an Irishman who arrived from Beachborough School in 1989. He sought to involve every single Ludgrovian in music, enthused everyone with the fun of singing, and moulded a first-class choir, which today supplements its school performances with charity concerts and singing at weddings.

It was a terrible blow when Ronnie died of leukaemia in 2001. His widow Hilary remains in charge of Ludgrove's Library, which she has revolutionised.

Ronnie Dowson brought verve to Ludgrove's music.

Today the music is run by Paul Bellingham and Debbie Clay, and with two choirs, a band, a string group and many other smaller ensembles no fewer than 150 out the 197 boys in the school learn an instrument from the seven visiting specialist teachers. There is almost no instrument (even bagpipes) which a boy cannot learn at Ludgrove. Music has finally been restored to the place it enjoyed under Arthur Dunn and Cecil Sharp.

Art

The widening of the syllabus has nurtured a number of Ludgrovian artists in the last 20 years: James Maconochie has had a number of exhibitions in London, Luke Martineau is well-known as a portrait painter, and George Lewis as a land- and seascape artist. Rupert Belfrage is a respected potter and ceramist, and Ian Bruce, who left Ludgrove in 2000, painted a remarkable Crucifixion in his last year at Eton, which today hangs in the Eton College Chapel.

Old Ludgrovian Ian Bruce's powerful Crucifixion

237

A devastating accident

Every year Ludgrove encourages one or two of its Old Boys to return for a gap year of helping out in the School, to assist with taking games and carry out a range of pastoral duties. In December 2002, two popular boys, who had just left Harrow, came to work for a term at Ludgrove; they were Fred Palmer (son of Old Ludgrovian, Peregrine Palmer) and Henry van Straubenzee, himself an O.L.

As they were returning in the small hours of the last Saturday of term, their car crashed into a tree in the Ludgrove drive. Fred was badly injured and, tragically, Henry was killed.

Ludgrove and Harrow were both devastated by this horrific accident, and the loss of a young man so full of promise, fun and enjoyment on the threshold of his life. The Harrow Chapel was full to overflowing for his memorial service.

Henry Van Straubenzee

Sports

Despite the considerable widening of the activity base to include such solo sports as skiing, Ludgrove has continued the tradition of excellence in team sports with which the school has always been associated.

Cricket: All Old Ludgrovian cricketers up to 1976 will remember having represented the School in grey trousers. White flannels were introduced for the 1st XI in that year. As if in celebration, Ludgrove's 1st XI was then victorious in all its matches for three years running!

Notable cricketers of the last 30 years have included Richard Pyman (nicknamed "Pumper" because of his whirlwind action), who captained the undefeated Ludgrove XI of 1981, and went on to play for Harrow, Cambridge and Somerset 2nd XI; Hugh Wilson who played for Wellington and, in the 1980 season, for Surrey as a fast bowler; and Peter Fane who, with Anthony Calder-Smith, put on 145 for the first wicket against Lockers Park in 1975, a Ludgrove record.

Some of Ludgrove's highest individual scores have been recorded in the last 30 years – by Ed Jennings who made 125 against Lambrook in 1993, and William Denehy, 104 not out against Winchester House in 2003.

Out of the Mouths...

Perhaps the most remarkable innings of all was played by Andrew Briers aged 9, who in 1999 played away in the Under-Ten side against Elstree. Anthony Bradshaw bumped into him in the corridor after the match when the following conversation took place:

"Hello Andrew – how many did you make today?"

"147, Sir."

"No, Andrew – not the whole side! How many did you yourself make?"

"147, Sir."

Other memorable moments have included David Wiggin playing against Heatherdown in 1973 and catching the last man on the boundary high above his head to win the match by 5 runs; Edward Chamberlin's outstanding side in 1987 touring Yorkshire, winning two of their matches and drawing one in spite of notorious all-night partying with the girls of Mowden Hall; Charlie Snow taking 8 for 5 in an Under-Ten match against Heatherdown in 1975; and William Beardmore-Gray directly throwing out the last Sunningdale batsman from third man in 1978 to win by two runs – Ludgrove's innings total had been 48!

Jos North in action

In the 1995 season Harry Walsh scored 426 runs. Fergus Eckersley nearly equalled this the following year with 410. But the outstanding batsman of modern times has been Jos North, who in 2002 scored 550 runs in 16 innings, the highest aggregate since Mike Griffith in the 1950s. In the same term he also won a scholarship to Radley.

The "Thatched" Pavilion

In June 2004 Ludgrove suffered an irreparable loss to its environment when the Thatched Pavilion, which since the time of Wixenford had formed the central feature of the whole lovely cricket field area, was burnt to the ground by vandals, together with all its contents of mowers, scoreboard, equipment and (most tragic of all) the old Wixenford Honour Boards. The whole school was in shock from the sudden loss of so

The pavilion before the fire…

…and after.

precious a landmark, which had been one of the most recognisable of all the features of the School to countless generations of Ludgrovians.

A tense moment in the Arthur Dunn Centenary final

Football: Over the years, Ludgrove's football has been run by Nichol Marston, Simon Warner, Gordon Milne and now by Andy Livermore. Today, teams represent the School at every level of ability. Many Ludgrovians have gone on to play for the 1st XIs of their public schools; and the Eton XI of 2002 included four OLs. The most talented side for the last 30 years was that of 2002, which lost only one match. It was notable that, in the Arthur Dunn Cup Centenary match between Shrewsbury and Charterhouse, the Carthusian side was captained by Tom Walker OL. How delighted Arthur Dunn himself would have been to see this!

Rugby: This became the major school sport in the Easter term from the late 1970s onward. Ludgrove competes with the best on the circuit, putting out five or six teams every Saturday of the term, and in 2003 the 1st

2003 was one of Ludgrove's most successful seasons for years.

XV were unbeaten in all but one of their matches. In 2000 Ross Jennings (OL 1986–1991), a graduate of Durham University, went on to Oxford where he gained a Blue and scored two tries against Cambridge at Twickenham. His brother Edward played rugby for the London Broncos and then with the Harlequins for several seasons.

Eton Fives: This is a most popular game. The Eton Fives courts at Ludgrove are considered to be the finest anywhere in the country, and the Final of the national championship for the Kinnaird Cup has often been played there. The IAPS Prep Schools Competition, for many years dominated by Highgate Junior School, has been won by Ludgrove five times. The best player in modern times is probably Ludgrove's Guy Smith-Bingham. In 2003 the Eton 1st Pair were the OL brothers Charles and Eddy Nissen,

Charles and Eddy Nissen won the 2003 National Schools Championship for Eton.

who took Eton to victory in the final of the national schools championship for only the second time in 35 years.

Golf: Ludgrove's splendid 9-hole golf course has introduced countless boys to the game down the years, and nurtured many excellent golfers such as Garth Milne, Andy Swanston and Sam Elworthy. James Rowland Clark won the Prep Schools competition, the Stowe Putter, in 2001, and with Alexander Cornwallis won the inter-schools trophy too that year.

Squash and rackets: Many who learned their squash from George Hughes-Games at Ludgrove have gone on to excel at Rackets and Real Tennis. His protégés include two Public Schools Racquets champions, Guy Smith-Bingham (currently British and American Amateur Rackets Champion) and Alexander Titchener-Barrett (currently National Under-24 Champion). But the most distinguished of all Ludgrove's racket players has been Julian Snow (the elder son of Alan and Dorothy Barber's daughter Theodora) who is today one of the best Real Tennis

Julian Snow

players in the world. He won the British Amateur Championship for a record 17th time in 2004 (beating Howard Angus' record of 16 times), has been British Open Singles Champion four times, British Open Doubles Champion twice and British Amateur Doubles champion 10 times. He has also been Open Champion of Australia and France, and twice of the USA.

Sports Day

One of the major innovations in the 1970s was the replacement of the traditional Fathers' Cricket Match by Sports Day as the central event of the Summer term. This was the brainchild of Stephen Graham. The first Sports Day in 1976 will not readily be forgotten: prepared by Stephen with military precision down to the smallest detail and the last blade of grass, the whole thing was consigned to oblivion by a torrential downpour on the crucial day. In spite of that first disaster, Sports Day has proved a huge success, one of the seminal events of the

Duncan Beardmore-Gray

Ludgrove calendar, with its gathering of parents, its picnics, brass band accompaniment, and the inter-sets mass relay, in which every boy in the school takes part, as the grand finale to the day.

An air-raid over Sports Day

Donald Shaw relates how, one day in June 1995, his business partner Tony Haig-Thomas invited him to go for a day's flying, which took in an air show at Dunsfold, where he was to give a display.

"Our route took us over Henley and Ludgrove. One of the young Princes was still at the School, and it was Sports Day. Everything looked quiet as we flew over in the morning, but on our return the lawns were covered with people enjoying their sports day tea. We decided to take a closer look, went down to about 600-700 feet and circled twice. The plane Tony was flying was a 2,000 h.p.Grumman Avenger, a US naval torpedo bomber. This is a huge, bulbous thing, dubbed 'Fat Charlie' by Tony and probably the noisiest aircraft ever designed. The sandwich-eaters must have been absolutely deafened; everyone wondered what on earth was going on, and the royal protection-squad swarmed out of the rhododendrons, their jackets bulging...

Luckily another of our partners, Johnny Birt, was a parent. He looked up, and calmed one and all by saying: 'Don't worry, I know exactly who that is; it's only Haig-Thomas and Shaw.'

So away we flew and everyone returned to their cucumber sandwiches!"

The Ludgrove Centenary, 1992

Ludgrove's Centenary Celebrations were held on a cloudless day in the Summer term of 1992, and were the highlight of that year. The event was attended by a large number of old boys and parents, including the Princess of Wales. The Rev. Nigel Cumming (1950-56) took the Chapel Service of Thanksgiving in the morning, followed by a huge reception on the Chapel Ground. The afternoon's entertainment included ascents in a hot-air balloon, sky-divers landing on the cricket pitch, a march-past in which Janet took the salute to the accompaniment of the Band of the Blues & Royals, and finally the cutting by Dorothy of a gigantic cake bedecked in the Ludgrove colours. It was a memorable day of happiness, fanfare and celebration enjoyed in perfect weather by over 2000 people.

Dorothy Barber cuts the Ludgrove Centenary cake.

The Princes

In 1990 Ludgrove received a visit from Diana, Princess of Wales, which resulted in the decision by Prince Charles and herself to send their two sons, Prince William and Prince Harry, to Ludgrove. William arrived in September 1992 and Harry in 1994.

Prince William arriving as a new boy

The Headmasters were emphatic that the two Princes would be treated exactly like any other boys throughout their time there, and that school life would proceed entirely unchanged. Indeed the only visible sign of their presence was an inspection of the School by Royal Security before William arrived: this led to the discovery in Valentine Stockdale's desk of an ingenious but potentially alarming 'race-track' for ball-bearings, formed from a complex entanglement of steel and wires. It was pounced on and taken away in a high degree of excitement for immediate forensic scrutiny.

During the Princes' time a succession of personal protection officers provided discreet security, and became fully integrated into the

Ludgrove community. Both William and Harry were there for five years in the mid-1990s – a particularly sensitive time for them domestically – and they both received all the care and support that Ludgrove could provide.

H.R.H. Prince William has contributed these vivid recollections of his years at Ludgrove

Ludgrove conjures up many memories – from fear of being put in a dormitory with a group of noisy eight-year-olds, to uncontrollable giggling in serious maths lessons. There was also the memory of Tuesday's and Thursday's grub, where we would all try to take just one more bar of chocolate without the monitor seeing us. I never got away with it!

And who could forget having your birthday at Ludgrove? Never mind the presents from your parents, the only thing I wanted was my ice-cream birthday-cake, topped with flake and covered with wine-gums. For one day of the year I would gain 150 more friends, and the noise of the whole school wanting some ice-cream cake overtook that of any football match. And in the background all that could be heard was the constant 'ping-ping' as Mr Marston would try to keep order with his bell.

I have many happy memories of my time at Ludgrove. It will always be a place that brings a cheeky smile to my face.

Both boys did well at Ludgrove: Prince William was in the school swimming team (he subsequently became Captain of Swimming at Eton, and played water-polo for the Scottish Universities in 2004 while at St. Andrews University). He was remembered as " a delightful boy – always the first to volunteer if anything needed to be done." Prince Harry was a good sportsman, who played in the first football and rugby teams, and was Captain of the 2nd XI for cricket.

The Princess of Wales at Ludgrove Sports Day

Happily, their years at Ludgrove were not marred by indiscreet revelations, intrusions by the press or unexpected events – with one exception. During William's first summer term, and only three days before Sports Day, another boy was revolving at speed on the lawn, whirling a putter round his head, unaware that Prince William was converging on its orbit. The result of the collision was a depressed fracture of the Prince's skull.

Prince William helping out on Sports Day

Janet and Pat Jones took him to Reading Hospital where

the injury was immediately treated, but in no time word of the accident had spread and, by the time Janet re-emerged, large numbers of the public had gathered on the hospital steps. The arrival of William's parents coincided with the descent of the world's press on Ludgrove, to report the incident, assess the damage and in particular to

Prince Harry with the Football First XI

try to find out the name of the boy who had apparently 'encompassed the death of the Heir Apparent' by the incautious swinging of a golf-club. In spite of the pressures, Ludgrove maintained total discretion, and to their great credit not one of the boys (briefed firmly by the Headmasters) divulged the name to their parents, friends or relations.

Both Harry and William went on to Eton in due course, and in appreciation of their care for the Princes, Gerald and Nichol were made Lieutenants of the Royal Victorian Order (LVO) by the Queen in 2002.

Alan Barber, 1905–1985

ATB had retired from the school in 1973. He and Dorothy were now living in the Garden Cottage by the Chapel Ground. It might well have been a difficult transition both for him and his successors. ATB 'was' Ludgrove. He had become a living legend there, imbuing the whole place with his personality and style, and now he was living almost literally on the doorstep of his successors. But, unlike many great leaders, he knew how to 'let go'. He had very little to do with the school after September 1973,

attended no school matches or Chapel services, offered no advice and confined his retirement to his beloved hobby of gardening (designating himself as "Head Gardener" to those who enquired). He looked after the farm, and left Gerald and Nichol to get on with everything, without scrutiny by their great predecessor in the Garden Cottage.

Alan Barber (left) enjoying a Test match at Lords in 1983 with his brothers Bertie (centre) and Philip

However, in 1983 Alan suffered a severe stroke which rendered him an invalid. It was tragic that someone so physically active all his life should be felled in such a terrible way. For more than two years he was nursed by Dorothy, in a way that tested love and devotion to their limits. But on 10th March 1985, just three months short of his 80th birthday, he died. At his memorial service in All Saints, Wokingham, Peter Borgnis gave an evocative and eloquent address; and Alan's life and achievements were summarised in a moving prayer by his old friend the Rev. John Eddison, who had preached so many times in the Ludgrove Chapel:

> *Let us remember with grateful hearts the life and work of Alan Barber –*
>
> *For the standards he demanded of himself and expected of others; and for his example of integrity, self-discipline and whole-hearted, single-minded devotion to his work…*
>
> *For his outstanding prowess at games, for his skill in imparting it to others…*
>
> *For his personal charm and loyalty as a friend; for his sense of humour and fun; for his innate understanding of boys, and for the fact that he never forgot what it was like to be young….*
>
> *For the living monument he created in the shape of Ludgrove….*
>
> *For the many memories he left behind to be cherished by his family and friends, and which will help to lighten their sense of loss, and colour their lives …with laughter and with love*

Tim Shaw, 1905–1986

Tim Shaw had retired in 1968. His first wife Peggy had died of cancer in 1965, when Jane Ramsay was among those who devotedly nursed her. In 1967 he married Isobel Graham, and lived out his retirement in Sussex. But in 1986, at the age of 81, devotedly nursed by Isobel, Tim also died of cancer.

At his funeral service, his nephew Donald, who had been at Ludgrove from 1947 to 1952, gave the following address:

> We have come here today to give thanks for the life of Tim Shaw. … Throughout his life he showed love and friendship in abundance; and if I add to these the qualities of courtesy, tenderness, loyalty and courage I am describing the character we would all wish to be – and he was.

Tim Shaw

Indeed Uncle Tim will always be remembered for his interest in people, and his happy knack of being able to put young and old alike at their ease and make them feel comfortable in his company. I personally am immensely grateful for his kindly understanding of homesick boys....

Ludgrove... was his life for forty years, and – together with Alan Barber – he helped it to gain the high reputation it continues to enjoy today...

May God keep him safe.

INTO THE NEW MILLENNIUM

What are Ludgrove's prospects as it moves into the 21st century and the third millennium? It faces many challenges. One is the political pressure on schools of this kind, and on the charitable status, which helps to sustain them. The late Paul Foot (Ludgrove 1945–50) expressed this trenchantly :

> I'm absolutely opposed to the private education system. I think a school like Ludgrove should be incorporated into a system which is available to everybody whatever part of the economic structure they come from. The fact that it's accessible to only a very tiny section of the population divides society: that's the central point. The resources, the facilities, the teachers and everything that flows from that are all better, and as a result private education becomes a central prop of the whole divided nature of our society today. And it also removes from the state sector the potential resources and influence for the good that such people could have. What 'comprehensive' should mean is that the people who have got confidence, wealth or ability will engage them fully in the state sector schools and pull them up by their bootstraps.

A second challenge is how to maintain the balance between the expectations of parents on the one hand – who today will settle for nothing less than the best of everything – and affordability on the other hand, in the face of the inexorable annual rise in the level of school fees.

A third challenge is that of greater public accountability to an ever-increasing number of official rules, regulations, standards and prohibitions pouring ceaselessly from both Westminster and Brussels – in Health and Safety, National Care Standards, Child Protection Policies, Training Qualifications, Criminal Records Bureau clearances, School Inspections, Employment Tribunals and many other matters. The questions which W.H.Auden famously asked in the 1940s remain, needless to say, beyond the scope of such official interventions :

> *Was he free? Was he happy? The question is absurd:*
> *Had anything been wrong, we should certainly have heard.*

"Was he happy?" Supper Night, summer term 2003

For Ludgrove however, these are indeed the central questions.

A fourth challenge is how long the system of 'boys only, boarding only' from the age of 8, will endure. As we have seen, only four such prep schools still exist in the country today. In 1990, the Headmasters sat down with the Governors to consider what sort of school Ludgrove would probably have become by the year 2000. They anticipated a very different place. Micky Wiggin, a Governor at the time, recalls the discussion:

> We felt that 10 years on, 50 per cent of Ludgrove would be day children; and of that number, 50 per cent would be girls; and probably half the boarders left wouldn't come to the school until the age of about 11. That was the way the world was going, and we felt sure that people would less and less want to part with their children at the age of eight. We then arrived at the new millennium, and you'd have said, if it had been minuted, what absolutely useless people we

were, because Ludgrove is still 100 per cent boarders, and still 100 per cent boys. Now I attribute that wholly to the way Gerald, Janet and Nichol have led the school and made it so successful. Above all it's a happy place – and you simply wouldn't get people today to send their children away to school at eight unless they were very sure that they were going to be happy.

Ludgrove's answer to all these challenges, and to many more like them, is to continue to provide excellence in all it does – as testified by the Report of the Independent Schools Inspectorate in March 2003, which concluded thus:

I.S.I. Report on Ludgrove, 2003

- *a very good ethos, where good care is taken of the pupils and standards of behaviour are high*
- *a dedicated and hard-working staff*
- *excellent facilities which support the teaching and learning, and the pupils' personal development*
- *a curriculum which enhances the wide range of activities*
- *boarding arrangements which enhance pupils' personal development, and provide them with a positive social experience*
- *an impressive record in placing pupils at prestigious senior schools*

Underpinning this excellence has been the way in which the Headmasters have managed so much change, growth and innovation in the last thirty years while preserving at the same time the school's traditional character.

The character of Ludgrove is integrally bound up in the beauty of its site. This is how Gerald sees it:

The grounds are such an important part of our atmosphere here. I've always loved the grounds – and the maintenance side too, just as my Dad did.

"Nothing ever looks lovely without somebody working on it."

I'm around the place all the time wondering: "Which pitches shall we have today? Don't the boys' gardens need a bit of attention? Shouldn't we be pruning here and there?" I suppose I'd really love to be a groundsman! Nothing ever looks lovely without somebody working on it. And the boys love the grounds too, the fact that they can run straight out and play anywhere they like in such safety and variety.

The Future

Nichol Marston retired in the summer of 2004, and Gerald and Janet will do so in 2008. Simon Barber, Gerald and Janet's son, is the fourth generation of his family to teach at Ludgrove. He and another master, Andrew ('Sid') Inglis, were appointed Joint Deputy Headmasters in the summer of 2004. They are moving towards the top of an institution, which in turn is now at the top of its class among English preparatory schools. Today there are no fewer than 52 names already down for the Michaelmas term of 2010, seven years hence. In the 21st century, parents seem as keen as ever for their children

Into the future: Simon Barber and Andrew ('Sid') Inglis

to go to board at Ludgrove at a tender age. There are clear attractions in a school close at hand where childhood can unfold and be enjoyed in a secure, happy environment with easy and regular access for parents, and Ludgrove's proximity to London is

undoubtedly a vital asset.

But the particular 'Ludgrove dimension' underpinning it all is the family atmosphere that pervades daily life there. A parent recently summed it up:

What comes over very strongly is Ludgrove's absolute love of small boys and of developing those small boys. It seems to me that children are under so much pressure these days to achieve results in everything they do from the earliest age. But Ludgrove boys are allowed a childhood. That, after all, is when so much of how to interact with others in life is learnt.

~

EPILOGUE: FULL CIRCLE

"A winning combination."
Good Schools Guide, 2003

The beauty of the School site evoked in the last chapter has always inspired Ludgrovians. Sir Shane Leslie was equally struck by the beauty of the old school in Hertfordshire, when he went there as a new boy in 1895. Almost half a century later, in 1944, he returned to the site, by then half-empty, its neglected buildings used as offices, and recorded these evocative memories of Arthur Dunn's school "in its first flush of youth":

> I found myself during wartime outside the gates of Trent Park near Cockfosters – once the seat of banking princes, the Bevans – and walked along lanes and around corners which I could have traced in my sleep.

Gateway and drive, Trent Park, c.1895

Passing old Trent Church and Norrisbury, I entered Hadley Common. The old gates of fifty years ago were still swinging, for here I first entered the world of school. At the bottom of the road lay Ludgrove School, in its first flush of youth on my arrival there in 1895. I was indeed in the first forty boys who attended that renowned academy. My number was 36, which I have considered my lucky number ever since.

I knew it only as a school of careering boys and swiftly moving masters, led by that incomparable leader of boys, Arthur Dunn. I cannot believe that forty years have passed since his death, for I sensed him rapidly coming past the gates, and I could see him as of old waiting to receive and cheer the boys after their holidays, Mrs. Dunn at his side and the baby Johnny in his arms.

I walked through the school yard and found every familiar mark: the little orchard; the famous Fives Court where so many players of Eton Fives had learned their first strokes; the rackets courts, once the Bevans' carriage house; the asphalt yard, and the last wicket still chalked on the wall. Over all hung, soundless and mournful, the school clock. The wooden fencing was down, admitting to the Cottage where dwelt Arthur's incomparable staff of assistant masters – Henry Hansell, Joe Smith, Oakley, Wells, Crabtree major and minor. The real scholar among them was Weatherhead, who had entered nuptial bliss and lived elsewhere. They were all athletes and joyous companions rather than 'ushers'. They lived in the imaginations and affections of the boys. To this day I can sketch the towering Hansell defending goals with $6^{1}/_{2}$ feet of graceful, leaping strength. I can see the cynical little bearded Weatherhead playing at forward, with Joe Smith acrobating with the ball at centre. They played like inspired schoolboys, but behind them stood a tower of strength, the strongest, bravest, straightest Englishman I could ever dream of meeting – "Oakers", full back for England. As he stood there in my mind's eye, he reminded me of prints of an old champion of England waiting in the ring.

Passing 'scugs corner' and the old fig tree into the playing fields – cricket to the left on the slope, football to the right on a pitch which Arthur Dunn had had levelled at immense cost and labour; but it was ground on which the Universities of Oxford and Cambridge had deigned to play. I remember enthusiastic boys and masters on their knees picking stones from the ground for days and days.

Today a few soldiers were kicking at a goal, and the old pavilion stood in tatters under the raids of time. Around it Henry Hansell had planted rose trees, which we boys used to rid of caterpillars to win his favour. Amid the wreck, one rose tree was still blooming! The Cricket Ground remained as ever, with tall trees around the top boundaries over which masters like Field and Weatherhead used to hit sixes to the hysterical delight of the gallery of boys.

How strangely peaceful it all seemed – not a sound by a man or boy stirring. I wandered for an hour communing with dead friends – masters I could see at every corner, and boys grown to manhood and dead long ago.

The buildings stand intact, used by a City firm for their clerks; but the boards with all our names have been taken away by the School to pastures new. The terraced gardens have been excavated into shelters, and the pond has been boarded off from the grounds. But the familiar trees are all there; only the familiar faces are all gone.

Ludgrove staff in 1896, Hansell (seated) left, Weatherhead (seated) right

The old Ludgrove has recently been converted into luxury flats. Well over a century after its foundation, what would Arthur Dunn think of the new Ludgrove today?

He would be struck by the beauty of the grounds and gardens, reminiscent of his own lovely site at Barnet before the Piccadilly Line reached Hertfordshire. He would be astonished by the size of the school, the scope of its activities and curriculum, and by

Science was not taught in Arthur Dunn's day

its five-figure annual fees. He would frown at the complexity of modern life compared with his day, and at how much of a Headmaster's time is taken up with bureaucracy and regulations. He would approve strongly of the fact that many Ludgrove boys still go on to Eton, though welcoming the variety of other public schools to which they also go today.

He would be perplexed by today's competitiveness, by the extent of the learning support, by the number of *exeats* the boys enjoy during the term, and by the whole world of information technology. He would endorse the 'hands-on' style of the Headmasters; he would be impressed by the much greater involvement of parents in the life of their boys at the school; and he would applaud the vitality of Ludgrove's music and drama, and of course its success on the games field, where he would look again for that elusive quality of "dash" in the boys, to which he himself attached such importance. He would be proud of Ludgrove's undoubted reputation for academic excellence, and of its determination to bring out the best in every boy no matter what his talents or ambitions.

But above all he would note with approval that – amidst all the changes that have occurred – Ludgrove still has the feel of a 'sanctuary of kindness', with the same happy atmosphere which he himself had always so keenly fostered; and that his foundation has been run for over 100 years of its 112-year history by no fewer than three generations of the same family, descended from his friend Bill Oakley, with a fourth recently appointed as Deputy Headmaster. He would conclude that those who run Ludgrove today are therefore aware of the great traditions of the past and are determined to preserve them.

Then he would go into the Dining Hall, and see around the walls the Honour Boards bearing the names of every boy who has ever been to Ludgrove; and over the main door his own splendid portrait, and inscribed on the Boards next to it the names of his own boys, whose faces he would see and whose voices he would hear again as if it were yesterday.

Then he might turn to the report on Ludgrove in *The Good Schools Guide* for 2003 which concludes:

"Ludgrove is a competitive school with high academic standards…with excellent pastoral care and wonderfully enthusiastic teachers, offering a wide variety of 'Boys Own' type activities plus high standards of behaviour. Manners are hugely important, and kindness to each other – these things don't change. It's a winning combination."

"These things don't change!" The phrase would strike a chord, and he would look again at the famous statement

The portrait of Arthur Dunn in the Dining Hall

from Ecclesiastes framed above his desk, and reflect that the things he himself always held to be of the highest importance in life never do change at all. He might have read the speech in the 1960s by that great advocate and jurist, Lord Birkett, and seen his favourite saying repeated at the heart of those simple words:

> The world has changed a great deal in my lifetime, and we must all adapt ourselves to change if we can. But I still think that there are some changeless things in the world that make or mar our happiness.
>
> I think that men and women who can choose their job, and find a daily pleasure in doing it are fortune's favourites; that a happy home life is the very greatest of human blessings; that there is infinite wisdom in the old words *'Whatsoever thy hand findeth to do, do it with thy might'*; that it is wise to have a hobby of some kind, and if it's a useful hobby, so much the better; that it is the highest wisdom to make friends, and to take every kind of trouble to keep the friendships in good repair, particularly as you grow older; that excess in all things is to be avoided; that it is wise to keep one's word, and not break promises; that a sense of public duty should be cultivated, if only as a safeguard against selfishness; and that it is wise to keep the mind alert by reading and by all the agencies that now exert themselves for our benefit. I think that it is wise to realise the value of a margin in all things, and not only in money matters; not to spend too much time on seeking mere pleasure; and not to live for the moment only. In the end, it is Life that teaches us all.

These precepts are thriving in the Ludgrove of today. As the school moves into the new millennium, they still lie at the heart of the Ludgrove spirit, a spirit which remains Arthur Dunn's greatest and most enduring legacy to his school and its story.

ENDNOTES

Chapter 1

[1] The author acknowledges the valuable background to this chapter provided by Donald Leinster-Mackay in his book *The Rise of the English Preparatory School*

[2] The Rev. Sydney Smith (1771-1845) Educated at Winchester and New College, Oxford, he became a fashionable cleric, famous for his wit and prolific correspondence.

[3] Visiting Professor of Economics at the Stern Business School, New York University

Chapter 2

[1] Sir Shane Leslie, *Men Were Different*, 1937

[2] Edward Grayson, *Corinthians and Cricketers*

[3] Sir Shane Leslie, *Men Were Different*

[4] The author acknowledges the help provided on the background to Ludgrove by Mr Brian Warren, Hon. Archivist of the Potters Bar & District Historical Society and Mr Hugh Bevan of Alton, Hampshire.

[5] From the Rev. F.C.Cass's *History of Monken Hadley*

[6] John Betjeman had briefly taught at Heddon Court in the 1920s, after coming down from Oxford. It was there that he wrote his poem *"Cricket Master (an Incident)"*

[7] Sir Gerald Tyrwhitt Wilson (Lord Berners) describing Mr Gambril of Elmley Prep School.

[8] Osbert Sitwell , Vol. 2 of his autobiography, *The Scarlet Tree,* 1946

[9] Duke of Windsor, *A King's Story,* pp. 56-57

[10] Kenneth Rose, *King George V*, London 1983

[11] Lord Home of the Hirsel, *The Way the Wind Blows* (autobiography), London 1976

[12] Edward Grayson, *Corinthians and Cricketers*

[13] The details of this case are taken from E. Majoribanks, *The Life of Sir Edward Marshall Hall*, London 1929

Chapter 3

[1] Trent Park was sold by Francis Bevan in 1908 to Sir Edward Sassoon, a merchant banker, MP and confidant of Edward VII. When Sassoon was killed in a car accident in 1912, the house passed to his son Philip, then aged 23. A millionaire bachelor, aesthete and society host, Sir Philip Sassoon remodelled Trent as the setting for lavish hospitality.

Chapter 6

[1] From the autobiography of the Marquess of Bath, Vol. 1, *The Early Years* , Artek Press

Chapter 7

[1] S. Sebag Montefiore, *My Affair with Stalin,* (Weidenfeld & Nicholson, 1997)

THE HEADMASTERS AND MAJOR EVENTS IN THE SCHOOL'S HISTORY

HEADMASTERS, DATES AND NUMBERS IN THE SCHOOL

Headmasters	Years	No. of boys	
		Year	Number
A.T.B. Dunn	1892–1902	1900:	63
G.O. Smith & W.J. Oakley	1902–1922	1922:	65
W.J. Oakley & F.A.H. Henley	1922–1934	1934:	45
F.A.H. Henley	1934–1937	1937:	74
A.T. Barber & T.W. Shaw	1937–1968	1968:	90
A.T. Barber	1968–1973	1973:	128
G.W.P. Barber & C.N.J. Marston	1973–2004	2004:	197
G.W.P. Barber	2004 -	2004:	200

KEY EVENTS IN THE STORY OF LUDGROVE

1892 – Foundation of the school in Barnet by Arthur Dunn
1894 – New football ground created. Eton fives courts constructed
1895 – G.O. Smith and W.J. Oakley join the staff
1902 – Death of Arthur Dunn. Succeeded by Smith and Oakley
1905 – F.A.H.Henley joins the staff
1922 – G.O. Smith and Miss Smith retire
1928 - T.W. Shaw joins the staff
1930 – A.T. Barber joins the staff
1934 – W.J. Oakley retires. Succeeded by F.A.H. Henley
1937 – Ludgrove moves from Barnet to Wokingham
        F.A.H. Henley retires, succeeded by A.T. Barber and T.W. Shaw
1938 – Construction of air-raid shelter
1963 – C.N.J. Marston joins the staff
1965 – Science teaching introduced
1966 – G.W.P. Barber joins the staff
1967 – New library and music-rooms built
1968 – T.W. Shaw retires
1970 – G.W.P. Barber and C.N.J. Marston appointed Assistant Headmasters
1972 – Ludgrove Charitable Trust formed. First Appeal launched (£70,000).
        First Ludgrove skiing trip organised (to Ischl, Austria).
1973 – A.T. Barber retires. Succeeded by G.W.P. Barber and C.N.J. Marston
1976 – First Sports Day held
1977 – Dining Room extended. First specialist classrooms built
1978 – 'The Great Fire of Ludgrove'. Ludgrove soccer team visits the USA
1980 – School numbers reach 170
1983 – New music block inaugurated. Second Appeal (£400,000) launched for new Sports Hall,
        Theatre and two new Squash courts

1984 – First computer introduced
1985 – Sports-hall inaugurated by Dorothy Barber
1988 – Old gym converted to dormitory and assembly-room
1990 – First School trip to France.
      Farm buildings converted into art and crafts centre
1992 – Ludgrove Centenary celebrations
1995 – Old squash court converted to specialist classrooms
2000 – G.W.P. Barber and CN.J. Marston awarded the LVO in the Queen's Birthday Honours
2001- Third Appeal (£800,000) launched for new swimming-pool.
2002 – New swimming-pool opened in March
2003 – S.W.T. Barber and A.C.T. Inglis appointed Assistant Headmasters
2004 – CN.J. Marston retires. School numbers reach 200.

Appendix 2

CAPTAINS OF THE SCHOOL
1898–2004

Year	January	April/May	September
1898	—	—	J.H.B.Lyon
1899	J.H.B.Lyon	J.H.B.Lyon	D.C.Stephenson
1900	D.C.Stephenson	D.C.Stephenson	V.A.Barrington-Kennett
1901	V.A.Barrington-Kennett	V.A.Barrington-Kennett	R.O.Bridgeman
1902	R.O.Bridgeman	R.O.Bridgeman	G.R.Mitchison
1903	G.R.Michison	G.R.Michison	H.F.Campbell
1904	H.F.Campbell	H.F.Campbell	R.Lybbock
1905	R.Lybbock	R.Lybbock	M.R.H.Murray
1906	M.R.H.Murray	J.Foster	H.K.Chester
1907	H.K.Chester	H.K.Chester	O.W.H.Leese
1908	R.Philipson	M.E.Impey	C.J.Dudley-Smith
1909	C.J.Dudley-Smith	C.J.Dudley-Smith	A.Lubbock
1910	A.Lubbock	A.Lubbock	D.G.Buxton
1911	D.G.Buxton	D.G.Buxton	Lord Settrington
1912	Lord Romilly	Lord Romilly	C.R.E.Fenwick
1913	C.R.E.Fenwick	G.E.Tritton	R.A.Hoare
1914	O.St M.Thynne	O.St M.Thynne	A.B.Money-Coutts
1915	A.B.Money-Coutts	A.B.Money-Coutts	A.B.Money-Coutts
1916	A.B.Money-Coutts	A.B.Money-Coutts	T.P.Burns
1917	C.V.Pilkington	C.V.Pilkington	C.V.Pilkington
1918	E.W.Thynne	O.J.Philipson	E.F.P.Gage
1919	E.F.P.Gage	E.F.P.Gage	D.J.C.Hill-Wood
1920	Lord Cloud Hamilton	E.F.Gosling	H.M.Douglas-Home
1921	H.M.Douglas-Home	H.F.Winn	A.B.J.Grenfell
1922	A.B.J.Grenfell	L.A.Gilliat	L.A.Gilliat
1923	L.A.Gilliat	A.R.Primrose	K.F.Malcolmson
1924	K.F.Malcolmson	K.F.Malcolmson	The Earl of Hopetoun

1925	The Earl of Hopetoun	The Earl of Hopetoun	S.Marchant
1926	S.Marchant	S.Marchant	P.Arkwright
1927	J.W.Strang-Steel	R.D.Dale	U.Browne
1928	U.Browne	G.H.Arkwright	G.H.Arkwright
1929	G.H.Arkwright	G.H.Arkwright	R.N.Jardine-Paterson
1930	C.N.Johnson	C.N.Johnson	E.G.Lambton
1931	D.S.Robertson	D.S.Robertson	I.A.Henderson
1932	K.Bell	K.Bell	J.M.Strang-Steel
1933	C.M.B.Davies	J.H.P.Curtis	J.R.Warrender
1934	J.R.Warrender	J.R.Warrender	C.W.Lambton
1935	A.D.Henderson	A.D.Henderson	E.H.Spooner
1936	E.H.Spooner	E.H.Spooner	A.C.Petherick
1937	A.C.Petherick	B.C.R.Dodsworth	B.C.R.Dodsworth
1938	B.C.R.Dodsworth	M.D.Hoare	M.D.Hoare
1939	A.J.B.Mason	W.Houston	B.E.Spicer
1940	B.E.Spicer	B.E.Spicer	J.F.Nixon
1941	J.A.Worsley	J.A.Worsley	J.R.Day
1942	J.R.Day	W.J.Collins	C.W.R.Byass
1943	C.W.R.Byass	J.I.Morrison	T.L.Wright
1944	T.L.Wright	T.L.Wright	W.S.R.Kenyon-Slaney
1945	W.S.R.Kenyon-Slaney	A.G.Thynne	M.H.Elliot
1946	A.Heald	A.Heald	J.V.Wellesley
1947	J.V.Wellesley	R.J.Cock	T.G.C.Holcroft
1948	M.R.Lee	A.M.Rankin	C.R.T.Laws
1949	J.A.Wolfe-Murray	J.A.Wolfe-Murray	N.M.Allfrey
1950	C.J.H.Gurney	C.C.Douglas Home	C.C.Douglas Home
1951	M.Dunne	D.C.L.Bathurst	B.E.Allfrey
1952	W.D.Heber-Percy	Lord Garmoyle	T.M.Stockdale
1953	N.F.Nicholson	N.F.Nicholson	N.C.F.Barber
1954	C.J.R.Elton	C.J.R.Elton	A.C.Farquhar
1955	A.C.Farquhar	F.M.R.Davies	F.M.Strang-Steel
1956	F.P.W.Elton	N.P.Cumming	Lord Dunglass
1957	M.G.Griffith	M.G.Griffith	P.J.R.Scott
1958	C.B.Strang-Steel	Lord Mornington	M.C.Goold
1959	F.H.S.Gilbert	F.H.S.Gilbert	W.W.Montague-Douglas-Scott
1960	J.N.D.D'Arcy	J.N.D.D'Arcy	R.S.Gosling
1961	P.R.Dunkels	T.Basset	W.S.Johnstone
1962	D.S.Cumming	A.D.Swanston	J.B.Faulkner
1963	J.L.Hobson	J.L.Hobson	C.J.Harvie
1964	C.J.Harvie	S.G. St Clair-Ford	C.J.Jennings
1965	C.J.Jennings	J.H.S.Witherington	J.H.S.Witherington
1966	J.A.L.Wethered	J.A.L.Wethered	F.G.Green
1967	F.G.Green	F.G.Green	M.M.Bishop
1968	M.J.W.Parsons	P.R.P.Champness	A.D.H.Hunter
1969	J.P.Etches	R.A.C.Toller	R.A.C.Toller
1970	P.M.Ainsworth	P.M.Ainsworth	Lord Loughborough
1971	Lord Loughborough	Lord Loughborough	J.D.Boldero
1972	W.A.S.Dale	W.A.S.Dale	P.W.A.Westerman
1973	C.A.J.Bromely-Gardner	N.G.C.Hamilton	T.M.Liddiard

1974	S.M.Stuart	C.N.S. Jackson	M.J.Orr
1975	P.J.Fane	P.J.Fane	J.M.Liddiard
1976	M.J.Menaged	E.J.Bryans	A.Brown
1977	J.P.Snow	J.P.Snow	M.C.H.Westerman
1978	A.C.H.Tatham	A.C.H.Tatham	M.Barbour
1979	E.C.Chamberlayne	E.C.Chamberlayne	R.A.Liddiard
1980	C.K.Blyth	C.K.Blyth	R.H.O.R.Dutton
1981	C.J.E.Lunt	C.J.E.Lunt	R.H.West
1982	A.R.G.Lunt	A.R.G.Lunt	E.G.Pope
1983	M.S.Shashoua	D.L.Martineau	G.G.Hulbert
1984	P.M.D.Allison	P.M.D.Allison	C.I.A.Cumming
1985	J.M.R.Norman	J.M.R.Norman	P.R.E.Stucley
1986	M.O.Pilkington	E.R.H.Clarkson	E.A.Chamberlin
1987	H.A.J.Turcan	A.N.C.Mordaunt	E.F.J.Fenston
1988	R.W.I.Fowler	O.J.Meakin	W.J.Armitage
1989	M.A.Kimber	A.D.T.B.Cooke	S.W.Brooksbank
1990	J.P.A.Longworth	M.M.Singer	A.V.Cooper
1991	H.M.Sherbrooke	C.R.N.Jennings	G.J.Smith-Bingham
1992	A.G.Menzies	B.R.Clarkson	F.P.P. von Westenholz
1993	J.G. Le M. Peck	T.S.Chamberlayne	I.D.P.Russell
1994	J.R.H.Bullock-Webster	J.M.P.Thompson	A.N.Dalrymple
1995	H.E.V.Walsh	F.A.L.Marx	D.H.R.Ker
1996	J.R.H.Gayner	A.M.N.Jennings	A.P.G.Burnand
1997	B.M.Stoop	O.G.Stanley	S.G.S.Morrison
1998	W.F.J.Eskdail	L.B.Ward	T.G.A.Sinclair
1999	T.C.Hill	A.J.Smith	C.G.Storey
2000	G.F.Northcott	H.S.Preston	T.D.Astor
2001	W.F.Sanderson	F.M.Drummond-Brady	T.F.Meade
2002	W.R.P.Lowry	S.C.A.Harbord-Hamond	F.R.Murray
2003	W.F.Powell-Brett	J.D.Bladon	N.H.B.Mills
2004	J.W.Garnier	E.P.C.Eddy	

Appendix 3

CAPTAINS OF THE CRICKET AND FOOTBALL 1st ELEVENS

	Cricket	**Football**
1894	E.H.Buxton	—
1895	H.A.Hurt	—
1896	P.Hammond	—
1897	H.R.D.Lacon	—
1898	R.A.Hurt	R.A.Hurt
1899	J.H.B.Lyon	J.E.P.Howey
1900	R.C.Byass	J.E.P.Howey
1901	V.Barrington-Kennett	V. Barrington-Kennett

1902	A.L.Maynard	A.L.Maynard
1903	A.R.W.Curtis	F.B.Lyon
1904	H.F.Campbell	C.W.Norman
1905	W.S.Cornwallis	R.T.Stanyforth
1906	F.M.Eastwood	F.M.Eastwood
1907	J.H.M.Dunn	J.H.M.Dunn
1908	R.J.F.Remnant	R.J.F.Remnant
1909	I.G.Menzies	T.Philipson
1910	J.M.Cobbold	F.G.W.Marchant
1911	A.H.Foster	A.E.A.Keppel
1912	D.M.Leese	A.H.Ferguson
1913	H.M.Clutterbuck	C.M.D. Venables-Llewelyn
1914	A.L.Grant	A.L.Grant
1915	R.G.R.Oxley	W.W.Hill-Wood
1916	W.G.Worthington	H.R.Philipson
1917	D.W.Hoare	R.D.Tollemache
1918	G.M.Crossman	J.C.B.Cookson
1919	E.F.P.Gage	E.F.P.Gage
1920	E.H.Allen	J.R.S.Arkwright
1921	A.B.J.Grenfell	The Earl of Erne
1922	C.H.Gosling	A.B.J.Grenfell
1923	A.R.Primrose	L.A.Gilliat
1924	Lord Milton	G.P.Campbell-Preston
1925	The Earl of Hopetoun	The Earl of Hopetoun
1926	D.C.Goschen	M.J.Gilliat
1927	M.Meynell	M.Meynell
1928	H.Birkbeck	N.F.Turner
1929	M.E.Parker	M.E.Parker
1930	P. Holdsworth Hunt	P.Holdsworth Hunt
1931	C.D.Clark	I.A.Henderson
1932	R.O.Stanley	J.M.Strang-Steel
1933	J.H.P.Curtis	R.A.Henley
1934	R.A.Henley	A.D.Henderson
1935	K.C.Boles	K.C.Boles
1936	E.H.Spooner	J.N.R.Hoare
1937	D.C.W.Bampfylde	A.C.Petherick
1938	M.D.Hoare	M.D.Hoare
1939	V.C.Boles	J.F.Nixon
1940	B.E.Spicer	T.A.Newton
1941	J.A.Worsley	J.R.Day
1942	I.P.E.Gay	I.P.E.Gay
1943	C.W.R.Byass	P.C.A.Munster
1944	T.L.Wright	I.R.Lomax
1945	M.G.C.Jeffreys	A.C.D. Ingleby-Mackenzie
1946	A.C.D.Ingleby-Mackenzie	T.H.H.S. Pilkington
1947	R.A.Eckersley	R.A.Eckersley
1948	A.M.Rankin	P.D. Hill-Wood
1949	P.D.Hill-Wood	C.Chelsea
1950	R.D.Carnegie	M.Dunne

1951	J.A.F.Wilson	J.A.F.Wilson
1952	D.C.de F.Edwards	A.J.Cordle
1953	N.F.Nicholson	R.I.Jefferson
1954	R.I.Jefferson	A.C.Farquhar
1955	G.P.D.Milne	G.M.Pope
1956	M.G.Griffith	M.G.Griffith
1957	M.G.Griffith	J.S.Olivier
1958	M.C.Gould	C.H.Cordle
1959	F.W.J.Cornwallis	R.A.Herd
1960	D.M.Smith	T.R.O'Connor
1961	T.B. St Clair Ford	A.D.Swanston
1962	R.P.C.Shaw	R.S.Crawley
1963	R.S.Crawley	J.E.A.Streatfield-Moore
1964	J.M.Shaw	N.D.D.Hoare
1965	J.H.S.Witherington	J.H.S.Witherington
1966	J.M.Pelly	D.M.Hamilton
1967	D.M.Swanston	S.V.Tweedie
1968	B.K.Graham	M.M.Hamilton
1969	A.G.Chichester	R.O.Lagden
1970	M.B.H.Evans	I.M.Hamilton
1971	M.W.Fane	P.H.Wilson
1972	J.G.C.Doyle	A.A.H.Tabor
1973	D.P.Wiggin	R.P.M.Uniache
1974	A.J.Naylor	T.Beardmore-Gray
1975	A.J.Naylor	A.W.Cohane
1976	E.J.G.Bryans	T.I.Fane
1977	R.G.S.Vaughan	C.W.Snow
1978	J.M.H.Ford	M.S.J.Whitley
1979	W.Beardmore-Gray	J.T.E.Illingworth
1980	C.K.Blyth	C.J.E.Lunt
1981	R.A.Pyman	A.R.G.Lunt
1982	L.J.Sheffield	F.W.Tulloch
1983	C.E.L.Simson	W.J.F.Carpmael
1984	C.I.A.Cumming	A.A.Haig-Thomas
1985	E.M.S.Hewens	R.S.A.Cecil
1986	O.J.M.Lane	J.J.Walsh
1987	E.A.Chamberlin	R.J.Bonsor
1988	N.G.Harrop	G.W.Deedes
1989	H.A.Kamerling	M.J.M.Konig
1990	A.G.V.Robins	C.R.N.Jennings
1991	J.O.E.Fraser	A.G.Menzies
1992	E.A.N.Jennings	R.R.Wigan
1993	E.F.Colquhoun	J.M.P.Thomson
1994	A.M.A.Andjel	H.E.V.Walsh
1995	A.N.Dalrymple	F.J.Eckersley
1996	C.H.C.Gordon	J.P.R.Dobson
1997	S.M.G.Milne	H.C.Annandale
1998	C.P.A.Nissen	T.C.Rowles-Nicholson
1999	E.F.J.Nissen	J.J.Warren

2000	P.W.Stoop	F.A.W.M.Cornwallis
2001	C.A.W.Stewart	J.M.D.North
2002	W.E.L.Hopton	J.F.N.Rogers
2003	W.P.N.Denehy	H.L.C.Nicholls
2004	J.R.J.Hopton	

Appendix 4

LUDGROVE SCHOLARSHIPS
1938–2004

1938	P.R.V. Walmsley	Third Scholarship, Rugby
1942	J.R. Day	First Scholarship, Harrow
1946	J.W. Hawkins	Scholarship, Dartmouth
1947	C.H.L. Bathurst	Scholarship, Eton
	J.V. Wellesley	Scholarship, Dartmouth
1950	C.C. Douglas Home	Scholarship, Eton
1951	P.M. Foot	Scholarship, Shrewsbury
1952	T.M. Stockdale	Scholarship, Eton
1953	N.C.F. Barber	Scholarship, Shrewsbury
1958	M.C. Gould	Scholarship,Wellington
1960	J.W. d'Arcy	Exhibition, Bradfield
	M.T. Swanston	Scholarship, Rugby
1961	T. Basset	Scholarship, Stowe
	R.B. Swanston	Music Scholarship, Stowe
1965	C.J. Jennings	Scholarship, Harrow
1966	R.M. Thomas	Scholarship, St. Edward's
1967	F.G. Green	Scholarship, Harrow
	J. St.C. van Hasselt	Scholarship, Radley
	A.P. Murray	Scholarship, Eton
1968	P.R.P. Champness	Scholarship, Eton
	A.D.H. Hunter	Exhibition, Fettes
1969	T.S. Sammons	Scholarship, Charterhouse
1970	R.A.C. Toller	Scholarship, Harrow
1972	D.A. Colver	Scholarship, Harrow
	W.A.S. Dale	Exhibition, Shrewsbury
1974	C.R.S. Graham	Scholarship, Wellington
1975	D.M.B. Parsons	Scholarship, Leighton Park
	I.S. Yorston	Scholarship, Wellington
	A.J. Naylor	Exhibition, Marlborough
1976	M.F. Biscoe-Taylor	Scholarship, Harrow
	E.J.G. Bryans	Scholarship, Bradfield
1977	J.P. Snow	Exhibition, Radley
1978	S.J. Scott	Scholarship, Harrow
	R.C.H. Bryans	Cuthbert Heath Scholar, Bradfield
1979	M.D.T. Tennant	Scholarship, Wellington

1980	A.M.J. Graham	Scholarship, Wellington
	E.P.H. Rylance	Scholarship, Wellington
	J.G. Ironside-Smith	Scholarship, Harrow
	J.P.M. Heald	Scholarship, Eton
	I.M.C. Henry	Scholarship, Charterhouse
	H.M.R. Lumby	Scholarship, Bradfield
1981	A.S. Justham	Scholarship, Radley
	R.A. Pyman	Scholarship, Harrow
1983	J.M. Godden	Exhibition, Wellington
	A. Wolcough	Scholarship, Stowe
	C.D.E. Scott	Art Scholarship, Bradfield
1984	P.M.D. Allison	Scholarship, Eton
	W.J.F. Carpmael	Scholarship, Oundle
1985	D.J.Y. Wreford	Scholarship, Stowe
1986	C.C.V. Kaye	Scholarship, Harrow
	J.C.B. Smart	Exhibition, Eton
1987	R.L. Heald	Scholarship, Eton
1988	M.T.Y. Wreford	Scholarship, Stowe
1989	M.A. Kimber	Scholarship, Eton
1990	J.R.V. Fowler	Scholarship, Radley
	C.H. Allison	Scholarship, Eton
1991	A.V. Cooper	Scholarship, Eton
1992	C.R.D. Connell	Exhibition, Stowe
1994	A.G.A. Milne	Scholarship, Bradfield
1996	R.H. Gillett	Music Scholarship, Radley
	C.H.C. Gordon	Exhibition, Harrow
	F.J. Eckersley	Scholarship, Eton
	R.M.D.W. Gilbert	Scholarship, Eton
1997	I.A. Bennett	Scholarship, Radley
1998	J.M. Corbet Burcher	Scholarship, Eton
1999	C.R. Scrymgeour-Wedderburn	Exhibition, Radley
2000	S.H. Crawley	Scholarship, Harrow
	H.A.P. Sewell	Sports Scholarship, Harrow
2001	C.D.F. Eccles	Exhibition, Radley
2002	J.M.D. North	Scholarship, Radley
	D.A. Douglas-Pennant	Scholarship, Eton
2003	W.P.N. Denehy	Scholarship, Harrow
2004	F.J. Tapner	Music Exhibition, Radley
	F.J. Tapner	Scholarship, Radley
	A.N.H. Style	Scholarship, Radley
	H.L.P. Royds	Scholarship, Harrow
	C.T.J. Royle-Davies	Scholarship, Eton
	J.W. Garnier	Scholarship, Eton

Appendix 5

LETTERS TO LUDGROVE:
1914–1918

This is a small selection from the scores of letters received by G.O.Smith during the First World War – from former pupils either fighting at the Front or who had been wounded; from the parents of boys who had been captured, wounded or killed; and from masters in action.

Sixty-five Old Ludgrovians were killed in the Great War. The deeds and deaths of many of them are recorded in these remarkable letters. Most are written in reply to the continuous letters of encouragement or condolence which G.O. himself wrote to Old Ludgrovian soldiers and their families throughout the War. One letter, from the brother of an Old Ludgrovian, describes in detail the Battle of Jutland, and is written from H.M.S. *Indomitable*, one of the battle-cruisers in the heat of the engagement.

All these letters express in vivid and moving terms the hopes, fears, courage and grief of those involved in that tremendous struggle. They are a poignant reminder of the horror and sacrifices of nearly a century ago.

(NB. Those who lost their lives are indicated thus: ¶)

EVENTS AT THE FRONT
Many Old Ludgrovians wrote from the Front, or from hospitals and homes while recovering from wounds

From Tom Vesey, OL 1896–1899

Princess Henry of Battenberg's Hospital, 30 Hill Street, London W.

Nov. 11 1914

My dear Mr. Smith,

Thank you most awfully for your letter. I am glad to say I am not bad. I was very lucky, the bullet hitting a compass I was wearing on my belt. This turned it and instead of going through my stomach, it went into my side and took some of the compass with it. I had an operation yesterday and they took out the remains of the bullet etc., so I should be fit again very soon. I am very glad of a rest as we had a very rough time there just lately.

Did you see George Boscawen has got the DSO? I am so glad, as he is such an excellent fellow. I hear there are only 350 men left in my battalion and v. few officers. The 1 Bn. Coldstream have only 180 men and no officers except the Q[uarter]M[aster]. But big drafts are going out this week.

The German artillery is wonderfully good and it is what they chiefly rely on, and their organisation is wonderful too. They showed no signs of demoralisation or retreating when I left Nov 1st. The papers here are mad I think. I suppose it is because they know nothing.

I hope Mr. Oakley is flourishing.

I have seen a good deal this last week of 'Tommy Atkins' – there is no word that is good enough for him. For courage & patience & everlasting cheerfulness in adversity I have never seen his equal.

All good luck.

Yours ever

Tom Vesey

P.S. Roger Coke's ship is the 'Indomitable', Mediterranean Fleet. Last I heard of him he was all right.

Give Freddy Gordon Lennox my love. I hope Ludgrove is as flourishing as ever.

From Arthur Curtis, OL 1899–1903

43 Belgrave Square, London SW.
Nov 19, 1914

Dear Mr. Smith,

Thank you very much for your kind letter. I am going on well, but am not allowed up yet, as pieces of breeches etc. continue to come out of one wound: it is rather a bore, as I feel perfectly fit. I was dreadfully sorry to see 'Twiggy' Anderson was killed: I did not know before that he was out. Poor Richard was sniped through the heart from 50 yards, and died almost at once. I am glad to say they got the sniper. I fear the Ludgrove toll is mounting. Charles Norman is wounded and a prisoner; his people heard from him at Crefeld [a PoW camp in Germany]. Jack Pelham I left quite well: he bound me up. Harry's old tub rolled into Devonport 2 days ago, and he goes to Winchester today: so I hope to see him soon. The fighting was very fierce, when I left. We lost 10 officers killed and wounded the last 3 days fighting that I was there and a captain was left in command of the regiment. I will come down to see you, if I may, when I am up and about: but of course I can't tell when that will be.

Please remember me kindly to Miss Smith and the staff.

Yours sincerely

Arthur Curtis

From Fred Arkwright ✟, OL 1894 – 1898

9 Mandeville Place, London W.
Dec.7 1914

Dear Smith,

I have scratched my head for some time before settling how I ought to address you nowadays. It was v. good of you to write to me to condole. I have a little hole in my foot, just at the root of the toes, but it is a small affair, quite clean and mending fast. I hope to go home tomorrow and to get back again in a month or so. I only fly as an observer and only do that as my poor old ears, legs and lungs are such a handicap to cavalry soldiering in winter time. It is v. exciting, and a duel in the air besides being the v. last word in new methods of war, is also the nearest approach to the old 'man-to-man' combat. It is astonishing, too, what one can see and how easy it is to find one's way about 8000 ft or more high.

Well done Ludgrove! 190 odd is a fine total.

I think all goes well and there can be [no] doubt about how it will all end, the doubt being when it will end. Of course no one knows, but I look at May 1 next as likely a date as any.

Our men are marvels. You would never believe it possible for men to suffer losses and hardships in the way they have done. Men who in peacetime are always a trouble and in trouble, and that I certainly looked upon as the scum of the towns and as 'gutless' wasters, have proved themselves heroes 100 times over. I'm getting sentimental.

Well – again many thanks for your letter. Good luck to you and the old school. Remember me to anyone to whom it would mean anything.

Yours ever,

Fred. G.A. Arkwright

🐜   🐜   🐜

From Rex Benson, OL 1899–1903

On active service
Dec 17th 1914

Dear Mr. Smith,

Thank you so very much for the box of chocolates which has come with Christmas greetings from Ludgrove. It was nice to get it from you apart from the fact that it is the most useful and practical box of chocolate I have seen – I shall carry it as an emergency ration. I have spent the day wondering what you are all doing and who is still there – you and Mr. Oakley and Stanborough and Blore, and is Mr. Brown still going strong?

I have been out the whole of the blooming old war except the first 5 days, which I missed, being on my way back from India, and have not fallen out up to date. Now it looks like stalemate and the longer we stay and don't try a push, the less we shall like doing it, when the time comes and we shall have to make one. For the first 3 months we had so much fighting that one became fatalistic and nothing mattered except killing these beggars and doing them in. We have now had a month's rest, which I am sure is bad for us. As long as you can stick it you want to be at it all the time with just the occasional 2 and 3 days out, to keep fit. I wonder how it is all going to end. Germany must be beat, but she has got 100 kicks left in her and if she administers each one we shall take 3 years. I hope to goodness that Asquith or the other Governments don't consent to a makeshift peace.

My respects to Miss Smith and very best of good luck to you all,

Rex Benson

🐜   🐜   🐜

From Jack Sclater-Booth, OL 1900–1904

The Royal Dragoons, 6th Cavalry Brigade, 3rd Cavalry Division,
British Expeditionary Force
Dec 17th. 1914

Dear Mr. Smith

Thank you ever so much for the chocolate you sent me for Xmas, it was so very kind of you. Just lately we have not been doing very much as we have been supposed to be resting and refitting after 6 weeks rather hard time in the trenches. It was rather beastly up there as we were continually shelled whether we were in the trenches or not: the German aeroplanes seem to do a

267

great deal of observing for their shell-fire. What happens is this. The German aeroplane comes over, sees our horses and goes straight back and reports the position, and you can bet within 20 minutes of the aeroplane going away the big shells come. One day they killed about 50 of our horses. Then in the trenches they plaster them with shrapnel all the morning and usually attack in the afternoon. They seem to me not to mind how many men they lose in these attacks and they come in thousands all en masse, and their losses must be apalling. They have several tricks which we have got to know now. One in particular is they all come out of their trenches unarmed saying they have no ammunition and come to surrender; then when they have enticed us to come out of our trenches to take them prisoner at a given signal they all fall down flat and a few Maxim Guns are fired at us. This I may tell you is often done. I hear they have made another raid on England at Scarborough, Whitby and Hartlepool. I personally think it is rather a good thing as it will wake people up a bit at home and get more recruiting as it is rather slack now I am told.

Since we have been resting I have been home on 72 hours leave. I went up to York where my father is commanding the 5th Reserve Cavalry Regt., the one that feeds us and the Scots Greys. They were all very cheery up there. Please remember me to Miss Smith and also all the other Ludgrove masters I know. Wishing you all a very happy Xmas and New Year.

Yrs. Very sincerely,

Jack Sclater-Booth

 за   за   за

From Derek Stephenson, OL 1897–1900

On active service
December 22nd 1914

Dear Mr. Smith

Ludgrove's very kind present has just arrived. It is most awfully kind of you and Mr. Oakley and all to remember me. It seems a very long time since we met for a moment in the Pavilion at Lord's at the Eton and Harrow. I wish you and all a very happy Christmas.

I have been very lucky all the time in the way of escapes, and have not been actually wounded, though I have been knocked down by a shell. We had a very hard time at first, during the retreat from Mons – no sleep, but since then we have been fairly all right.

During the retreat, at halts, men used to fall off their horses asleep, in inches of dust. The weather has been beastly for the last month, but fortunately the 1st Corps has been resting. When we first left the trenches east of Ypres, there were, I think, only 727 out of 4000 of the Guards Brigade left. My brigade of artillery is affiliated, as they are pleased to call it, to the Guards. We were meant when the 42nd Brigade was mentioned in despatches on Oct. 31st – they made a misprint, which was rather sickening! We had the benefit of that attack of the Prussian Guard on the 11th Nov., when our infantry broke and ran right through the guns and we were left more or less alone. We put gunners out in front of the guns to act as infantry. In fairness to the infantry, I must say that they had been so long in the trenches that they hadn't a kick left in them, and so when the bombardment – with which the Germans favoured them and us before attacking – began, it was too much for them.

I had a gun in an angle of the trenches for 3 days and nights, with the Germans in a wood 70 yards away. I was afraid they'd try and rush it, as British infantry would have done, but luckily they didn't.

I hope we get back in time for next cricket season.

The first man of the Prussian Guard we saw we thought was a freak, he was so tall! But they all seemed like that, and it was v. funny to see the gigantic prisoners led in by tiny light infantrymen.

I shall hope to come down to Ludgrove when I come back, if I may. I met that extraordinary person, Booth, who belongs to the Royal Marine Motor Reserve! – a corps which I never heard of before, did you?

I hope Ludgrove is as flourishing as ever – I am sure it is. Please remember me to A.N.B. ['Bunco' Brown] and tell him I get the Navy League Journal even out here !!!!

Yours sincerely

Derek Stephenson ¶

THE WOUNDED

G.O. wrote to every Old Boy who had been wounded. Many of their parents replied.

From the father of Oliver Leese, OL 1903–1907 (later Lieut.-General Sir Oliver Leese – see Chapter 7)

Hotel Imperial, Cork
1 Nov. 1914

My dear Joe,

Thank you so much for your letter which gave Oliver great pleasure.

He is doing very well and I hope to bring him home on Wednesday.

He was badly hit in the neck by a bit of the cover of a shrapnel and it went down 10 in. into his back, just missing the spine by great good fortune.

He is extremely cheerful which has helped him very much and I hope will be fit again soon though I think it will take a little time. He was hit at 5 o'clock on his first day under fire – very bad luck as later in the night they had a grand bayonet charge and did a fine performance. This annoys him much.

I have watched the Ludgrove toll with great sorrow but much pride. It is a dreadfully sad time and the loss of these boys, many of whom are even now not much more than children, is very distressing. Still it is just these boys who show the true spirit of the nation.

Yours sincerely,

W.H. Leese

✤   ✤   ✤

From the mother of W.H. Wynne Finch, OL 1902–1905

11, Bruton Street, London W.
Nov. 4th, 1914

My dear Mr. Smith,

I am so touched by your kind recollections of the boys. Billy was wounded on Sept. 25 and got home to Woolwich Hospital on the 28th. He is wounded in both legs. While clearing houses of Germans during the night they secured 150 in the house. The white flag trick was played but luckily a corporal saw in time and despatched the German officer who had pulled out his revolver and shot Billy.

Then B. went on to clear a second house and had just burst in the door when he was shot from the window close by. The bullet pierced the magazine of his revolver which exploded and lacerated his right leg and two bullets through his left leg. Both above the knees and luckily no bone was touched – so we hope, though slowly, he will be quite sound again.

He is better today and wonderfully cheery.

John has got through wonderfully from the beginning, and got his mention [Mentioned in Dispatches] till he was ill with dysentery from the Aisne and is now Adjutant to a Convalescent Camp near Rouen waiting to go up again. These are fearful times. How many of your boys have been fighting, I am sorry about George Naylor Leyland ⚑

Please remember me to all I know at Ludgrove and to your sister.

Yrs. Sincerely,

Maud Wynne Finch

❧ ❧ ❧

From the father of Viscount Clive ⚑, OL 1894–1898

Powis Castle, Welshpool.
10th November, 1914.

Dear Mr. Smith,

Please excuse a dictated letter as I am in bed with a chill.

I am most grateful for your kind letter, and I am glad to be able to tell you that the report that Clive was wounded is unfounded, and that he is quite well. We have information from a friend who saw him on Sunday last; he had been sent over officially. His Regiment and whole Division had the most terrible experience between the 26th and 29th of October. They were fighting incessantly from the 22nd, but the worst came between the 26th and the 29th when the Germans brought up their huge siege artillery, and many of our trenches were completely blown away. Our men were not properly supported there with artillery, for what reason I do not know, but they gallantly held their own; they were fighting 4 to 1 infantry and at least 5 to 1 artillery against them.

The Colonel, Bolton, who must be a magnificent fellow, led 2 companies into the forward trench where the German artillery literally buried them. He with several officers and men appear to have been dug out by the Germans and taken prisoners. It is impossible to know exactly what happened except that we know that many of them were buried more than once.

Clive's Regiment (the Scots Guards) have suffered terribly. They have only 7 officers and 350 men left out of 1,100. Except for the grief that he feels at the loss of so many of his friends he really writes in very good spirits.

Yours truly,

Powis

P.S. I send you copies of his letters dated 27.28 Oct as I think they will interest you. Please return them. Poor Gibbs mentioned was killed next day, by the same shell which severely wounded Lord Dalhousie and Capt. Kemble also mentioned as all right by Clive. This shell knocked over 25 men as well [as] killing many. P.

❧ ❧ ❧

From the mother of Fred Arkwright ¶, OL 1894–1898

Willersley, Cromford, Matlock.
Dec. 3rd

My dear Mr. Smith,

I do think it kind of you to write so kindly enquiring after poor old Fred. I am thankful to say that we hope his wound is not very serious; he was shot while flying 5000 ft. altitude by a shrapnel bullet in the foot. The bullet was extracted last Sunday (he was wounded [on] 27th) and that is about all we know at present, except that he is now on his way to London! I hope the bullet will not have broken any bones – but I'm rather afraid. We can only feel so very thankful it was no worse. Since the end of Oct. he's joined the Flying Corps and has been doing some good work as an Observer.

I hope we shall get him here before long – as I have a hospital here (in the house) of 14 beds for wounded soldiers all full now, with a fully trained surgical staff, assisted by me! It is most interesting work and gives one so much to do and think about which I find most helpful in these awfully desperate times. Richard did not pass his medical for active service, but rejoined his Regt (he'd been on _ pay for 9 months) and is working hard at Windsor, training men in signalling and musketry.

Again very many thanks –
Yrs very sincerely,

Rebecca O. Arkwright

P.S. I have just heard from London that Fred has arrived at the nursing home (where he was after his accident) 9 Mandeville Place W. and is doing well.

THOSE WHO FELL

Many heart-rending letters were written by parents whose sons had been killed.

From the mother of R.J. Lumley ¶, OL 1904–1907

Middlethorpe Manor, York.
Oct 29th 1914

Dear Mr. Smith

I must thank you for your kind letter of sympathy from you and your sister. We have indeed had a crushing sorrow, for darling Richard was our great joy. He was doing so well. He passed quite well into Sandhurst and out at the end of his 2nd term with excellent reports, and on going into his Father's old regiment he was welcomed and popular both with officers and men. Both his squadron leaders thought so highly of him, and you know how bright and joyous he was. Life was opening out with every prospect of happiness. When I said goodbye to him at Aldershot in August he was all keenness and anticipation, yet fully recognising the risks and the challenges without recklessness. His letters and diary are very interesting. We can feel this comfort that the only anxiety and sorrow he gave us were in these last months, and in spite of the sorrow of his death we can feel proud that he has laid down his life for his God, King and country in the best of causes and we feel sure not in vain.

I feel that you are mourning the loss of many of your old pupils. Forster, Naylor Leyland and others. It is the flower of England's youth but we are going to win against what I only look upon as the spirit of evil.

All Richard's tutors and squadron leaders, besides his friends, write so well of him. My second boy Roger goes up for Sandhurst (instead of Oxford) in November, but I do not think will be allowed to go to the front. He is the only Lumley left to carry on and though he is very keen and is sure to pass well he is really more fitted for public political life than soldiering, but he wishes intensely to go. I am sending you a copy of Richard's last photo taken after the levee. It is nearly as good as the original big one.

With kind regards to Miss Smith

Yrs. very sincerely

Constance Lumley

⁊ ⁊ ⁊

From the father of J.F. Burbury ⁊, OL 1905–1909

2nd Corps Railhead
March 7

My dear G.O.

I was home for 3 days last week, and saw there was a very kind letter from you, and though no doubt my wife will write you, I must send a line myself, as I had seen the boy the last 3 months of his life and she hadn't. You wouldn't have known him; he was my height and as hard as nails, and in another 6 months would have been bigger than I am in every way, with his baby face not much altered on the top of all. He came on in the most wonderful way in his 3 months out here, and I don't believe had an unhappy moment: everyone out here is full of cheer and laughs with very small provocation. He was hit by a bit of shell in the head, and though he lived 12 hours was never conscious, thank God. I, who am on a railway staff job, and was about 10 miles away, borrowed a car and ran over as soon as I heard, but did not see him alive, which I do not regret. I saw him, and his face was the face of an angel, and I would rather remember him so. We have no business to pity them if all are like that. A man in his platoon gave him as good an epitaph as a man can want: 'A plucky youngster, and a real gentleman'.

More than anything I regret one thing, and that is that he did not get his week's leave, which was due in 2 days time and he had been counting the days to it, dear old man. But he had no regrets really: his face proved that. I saw a lot of him since November, as the Regt. were just in front of me, and when they were in reserve I had him daily. I live in a van and he used to come and spread himself in it.

Yours ever

R.W. Burbury

⁊ ⁊ ⁊

From the father of three boys, the youngest of whom, R.D.Tollemache, was at Ludgrove during the Great War. His brother David was killed, but a second brother served in the Royal Navy and survived the war.

The Royal Automobile Club, Pall Mall, London, S.W.
January 1915

Dear Mr. Smith,

I now grieve to tell you that I have received confirmation that my dearest son David was killed at Givenchy on Dec. 22nd. It is confirmed, what I told you, that his last words to his men were just before he was shot down a few yards before the German trench which they were attacking 'Come on men, keep your spirits up. We will shift them out of it'.

Please be so kind as to break the news to my 'little Rupert'. He has a tender little heart so you will know best when and how to tell him. Give him my very best love and tell him he must be brave like his brother and proud that he should have met his death so bravely. I am very sorry to have to ask you to convey this sad message but I know you will make it as light as you can for my dear little son.

Yours sincerely

Douglas A. Tollemache

fa. fa. fa.

From the mother of V.J.Ferguson ❡

Polebrook Hall, Oundle, Northamptonshire.
Sept. 5, 1918

My dear Mr. Smith,

We are so very grateful for your kind letter, and thank you so much.

The loss of our darling John is a heart-rending and heart-breaking grief to us, and hard, very hard to bear. To know we shall never see him again fills us with anguish and despair. Our only comfort is to know that his life here, and his Ludgrove and Eton days, were very happy, that he was proud and glad to go to France, and that his death was instantaneous and painless. For him we know all is well, but for us left behind, without him, all is sorrow and misery.

It seems so cruel to think of all those gallant boys all giving up their bright young lives so soon. Keppel, Wodehouse and my John, who were at Ludgrove together, all passed on, and I feel there must be great work for all these splendid boys in the next world. I will send you a photograph – again so many thanks to you and your sister,

Very sincerely

Margaret Ferguson

fa. fa. fa.

From the mother of G.V. Naylor Leyland ❡

Hyde Park House, London S.W.

Dear Mr. Smith,

Forgive me for not writing before but even now I can not write without tears and I am in such grief. Think what it is for us to know that our dearly loved Georgie can never return to us again. It is such agony, I wonder I go on living, but I try for Edley's sake.

If ever there was a perfect character it was his – so noble, brave and loving. He died a hero's death if ever any man did. His magnificent bravery made him indifferent to the most awful dangers and so at last his dear precious life was taken. I will send you an account of my darling's death soon.

I am in such grief I can not write more. Thank Mr. Stanborough and Mr. Blore for their kind letters, and I will write to them both later. I know how George loved you all, but my heart is breaking.

Yrs. v. sincerely

J. Naylor Leyland

MASTERS

Several members of Ludgrove's staff also went to the Front

From Charles Eyre, recording the death of Wilfred Bird

2 KRA, B.E.F.
May 11th 1915

Dear Joe,

Just a very few lines to tell you sad sad news about poor old Wilfred Bird. By the time you get this, you will probably have seen his name in the papers. He was shot through the head while leading his men in an attack on a German trench, and fell without another word. It is perhaps the death one would most prefer to have – absolutely painless. To be shot by a stray bullet in a trench or on a working party by night or by a stray shell miles behind the lines – these are the things we all dread. But to die at the head of your men, while they are looking towards you for guidance and inspiration, that is a great thing and I do believe that Wilfred – in fact I know, he told me so – that, if he had to die, he would have preferred to die so. His captain told me that he was carrying out his orders to the letter, when he fell. He took his men over our breastworks, across an old disused British trench, through our barbed wire and was leading them over the 300 yards of open ground, when a Maxim [gun] caught him. His body, I believe, is still there, though one of the wounded brought in his wrist-watch which is being sent to his father, to whom our C.O. has written a letter.

Every officer who left the breastworks that day was killed or wounded. In spite of disguises – Wilfred was wearing webbing equipment and carrying a rifle with bayonet fixed – the Germans seem to spot officers at once. I can't write more: but I thought you would like to know something. After all, the loss is ours, not his.

Give my love and sympathy to all at Ludgrove.

Yours ever,

Charles Eyre

      🙛   🙛   🙛

Ludgrove's music master, Henry Balfour Gardiner, kept in touch with his colleagues.

Censor's Office A.P.O 4, B.E.F., France
May 27, 1916

Dear G.O.S.,

May I have a p.c. with Wilkinson's address on it?[1]

C.K.S. sent me a long letter, mostly about Ludgrove, and I read it with interest and with envy. He enjoys being there, and I sincerely hope, for his sake and yours, that he will not be called away for military service before the end of the term. It would interest me to see whether he gets any appreciable results out of the singing class – you are no doubt aware that he is one of the best choir trainers in England, and has the best choral society in the South of England. But of course the teaching of small boys presents special difficulties.

I do seven hours grind here every day, and am gradually acquiring some sort of idea of the organisation of the British Army and of what goes on at the front. We had an extraordinary bit of luck the other day. Owing to mist, an aeroplane could not be clearly discerned from one of our flying stations, but when it got lower, it showed a white light. Our men answered this, on the chance, by showing a red one, and in so doing were lucky enough to hit on the signal prearranged by the Germans for their returning aeroplanes. The German machine was a brand new one, of the latest pattern, with a machine-gun, and the occupants were so astonished at landing in the English lines instead of their own that they made no resistance.

Must close.

Best wishes to all of you

H. Balfour Gardiner

[1] *Possibly referring to G.J.Wilkinson, an OL who was later killed*

❧ ❧ ❧

Frank Henley himself wrote several times in the most vivid terms about life at the Front.

Headquarters ASC. 60th (London) Divl. Train. B.E.F.
Saturday Sept. 16, 1916

My dear Joe,

It is quite a change – & one for which I am pleased – to address an envelope to Ludgrove again, as I much miss my correspondence during the holidays. Many thanks for your letter of the 10th. I am so terribly sorry to hear that you have really almost given up all hope about poor little Wilks [Could this be the G.J. Wilkinson referred to by Balfour Gardiner?]. I got a letter from Brown in which he said Wilks's mother had great hopes that he was a prisoner and I had pinned great faith in it: I only trust our worst fears may be groundless. What a funny thing that your letter to his mother was returned. B-Gardiner seems to be the one who is best acquainted with details concerning him. It is a wretched business altogether, but we must still hope for the best. Poor little chap – as a prisoner – moreover in the ranks. I am afraid life will be very hard. You should see the German prisoners here. They do not overwork themselves road mending and probably live like fighting-cocks compared to what they lived like in the trenches.

Yes – the Zeppelin must have been a wonderful sight. Margaret slept all through it, but she tells me the village people say that Shenley was brilliantly illuminated by it. It will get the wind up others perhaps! – though I am afraid we must be prepared for further efforts as you say. It is sickening for you having to begin all over again as it were, with new hands at the head of the school, but I hope they will soon get going and realise their responsibilities. […].

I trust the advent of Roumania will soon have the desired effect, though my feelings about the war are very like a barometer![1] I cannot see daylight yet, though I shall be more disappointed than I can say – to put it mildly – if I am not meeting the 5.50 on May 3rd (?) 1917! I think everyone is counting on April or May now. I am afraid the year and the Hun are too far advanced now to enable us to hope for an earlier date. Please thank Miss Smith for her kind messages. I am already taking precautions against the winter, but if we do move forward I don't suppose the dirty Hun will have left us much to write home about – favourably anyhow!

[…]

It is lunch time so no more except the very best of luck to Ludgrove and may you and Miss Smith & Oakley have no worries.

Yours Ever

Frank Henley

[1] *In 1916 the Russian successes on the Eastern Front encouraged Romania to join the war against the Central Powers (Germany, Austria-Hungary, Bulgaria and Turkey). This forced Germany to open a new Balkan front.*

❧   ❧   ❧

Headquarters A.S.C., 60th (London) Divisional Train, B.E.F., France.
Thursday Sept. 21, 1916

My dear Joe,

I simply cannot let the day go by without writing and telling you how much I am thinking of you all this afternoon and to send renewed wishes for one of the very best of terms.

Margaret tells me she intended going over to see you all yesterday (Wednesday). So if she did I shall no doubt hear all you have been doing and how Ludgrove looked, in due course. I wonder if you have been doing anything to the place during the holidays? I hope I shall get a Divsn. List in a fortnight or so – it will be interesting to see how many of the names I know.

I had a long letter from [Balfour] Gardiner the other day – apparently he has fallen on his feet properly and has a piano and time for compositions! – rather different to the beginning of his martial career. I am afraid, like you, he holds out very little hope of our ever seeing poor Wilks again but until it is definitely certified I shall continue to hope for the best. I saw such a lot of German prisoners this morning – a dirty looking lot of rascals – but one and all well shod. They work – or pretend to – on the roads. Gardiner talks about 'thinking of taking his leave on the 27th' – lucky devil – I do not suppose we shall get any this side of November. I long for it in every way of course, but I do rather dread the return. We are now in a regular clockwork groove and the days are going so extraordinarily fast – in fact it is difficult to remember the day of the week and the date very often! [...] Now and then I run across people we know slightly, but I expect the majority of our mutual acquaintances are in the other Division. I was much amused to see the photograph of Worthington, Gordon-Lennox and Leveson-Gower in the Tatler doing war work – no doubt you have seen it.
It is now 4.30 and I can picture you going through a dreadful hour with the new parents. I hope the new boys will be a good lot and give you no worry. I can hear you too saying 'Classical School at 10' tomorrow morning!

The news is still jolly good I think but annoyingly slow – I hope the big crack will come soon, but even if the Huns shorten their line I don't see how it is going to do anything but protract the blessed war. I wonder if you have gathered anything of real importance today to cheer us up?

My best wishes to you all especially Miss Smith & Oakers. Love to the boys –
Yours Ever

Frank

❧   ❧   ❧

Headquarters Co. A.S.C., Wheel Echelon, 60th Divisional Train, Salonika Field Force.
Thursday 22 November 1917

My dear Joe,

Very many thanks for your letter of the 6th – the latest I have had so far. Yes – in many ways we are lucky to be here – the scenery is fine and our camp (of this Wheel Co [transport company]) is the best in the Train. But they tell me the summer is the devil, and if we get through it without malaria we shall be lucky. Cheerful isn't it! Well, my 'house' is finished at last and we (my brother-in-law & I) are in it. Every blessed brick laid by ourselves and only a 'Wheeler' to nail on the corrugated iron. I very much wish you could see it, but one day I will show you a photograph of it. At present I am making a formal garden in my spare moments. The centre is sunk and it is paved everywhere.

I go out on convoy nearly every day 25 miles – my word I am tired at night at the end of it, as I have to keep cantering up and down the convoy cursing drivers and seeing the mules are all right etc the whole time. When we halt for 10 minutes breather I collect bulbs etc. Lovely cyclamen, Xmas roses, lilies etc all growing wild. [...] The news in the rag we get here is good – especially about the submarine strangle – very clever that if it is as true as they say.

Now to bed as I have an early day tomorrow. My love to Oakers and kindest remembrances to Miss Smith.

Love to the boys
Yours always

Frank

I have great hopes about being back in January.

Ludgrove's Contribution
From the Duke of Devonshire (Father of the OL, Andrew Cavendish)

Devonshire House, Piccadilly, W.
Nov. 14, 1914

My dear Smith,

I am most grateful for the cheque you sent me for Princess Mary's Fund and I hope you will tell the boys how very much I appreciate their help and kindness. The Fund is going well, but apart from the question of amount, we have abundant evidence to show that a considerable proportion of the money subscribed comes from those who have really denied themselves something to make their contribution. I know that this is very true in the case of the Ludgrove boys and a gift in such circumstances has indeed an enhanced value. The present is to be given to the officers as well as the men and I expect a good many pipes will be smoked on Xmas Day by 'men' who only a few years ago were very happy boys at school.

We all know the terrible sorrows which the war has already produced, but we also know that the sacrifices made today are for the happiness and glory of future generations.

Whatever may be the call in times to come, it is certain that the response will be the same as it is now and the same spirit of duty and devotion will be there.

Princess Mary will be most grateful, and when I see her I shall tell her how you have helped her Fund.

Believe me
Yours v. gratefully

Devonshire

JUTLAND

This letter was written by Lieutenant H.D. Tollemache R.N., brother of an Old Ludgrovian, R.D. Tollemache, after the naval battle of 31st May 1916. It is included for its historical interest and vivid descriptions.

H.M.S. Indomitable, c/o G.P.O. London
Monday June 6th 1916

My dearest Mummy,

I expect you are dying for a letter and getting fearfully down in the dumps after reading the newspapers. It certainly was a tremendous scrap. We had in this ship four separate actions. Our Squadron, the third Battle Cruiser Squadron (Invincible, Inflexible and Indomitable) were detached from the remainder of the battle-cruisers to start with and joined up later. The first show we had was at about 5.30 p.m. when we came across one of our light cruisers being attacked by four German light cruisers. She seemed to be keeping them at bay splendidly, but she could have been done in eventually if we had not put in an appearance. I don't think the Germans saw us coming until we opened fire and then we let them have it in the neck. One blew up and sank and two others were burning badly; the fourth pushed off at top speed and we left them being chased by two more of our light cruisers who arrived on the scene. I don't know what happened to them.

We did not wait to see but pushed on at full speed and joined up with the other battle-cruisers taking station ahead of the line with the Invincible leading. We opened fire again at about 6.15 and the battle-cruisers were now engaging the enemy's battle-cruisers and also the van of the battle fleet. About five minutes after we had opened fire the Invincible went down. It was a terrible sight, we were next but one astern of her. A salvo struck her right amidships. There was a great sheet of flame and an explosion which must have torn her in two. She sank in fifteen seconds with her back broken and her bow and stern sticking up like the arms of a V. Poor Leo Johnstone went down in her. Stewart, Admiral Hood's Flag Lieutenant, was on leave and so escaped. The Queen Mary and Indefatigable both sank before the Invincible. The Indefatigable took about three minutes to go down but the Queen Mary simply vanished in a cloud of smoke and debris and disappeared.

One of the most magnificent spectacles that have occurred since the war was the attack on the enemy's fleet by our destroyers. Nothing stopped them if they could possibly go on. I think this ship must be charmed. We had six torpedoes fired at us in the space of about twenty minutes and not one hit. Three passed right under the ship – you can see the track easily – one ran right alongside and kept up with us about twenty yards off. You could see the propellors going round and the red explosive head. Salvo after salvo straddled us but we never had one direct hit. The other ships could hardly believe us when we said we had not been hit, some of them said that they expected to see us go under any minute.

Our only casualty on returning to harbour was a case of mumps. Of course we had slight damage from splinters of bursting shell but that was nothing. I have got a little bit of German shell which I found on deck – my first war relic! We saw a lot of our salvoes telling on them, they were nearly all on fire (the battle-cruisers). We ceased firing at 7.0 p.m. and at 7.15 repelled a destroyer attack. It was a fine night. The Germans made a smoke screen and suddenly out darted the destroyers from behind it. They were closing at the rate of 1200 yards a minute [approximately 40 m.p.h.] but they never delivered their attack. The Inflexible and ourselves loosed off at them like blazes and they soon turned tail (a very different attack to that which our destroyers made). We think we put about five under.

At 8.15 [p.m.] we again got into action with their battle-cruisers. It was a short sharp action and their leading ship soon stopped firing and fell out of line. Their second ship was badly on fire and none of the others were firing with all their turrets. We continued firing until it came too dark to see them. That night was the most anxious time of the whole lot as with the mist and dark you could only see a very short distance, and at any minute we might have run into them at point blank range and it would simply have been a question of who could get off their first broadside. Of course we remained closed up ready for instant action and I think we all felt it more than all the fighting we had gone through the day before. At about 2.0 a.m. we sighted a couple of Zeppelins. We let off a couple of 12" at them and our light cruisers engaged them, but I am afraid they must have given our position away to the German fleet. I wish to goodness we had some [airships]. Their value for scenting is inestimable. We continued patrolling all that day and at 5 p.m. the fleet went through the solemn ceremony of burying those who had been killed in action at sea. We passed over the scene of the action that day. There was wreckage everywhere and hundreds of dead fish! We passed two wrecks of ships with their bows down and their sterns sticking vertically up in the air, one about 100 feet out of the water. We also saw a lot of dead Germans. When we got back to harbour we coaled and ammunitioned at once and now we are all waiting again for them to give us another lap. I do not think it will be long[1].

Poor darling you must have been a bit anxious when my telegram never fetched up. Is there any chance of the family coming north later on, it would be lovely. You could see all the ships. I don't expect leave for ages. It was rather funny because we had some Army officers from the front paying a visit to the fleet during that show. The story goes that one of them said he would rather do eighteen months in Flanders than another five minutes of that action! You know Sims' appointment to the Lion [Beatty's flagship] was cancelled. He would have been in the Queen Mary, only he is on sick leave. Goodbye my darling, best love to all at home

From your devoted Boy

[1] *Editor: In fact the German High Seas Fleet never ventured into the North Sea again. Following the Armistice in 1918 the remaining fleet, including 11 battleships and 5 battle-cruisers, was escorted by the Royal Navy to Scapa Flow. However, the German crews deliberately scuttled their ships rather than allow them to be used by the British.*

The following signal was sent to Admiral Beatty, commander of the Battle Cruiser Fleet, by Admiral Jellicoe, C-in-C of the British Grand Fleet:

Please accept my sincere congratulations on the action of the forces under your command under the difficult and disadvantageous conditions of light which existed for you. Your ships inflicted very severe damage to the enemy. Words cannot express my deep sympathy with the relations and friends of the gallant officers and men who have gone under.

Admiral Beatty signalled to his ships:

I wish to add my own congratulations to those of our C-in-C and my great sympathy with the relatives and friends of those who died so gloriously. I am even prouder than ever of my command. No Admiral could wish to be better served. I thank you.

Admiral Sir David Beatty succeeded Jellicoe as Commander-in-Chief later in 1916. H.D.Tollemache continued his career in the Navy and during the Second World War was posted to Washington as Combined Operations representative with Britain's Admiralty delegation to the USA.

Appendix 6

THE ROLL OF HONOUR: OLD LUDGROVIANS WHO GAVE THEIR LIVES IN TWO WORLD WARS

1914–1918

G.R.L.Anderson
N.F.E.Anson
F.G.A.Arkwright
G.C.Armstrong
G.S.Bailey
D.S.Barclay
G.W.Barclay
A.H.Barrington-Kennett
B.H.Barrington-Kennett
V.A.Barrington-Kennett
W.H.Beaumont-Nesbitt
W.S.Bird
G.W.Birkbeck
G.E.Boscawen
V.D.Boscawen
F.Bowes-Lyon
T.R.Bruce
J.F.Burbury
A.H.R.Burn
R.F.T.Burrell
F.D.E.Cayley
N.G.Chamberlain

H.K.Chester
Viscount Clive
Sir R.J.Corbet Bt.
A.Crum-Ewing
L.K.Digby
A.G.S.Douglas-Pennant
C.J.Dudley-Smith
J.H.M.Dunn
J.S.Dunville
F.M.Eastwood
J.W.E.Egerton-Green
W.A.D.Eley
V.J.Ferguson
A.H.Foster
J.Foster
J.Goschen
R.T.S.Gwynne
P.S.B.Hall
R. Hall Watt
J.C.F.Harter
J.E.Impey
A.E.A.Keppel

G.R.Lane
W.W.Laurie
N.J.B.Leslie
R.J.Lumley
F.G.W.Marchant
G.H.F.Maude
W.A.A.Middleton
W.A.Mitchison
G.V.Naylor Leyland
W.L.O.Parker
F.P.C.Pemberton
A.J.Renton
G.H.T.Ross
D.C.Stephenson
Sir R.V.Sutton Bt.
C.E.H.Tempest-Hicks
A.Trotter
J.L.D.Venables-Llewelyn
G.J.Wilkinson
E.G.Williams
E.Wodehouse

1939–1945

J.B.Arkwright
J.R.S.Arkwright
G.N.Beaumont
M.J.Beaumont
J.Birkbeck
J.J.Boldero
R.L.Bradford
R.P.H.Burbury
Lord Frederick Cambridge
Viscount Carlow
A.P.Cliff-McCulloch
J.M.Cobbold
R.N.Cobbold
The Hon. J.P.Corbett
The Earl of Coventry
C.W.G.Coventry

The Hon. G.C.Douglas Home
The Earl of Erne
C.R.E.Fenwick
N.A.St.G.Gibbes
J.P.A.G.Graham
The Hon.J.Hamilton-Russell
The Hon.J.Hamilton-Russell
The Hon.D.C.Hamilton-Russell
D.W.Hall
G.L.Hare
The Marquis of Hartington
D.R.F.Haviland
Lord Edward Hay
A.J.E.Howey
T.A.K.Hickman
The Hon. D.H.Joicey

J.Monroe Hinds
R.N.Orr-Ewing
C.W.Parish
E.G.Pelly
Sir L.F.Phillips
G.S.Salt
E.G.A.Sotheron-Estcourt
J.M.Spooner
The Hon. F.A.Stewart-Mackenzie
J.M.Strang-Steel
A.G.Strickland
J.D.A.Tharp
R.C.Twining
H.F.Wickham Boynton
The Hon. A.E.Winn
W.G.Worthington

Appendix 7

THE McCORMICK-DUNN LETTERS

Richard Barber writes: The following correspondence came to light after a visit I made to Chicago in 2002, when I was shown around the Chicago Tribune Building in the heart of the city. It was only on my return to England that I discovered to my astonishment that its most famous proprietor and editor, Col. Robert McCormick, had been at Ludgrove; that indeed he and his brother Medill had been the second and third boys to enter the new school in 1892; and that there exists in Chicago an archive of his correspondence with Sir Shane Leslie and Helen Dunn which has never been published until today.

I am deeply indebted to Mr Eric Gillespie, Director of the Robert R. McCormick Research Center at Cantigny, Ohio, for permission to publish this correspondence. It shows a sensitive and generous side of the Colonel's character that is seldom mentioned in accounts of his life. It describes a charming, affectionate relationship, which grew up through these trans-Atlantic letters between a famous American and an elderly English lady. It was a relationship based on their shared love for the old school her husband had founded, of which Helen was so proud, and at which Robert McCormick had been so happy as a boy over half a century earlier. It also reveals some trenchant social attitudes of the day, and reflects something of the atmosphere of grim austerity in post-war London, of which Helen Dunn is a colourful witness.

It is sad that, despite all the warmth and generosity of this correspondence, Col. McCormick and Helen Dunn never met.

From Sir Shane Leslie to Robert McCormick

30th June 1947

Dear Col. McCormick,

Could you put me in touch with a couple of American McCormicks from Chicago who were at Ludgrove School in England with me during the 1890s over 50 years ago? Old Ludgrovians are presenting some books to Mrs Arthur Dunn for her 80th birthday next month, and we should like to include the McCormicks who were there. The Headmaster, Mr Arthur Dunn died in 1902. The subscription is limited to £2 but we would like to get in touch with all survivors.

Compliments

Shane Leslie

From Col. Robert McCormick to Sir Shane Leslie – 11th July 1947

Dear Mr Leslie,

I am delighted to send two pounds to join my old schoolmates in a present to Mrs Dunn. I remember her with great affection and great esteem.

I have been back to the school a couple of times, the last I believe in '33.

In '15 I had a telephone conversation with Hugh Buxton, and for some years after that corresponded with Pelly, then a retired Brigadier-General. I have a picture at home of the boys of the school, but of what year I do not recall. I will look at it this evening to see if I can recognise you.

My brother, Senator McCormick, died in 1926. There was another American boy at the school, but his name escapes me and in all events I have never seen him since.

Yours sincerely

Col. McCormick

ᙏ   ᙏ   ᙏ

From Col. McCormick to Sir Shane Leslie – 6th August 1947

Dear Sir Shane,

I perceive you have a handle to your name. I didn't know it.

May I trouble you a little more? My friend Pelly retired as a Brigadier-General before 1914. How come this 66- or 67-year-old retired General is living at Windsor Castle?

Can you give me some details of Barclay being eaten by a lion? Was he hunting it? Was it one of the man-eating lions from Kumaon – or what?

I remember him as an awfully nice little boy.

I think I place you now. Weren't you the youngest boy in the school?

I wish we had known of each other in 1934-35. We could have talked of Ludgrove.

Sincerely yours

Col. McCormick

ᙏ   ᙏ   ᙏ

From Sir Shane Leslie to Col. McCormick – 14th August 1947

Dear Col. McCormick,

Your letter finds me in a country of which Chicago was once spoken of as an important suburb! If you are ever in Ireland, I hope you will look in here where we live on the actual border.

You ask me about poor Barclay's fate. He was a great hunter, but this was a tame lion which he brought back to Norfolk. I forget the details, but they were the reveries of Daniel's den. Theo Pelly is one of the retired warriors who are accommodated in Windsor Castle. The first War took many of the Ludgrovians, but the surviving ones have done pretty well – a Viceroy, an Ambassador etc. The only Ludgrovian to reach a sticky end was Hall Minor who was shot by an actress in bed (it is described in the life of Marshall Hall K.C.)

We shook hands in January 1895 and I hope perhaps again.

Yrs sincerely across the years

Shane Leslie

ᙏ   ᙏ   ᙏ

From Helen Dunn to Robert McCormick – 3rd August 1947

My dear Bob or Bertie,

Is this right? I think we had a nickname for you, but would you like me to call you Bob or Robert?

I was so delighted to get your letter to Shane, which he sent me on for me to read two days ago.

I must write to you to thank you for it too for remembering me so nicely, of course I have never forgotten a single boy; if I saw your photos I could tell who everyone is. You were about the second boy. Theo Pelly was the first, he came to London alone in April 1892 for two or three weeks, then along came Gerald Gurney who was very fond of caterpillars; and Medill (your brother) and a rather nasty American boy called Hoadley for a very short time – greedy and not attractive.

Of the first four we always liked Theo and you best! And we were photographed with you all. Then came Hugh Buxton, Knyvet [Buxton] who was killed in India at polo, Trevor Barclay who was killed by young lions at their place in Norfolk. Also Blackwood, G.L.Baxter, Nikko Wood – and afterwards Mike Palairet (son of Sir Michael).

I wonder if you remember Mr. Crabtree – he came to the party, and is very lame.

How I should love to see you again and pick up the old days.

I went over to see Theo Pelly and his wife yesterday. He is a Knight of Windsor and lives in a delightful building up 37 steps of the main Gateway of Windsor Castle, has a certain amount of duties, no rent or rates, and a pension but no servant. He and his charming wife do all the housework, and he also mends old violins and 'cellos, and has a string quartet twice a week. He looks very young, but has two girls, one married with two children, and one working in Switzerland, both pretty.

You will like to hear that Ludgrove now has 99 boys and has never had a break.

Alan Barber, the Yorkshire cricketer, and his wife are charming.

Both my great-nephews have been there and both my grandsons, and many friends.

Nurse Broomfield is still going (84), and came to the wonderful party they all gave me at the Dorchester on July 10th.

Hugh Buxton is now very thin, and in fact we are really all starved here and have been for years, and people of 80 are like 120 – and people of 60 are 80; only the youngest have enough to eat.

It is awful, and no one realizes we won the war in the first year, for had we not kept on when France let us down we should all have been under German rule now. Of course you have all been a great help, but the first year when we were alone turned the scale.

Now all but the rich have been starving for 8 years. I have lost three and a half stone, and am now only seven stone. We have hardly enough to eat, can never entertain, lack our own butter, tea, sugar, meat and other things, and no one has any servants; people of 70 and 80 wash up, clean the kitchen, clean the car etc. – people of the highest class.

Now do tell me – are you married? And how did Medill die, and are you as uncomfortable as we are?

Many of us pray to die, but we do it smiling.

I have a grandson at Eton[1], and a charming granddaughter of 10; my elder grandson at 18 left Eton and was in the Guards and was promptly killed in England by mistake in signalling[2].

Now I must stop,

With my love and thanks for your charming letter from Sir Shane Leslie who sent it to me.

Your old affectionate friend

Helen Dunn.

[1] *Ned Boldero*   [2] *Ned's brother John, killed in 1944*

From Robert McCormick – 23rd August 1947

Dear Mrs Dunn,

It is indeed wonderful to hear from you. It is more than fifty years since I have seen you.
I suppose the Knight of Windsor is quite a person. I never heard of the rank before.

I remember Pelly, the Buxtons, Barclay and Gurney best; and the master from Tasmania who was also a clergyman.

At first I thought I did not remember the nurse, but now I recall her singing at prayers. I also recall the gardener who bowled to us and also played in the Salvation Army band.

It's depressing to read of conditions in England. Everything is frightfully expensive here, but there is no shortage.

There are two bad possibilities in front of us: this unprecedented drought may bring on something like a famine. The next election may bring in a labor (1) government, and then the whole world will fall. Medill died of stomach ulcers in 1926. His son was killed in a mountain accident. He had two daughters, each of whom has a boy and a girl.

I am twice married. My first wife died in 1939 and I married again two years ago.

I remember the name "Hoadley" but I hardly recall the boy. I have never seen him since.

I will never forget how sweet you were to lonely little boys.

Yours very affectionately

¹ *Editor: At that time the USA had a Democrat administration under President Truman. McCormick, a staunch Republican, must have feared something even 'worse'. He need not have worried. In 1953 Truman was replaced by the conservative Republican, Dwight D. Eisenhower.*

From Helen Dunn to Robert McCormick – 13th September, 1947

My dear Bertie,

I was so pleased to get your letter. Hugh Buxton was at the party, and is now very thin and dark instead of a gorgeous head of fair hair. Terence Barclay was so badly injured by tame lions, which his father kept in Norfolk in the park, that he died of wounds. Hoadley was a "wash out". Theo Pelly is poor, but happy and well. I am sorry about Medill, but he has escaped an awful time.

The War (though we won it) has completely ruined our lives. We are now just starving slaves, with no real joy in life. We can't even have friends in to meals unless they bring their own food. Nothing is free, and if it is you can't get it. Now, if petrol is stopped, the only thing left, which was to go and see our friends, is finished. The winter is facing us all. No one can get a house. No one is allowed to build one, and when you come to find that we really won the war alone in the first year, it seems hard that we should suffer most. When France failed, had we given in before outside help came, Germany would now rule Europe.

I don't suppose you can do anything. All our lovely old houses are empty or given up to offices; their owners of 600 years are living over shops, or in cottages with no servants. Of course the very rich can manage, but ordinary people would prefer death to such a life.

If you came here, this would not strike you at once, but only if you went into things. But we are all brave as usual, though I am getting worn out and sick of it. Now we may not even go abroad if we wish to. The so-called lower classes are behaving atrociously, thinking only of themselves, while the upper are bearing the whole burden.

Churchill could save us now if we could get him and Lord Woolton back.

I must not go on like this, but we feel very bitter at being allowed to be slaves. We want petrol for private cars terribly badly – for people to see their children at school, get a breath of fresh air, visit ill people and lonely ones, go to Church etc.

I must stop, Bertie, and forgive this – it is not an ordinary grumbling letter, as I tell you we are being very brave and I hope it will come out all right, but we want all the help that we can get.

I am so dreadfully sorry that things are bad with you. Every German ought to have been killed before they started this war – and I believe, if they could, they will always start a war. They are a beastly nation – not human beings at all. I should love to see you if ever you come over and if I'm still alive which I sincerely hope I shan't be – as I have had a terrible sad life.

I am glad that you are married; it is impossible to live alone as I am proving, and Johnny[1] was killed 31 years ago today. My elder girl[2] is in a home from overwork, [but] has a perfect husband. Their home bombed from top to bottom, full of lovely things. Their older killed at 18 in this war by a mistake in signalling. Please be careful what you repeat in this letter, Bertie. My love and deep love for what you said about my husband.

Yours affectionately

[Helen Dunn]

[1] *Johnny Dunn, Arthur and Helen's son, who was at Ludgrove and was killed in the First World War, in 1916*
[2] *Margery, who married Harold Boldero, Treasurer of the Royal College of Medicine.*

Helen's younger daughter, Mary, became the Hon. Mrs Andrew Shirley.

From Helen Dunn to Robert McCormick – 27th December 1947

My dear Bertie,

Do I still call you this, or do you still hate it? If so, what?
I am delighted with the photo, and I only have a very bad one of it, and I have filled in every name with great ease and also destination.

A few weeks ago, just for amusement, I wrote out the first 200 boys at Ludgrove with us – 1892-1902 – with all their initials, from memory. I am going on one day to correct my mistakes. There will only be about eight.

Your name is second on the board. You should go there next time. It is Ludgrove, Wokingham, near Reading. Very ugly but airy and excellent, and the heads, Mr and Mrs Alan Barber, delightful. 90 odd boys, all first class, including the Duke of Kent, and most of the peerage, not Roman Catholic.

[…]

My country home commandeered and half my money gone, and as for food well you won't believe it but I have not seen a ham nor a piece of cold bacon for 12 years.

We have about 1s 3d worth of meat, no eggs unless we have a friend with fowls. I think we shall all eat seaweed soon.

Well I wish you a very happy year, and stick to England please. We are worth it. Ludgrove alone lost 48 boys in this war.

Yours affectionately

From Robert McCormick to Helen Dunn – 15th January 1949

My dear Mrs Dunn,

Your welcome letter arrived the same day as the proof of the story on Ludgrove. Of course it is intensely interesting to me. Our Sunday editor found it the same. I don't know how much our readers will understand it. They know about Kings because of the Bible, Shakespeare and the news, but the peerage is quite alien to them.

I believe I learned more about the peerage from George Baxter, Shane Leslie and the Duke of Hamilton in the few hours I had with them than I ever knew before, because I haven't been much in England since my childhood.

I am sorry I did not know where you were when I was in London. They gave me such a busy run-around I did not have time to look you up.

[…]

Here are some fleeting memories:

• Mr Hale from Tasmania made it very plain that he was not an Australian
• Whichever one is Woods, I think he had an American mother, and rather a common one at that. He used bear-grease on his hair.
• Either Baxter or Barclay boasted of some ancient Scot who rode from Land's End to John O'Groats, whereupon Knyvet Buxton said he must have used a "bone-shaker" – referring to the old wooden bicycle at the school.

Continue to call me "Bertie". The name pretty well disappeared in my college days, giving way to the euphonious "Rubberfoot" based on Rutherford. I am commonly known as "the Colonel", a very useful moniker as it can be either familiar or formal.

I was really a long time in the army, from 1915 to 1920, and on the general staff after my retirement for another 10 years.

The ham question is a very simple one. There will be one on the way to you shortly.

Our government is following yours into socialism, but when they ordered the killing of pigs and the burning of grain I refused. In construing our Constitution, the courts are superior to the Legislative. They did not dare prosecute me. So for the present I am living high.

Our future does not look so bright. We stopped the New Deal in 1946, but after that the Republican party went to pieces, and there seems to be no organised resistance to it now.

I do not think collapse can come in my time. My sympathy is with the middle-aged. Our daughters are quite prepared for the future. One of them, who took a course in nursing during the war, kept it up after the peace and now carries a certificate. They are so short of nurses here that she is constantly called upon at the hospitals, to the exasperation of her mother who has now sent her to Mexico City to visit a schoolmate, from where she will go to our house in Florida with her sister for the rest of the winter.

The girls are enormous for the eyes of our generation, and can take another year catching up with their growth.

I do not know why I have survived all of my contemporaries, because I have done everything I could to get killed, including two years in the old Wild West, a year exploring the Arctic, polo, fox-hunting, mountain climbing and two wars. I guess I was born to be hanged.

Yours affectionately

From Helen Dunn to Robert McCormick – 31st January 1949

My dear Bertie,

Thank you so much for your delightful and most interesting letter – so full of vitality and humour. I really did enjoy it, for which reason please do not try hanging, or I shall not get another. A duel with an Italian Count or a Spanish Grandee would be a more thrilling death if you want it!

I had no idea that you were writing about Ludgrove – please send it to me when done – do you want any more tid-bits?

Mr Hale went to Australia because he wanted to marry my handsome sister and she said "No". She is married and has several children and is very happy as far as I know. How interesting it is to talk about it all, and so refreshing to me.

We produced a great many peers, but they wanted to come, we never hunted them. Arthur liked the old-fashioned English Gent type. My own mother went back to 1500, but no title. Arthur's family very old too, but what does it matter when character and ideals are so far more important.

My daughter Mary, who married the son of a very "old" Earl Ferrers, says that everyone is snobbish over something (my mother was not, over anything) – that there are blood snobs and dress snobs and music snobs etc. You are so like her, she is so amusing and clever and has written the whole "Lady Addle" series, quite classic here.[1]

With regard to Wood – not Woods – there were two – the one in the photograph is Nicholas Jarvis Wood, rich, attractive, lived in Kent - quite all right socially - but grew up a spendthrift and racing-mad, and died young. The other Wood was awful – landed us with an account for the term – bills for suits at Stimsons in Hanover Square (still going) – all flannels – books – and then wrote to say he would return on a certain day, but we, having lost £80 in one term, said No, not till the account is paid – and never saw him again – our only bad debt.

Don't speak of America going down, if she keeps up her high aims she will come to be possibly the greatest power. Think of your statesmen, and compare with our appalling government. We have about 5 good men on both sides – Churchill top (his book is magnificent, but no leader now), Eden, Bevin, Cripps. Attlee can't lead for nuts. We want a Salisbury back in the Commons. Some of the young members are very good – Lord John Hope (Ludgrove), son of Lord Linlithgow – Lord Montagu of Beaulieu – and many others. England is being dragged through the mud and does not know it.

Thank you enormously for the prospect of ham – it will be a real treat and help. We now have one slice of bacon per week – too small to eat, so mince it up for flavouring!

I must stop, though I enjoy this letter, and I'm so glad you have a charming wife and two girls – a home in fact. […]I am poor and very lonely. My country cottage commandeered. I think I will fight a duel and die with honours. Keep well Bertie, and build up the country and the world, and give a thought for Britain for Arthur's sake whose motto was "Whatsoever thy hand findeth to do, do it with thy Might"

I shall probably give away the Arthur Dunn Football Cup this April.

Yours affectionately

[1] *Helen Dunn's younger daughter Mary (1900-1958) wrote the satirical book* Lady Addle Remembers *and three more in the series, under the name Mary Dunn. They were published in the years 1936-1947 and became best-sellers. In 1986 they were republished as paperbacks under the Black Swan imprint, with introductions by the journalist and broadcaster Simon Hoggart.*

From Col. McCormick's secretary to Mr Piedmont, Purchasing Dept. – 18th January 1949

Dear Mr Piedmont,

Please purchase a ham (I think ARMOUR would be the best) weighing not more than 15 pounds, which Colonel McCormick wants to send to:

Mrs Helen Dunn
5 Grosvenor Court
Sloane Street
London SW1
England

Mrs Dunn was one of the Colonel's teachers – or wife of one of his teachers – when he was a lad in school at Ludgrove, England.

I suppose the ham will go by regular Parcels Post.
Sincerely

From Bill Fulton, London Correspondent, Chicago Tribune ("The World's Greatest Newspaper"), 85 Fillet Street, London EC4

Dear Colonel McCormick,

I called on Mrs Helen Dunn today and presented her with the tinned ham which Charlie James sent to me for delivery.

She was delighted, saying "I haven't seen or smelled or tasted ham since before the war."

I found her very bright and spry, although she is recovering from a sprained ankle she suffered some time ago. She showed me some of the pictures of Ludgrove in her album.

Mrs Dunn wanted to know all about you, and asked whether you still had the sense of humour you had as a boy. I replied in the affirmative.

I believe she will write to thank you personally for the ham, which is really a great treat (the meat ration has just been cut again), and she hoped to be able to dig out a copy of an early school picture in which you are sitting in the front row.
Sincerely

From Helen Dunn to Col. McCormick – 25th March 1949

My dear Bertie,

I must begin this today even though I finish it tomorrow.

Thank you more than I can say for the wonderful present. I have not been near one since before the war, and am more than grateful. It is dreadfully difficult to find things to eat when you are only 2 – and your ham was an unforgettable treat.

I so enjoyed seeing Mr. Fulton, he is so nice and it was a real pleasure seeing him – he thinks no end of you! I wish I could see you again.

March 26th: I have thoroughly read the Story [the Chicago Tribune story about Ludgrove published after the Colonel's visit there in February] and have much enjoyed it – had I known he was writing I could have supplied some short, amusing tit-bits – but it is lovely and I like "the

Buggy" which was quite true, only it was an ordinary shooting dog-cart, and he was so poor that he had to come round to my father and borrow table, cloths & spoons & forks!

We made quite friends, Mr. F[ulton] and I, and he showed me his very pretty wife's photo and child.

Next Saturday April 2nd – the Final of the Arthur Dunn Cup will be played – Old Carthusians and Old Salopians (Shrewsbury) – close to London and I shall present it.

Mr. Fulton told me how you met our Queen[1] (I have known her since she was 8 – I went to her wedding.)

Have you a small photo you could send me, or a snapshot of you?

My love and thanks, and if I find any interesting photo I will send it to you.

Yours affectionately

Helen Dunn

[1] *The late Queen Mother who, as Lady Elizabeth Bowes-Lyon, married the Duke of York, later George VI*

From Helen Dunn to Col. McCormick – 9th April 1949

My dear Bertie,

Thank you so much for your last most interesting letter, and also now again for the best ham that has ever lived.

I had not eaten it when I last wrote, but Mr. Fulton told me exactly how to deal with it and it is really superb. I cut it as I have been taught, like a wafer, and we managed to glaze it – thank you many, many times.

We are all terribly upset about the Budget – having hoped for some small relief – life here for poor gentry is impossible. Incomes practically halved and everything you touch gone up – all due to our really idiotic Government.

However our London Municipal elections are wonderful. The Socialists who waste our money are all but out – possibly quite. If only the next General one does as well we may be saved yet.

Do keep your Socialists-Communists out if you want to be free. We have about as much freedom as a Dartmoor inmate.

Base-ball! I vaguely remember Arthur trying this, but have forgotten how it is played. Last Saturday April 2nd I gave away the Arthur Dunn Amateur Football Cup for Public Schools. It is an enormous success and is true football, no sneaking pro tricks which I have seen – lovely runs, charges, passes and headings. I could hardly breath [sic] for excitement. Old Carthusians won by 2 goals for the 13 th time v. Old Salopians – Alan Barber and his wife were there as Alan is a Salopian. Our beloved and wonderful Sec. Major Jack Stuart retired after 20 years of hard work and great success, and I arranged secretly that after I had had my 3 cheers we should give 3 for him – to his great surprise and pleasure.

Now we have an Old Wykehamist as Secretary – Arthur always wanted this Cup, and my brother Norman Malcolmson started it in his memory. All gate money goes to charity, the feeling of friendship is wonderful.

The Baxters. I am glad you are going to see them. I remember dear George so well, but had not heard about their little girl. I am deeply sorry about the sadness and horror of it and their loss.[1] Please give him my love.

H.M. Our Queen. I am glad you liked her, all her family are my friends (I had 2 heavenly fortnights at Glamis [Castle]) […]

Now I must stop, but somehow I do enjoy writing to you.

My love and renewed thanks, I shall have to write again when the photos come.

Yours affectionately

Helen Dunn

[1] *In 1948 George Baxter's only daughter Susan, aged 12, was killed in a riding accident near Glamis, in Scotland*

&. &. &.

From Helen Dunn to Col. McCormick – 4th May 1949

My dear Bertie,

Thank you so very much for your photograph. I am more than delighted with it, and so proud of it that I am devising a very specially nice frame for it. Its fate is not to be put away in a drawer but to hang on my wall.

I think it must be very like you – the eyes are the same as in my first group at Ludgrove.

My girl Mary Shirley was also very pleased to see it, and we both felt how very vital you are.

Do you remember Arthur's favourite verse in his room – "Whatsoever thy hand findeth to do – do it with thy might", and you look like that. Another man I know, Lord John Hope, now of Linlithgow, saw it hanging up and told me it had influenced his life. Oh how we want it here, but I do think we English have got very tired and weak for want of food and perpetual want of freedom.

The ham was fit for all the kings of the world. I have never tasted a better. Not only did I and mine enjoy it immensely, but I was able to have 2 people to lunch and to cut off some good thin slices for a great friend of mine who always gives of his best to others. My father always made us cut ham very thin as you get the full taste.

Yesterday I looked out of the window and saw Shane Leslie striding along in a lovely green kilt.

I will stop or you will be bored, but I enjoy writing to you and getting your letters on any subject, and I am so delighted in every way with your picture. If you ever come here, do let me see you.

Many thanks and my love

Yours affectionately

Helen Dunn

&. &. &.

From Mary Shirley (née Dunn) to Col. McCormick – 19th July 1949

Dear Col. McCormick,

You were so kind to my mother, and so interested in Ludgrove, that I feel you would like this brief line to tell you that she died quite suddenly on 1st July while staying with her sister, Mrs Bevan.

She had no pain and no long illness, for which we are very thankful.

My husband and I came down here [an unidentified address in France] for a brief respite before I plunge into the task of executorship. We find France, as always, very lovely, very welcoming to people who love and understand it, as we do, and full of beautiful food.

If you are ever in London we should be so pleased if you would look us up. My husband is Managing Director of the Times Book Club, so you could always connect with us in that way.

Very sincerely

Mary Shirley
(Hon. Mrs Andrew Shirley)

&. &. &.

From Col. McCormick to Mrs Shirley – 27th July 1949

Dear Mrs. Shirley,

Bill Fulton carried a dispatch covering the death of Mrs Dunn.

She had a long, interesting life, although alone for many years.

I am starting around the world by plane in March. I probably will not go north of Barcelona because of the season of the year. If I should change my plans I shall certainly look you up in London.

Sincerely yours

Robert McCormick

Appendix 8

FROM THE BOYS' BOOK OF CRICKET BY FRANK HENLEY, 1924

CHAPTER XXI – "DO'S AND DON'TS"

"This List should be framed and hung on the wall of every cricket pavilion throughout the British Empire" – Sir Pelham Warner

I. When Batting

– DO'S

Do (1) put the left foot well up to the bat. If you don't, you lose balance and power and many extra runs.

Do (2) play with as straight a bat as possible when you know you should.

Do (3) take the bat back as straight as you can. A flourish or a faulty back stroke puts every shot out of gear.

Do (4) get your left shoulder well forward in line with the ball.

Do (5) call "Yes", "No" or "Wait" when it is your call.

Do (6) play yourself in before having a risky "go". You will get a sight of the ball in an over or two.

Do (7) play for your side all the time. Ten runs in half an hour are often worth ten times as much as twenty in ten minutes or vice versa.

Do (8) get to the pitch of the ball if you are going to have a "go", and hit straight and as hard as you can.

Do (9) run the first run as fast as possible. You can often get a second one by doing this.

Do (10) ground your bat when you are running in. You can gain a full yard in this way.

Do (11) watch the bowler's hand as he delivers the ball, and keep your eye on the ball at all times.

– DON'TS

Don't (1) make up your mind, before the ball has been bowled, what sort of shot you are going to play.

Don't (2) think it is "time for you to hit another four". You will only blame yourself on your way back to the Pavilion.

Don't (3) say "Will you?" when it is your call. This confuses your partner who is waiting for a decision from you.

Don't (4) play "cow shots". They are fatal in nine cases out of ten.

Don't (5) get impatient at not scoring. Wait till the right ball to hit comes along; you probably won't have to wait long.

Don't (6) run down the middle of the pitch or cross your partner. You may spoil the wicket for the rest of your side.

Don't (7) hit with a flat bat balls pitched up on the leg side.

Don't (8) move the right foot back when making a forward stroke.

Don't (9) kneel down or bend the left knee too much when playing forward.

Don't (10) run away. Many fours are lost in this way. You may be bowled off your legs.

Don't (11) call "Yes" when you cannot see the ball.

Don't (12) call "Yes" just because you have hit the ball hard. It may be going straight to the fielder.

Don't (13) play forward or back with a crooked bat.

Don't (14) throw your head back when making forward strokes.

Don't (15) put your left leg in front of straight balls which are well pitched up, in an endeavour to hit them to square leg.

Don't (16) go out to bat without gloves.

I. When Bowling

– DO'S

Do (1) keep your arm up. It will make all the difference to the "life" in your bowling.

Do (2) always bowl straight and well up to a new batsman. He is just as anxious not to make "0" as you are to get him out. A full pitch to leg or a short ball is what he's hoping for.

Do (3) use your head. To "serve up anything" is not likely to get a batsman out.

Do (4) pitch the ball up. Thus you will make the batsman play at the "blind spot", whereas he can step back and watch the short ones.

Do (5) always bowl well within yourself, i.e. do not try to bowl faster than you can. Otherwise you will lose length and direction, and many runs for your side.

Do (6) try to bowl at least five balls in every over with the object of hitting the wicket.

– DON'TS

Don't (1) bowl before your fieldsmen are in position.

Don't (2) bowl to leg if you can avoid it. It means runs or byes to the opposite side; also it may injure your wicket keeper.

Don't (3) play tricks with your run up to the wicket. You lose step if you do, and will experience a lack of confidence.

Don't (4) think you can't get a batsman out. It should be a struggle between you and him all the time.

Don't (5) blame the fielder if he misses a catch. It is very disheartening for you, of course, but he has not done it on purpose, and to blame him may only make him miss another.

Don't (6) show the batsman you are going to bowl a slow or fast one. A cleverly disguised ball is a very dangerous one.

Don't (7) try "fancy actions". Your own probably suits you best.

Don't (8) try to persuade your Captain to give you "just one more over" unless you have a particular reason for doing so.

Don't (9) ever give up trying. It demoralises your whole side and gives the batsman confidence.

Don't (10) bowl slackly in practice. You will never get your length, and will not use the proper muscles if you do.

III. When Fielding

– DO'S

Do (1) be on your toes all the time, even if there's the temptation to take things easily. You cannot start properly unless you are alert.

Do (2) back up everything. Even if there is the probability that the ball will not be thrown in at your end, it is your duty to move directly the stroke is made, so that you may cover the man you are backing up.

Do (3) move quickly when and where your captain tells you. He has a lot to think about in order to get the best out of his side, and a slovenly fielder may easily spoil an XI.

Do (4) keep the tips of the fingers of both hands down when meeting the ball.

Do (5) try to get into position before a catch arrives, so that you can, if possible, be standing still when you make it.

Do (6) allow the hands to "give" a little when you make the catch, so as to allow it as small a chance as possible of bouncing out again.

Do (7) get your legs behind the ball.

Do (8) try to throw in a quick return from cover point by keeping the throwing hand under the shoulder. This saves much time – though it requires a great deal of practice.

Do (9) run in to meet a ball which is coming slowly towards you. Don't wait for it to reach you.

Do (10) walk in a few paces as the bowler delivers the ball, if you happen to be fielding at Cover or Extra Cover. This will ensure your being on your toes.

– DON'TS

Don't (1) move from the place where your captain has placed you, even though a ball may have beaten you by 4 or 5 yards.

Don't (2) get slack or sloppy in the field. You never know when you may win a match for your side by stopping a four or making a catch etc.

Don't (3) throw the ball in to the bowler along the ground. It is an effort for him to pick it up, and he has quite enough hard work to do.

Don't (4) throw in half-volleys. Long hops or catches are best.

Don't (5) throw in unnecessarily hard, i.e. when there is no occasion for it. You may damage your bowler's hands, or give away overthrows.

Don't (6) appeal for l.b.w. when you cannot possibly see.

Don't (7) point the fingers at the sky when you are shaping for a high catch. Keep the hands in a horizontal position and overlapping.

Don't (8) grab at the ball before it reaches you. Let it come into your hands, and watch it until it gets there.

Don't (9) back up by only a yard or so the man you are covering. Stand at least 6 or 8 yards or more from him.

Don't (10) try one-handed catching when two hands would be safer. "Gallery" catches don't count any more than safe ones.

F.A.H.Henley – April 1924

LITERARY SOURCES

The extracts from *The Scarlet Tree* by Osbert Sitwell are reproduced by kind permission of Macmillan Publishers Ltd and the estate of Sir Osbert Sitwell.

The extracts from *Mr Home Pronounced Hume* by William Douglas Home are reproduced by kind permission of Mr James Douglas Home.

The extracts from *The Early Years* by Alexander Thynne, Marquess of Bath, are reproduced by kind permission of the author.

The extracts from *My Affair with Stalin* by Simon Sebag-Montefiore are reproduced by kind permission of the author.

PICTURE CREDITS

The author and publishers would like to thank the individuals and organisations listed below for their permission to reproduce the pictures supplied. All other photographs and illustrations come from the Ludgrove School archives or from the Barber and Shaw families:

Chapter I
Pages 4,5 Rugby School archive; 6,7 Illustrated London News Picture Library
8,9 from *A History of Elstree School,* 1978; 10 Punch Cartoon Library

Chapter II
Pages 16,17 from *Finchley and Whetstone Past,* 2001; 18 Hugh Bevan Esq.
23 from *A History of Elstree School;* 24 The University of Georgetown, Washington D.C.; 36 National Portrait Gallery: 39 Talkback Productions; 40, 41 (top) The English Folk-Dance and Song Society; 47 Normile Baxter; 49 (R.McCormick) *The Chicago Tribune,* (Daniel Jones) University of Leiden, Netherlands.

Chapter III
Page 57 (Sir Osbert Sitwell) National Portrait Gallery; 58,59 National Portrait Gallery; 61 from *Finchley and Whetstone Past*; 63 Bridgeman Art Library, on behalf of the MCC (oil painting by A.Ludovici c.1899); 71, 77 Imperial War Museum; 90 (top) Roland Pym; 90-95: the illustrations were specially drawn for this book by Roland Pym; 96 The Bodleian Library

Chapter IV
Page 100 The Earl of Home; 110 the estate of Robin Milford.

Chapter V
Page 112 (above) Illustrated London News Picture Library; (below) the late Duke of Devonshire; 113 Illustrated London News Picture Library; 114 (above) The Earl of Harewood; 122 Mary Evans Picture Library; 123 London Transport Museum; 125 (above) Captain N.Dalrymple-Hamilton; (below) David Shaw Esq.; 126 *Wokingham Times*; 131 Punch Cartoon Library.

Chapter VI
Page 135 The Tate Gallery; 153 The Earl of Harewood; 155 Imperial War Musuem; 159 Sholto Douglas Home, Tara Douglas Home; 162,166 (top) The Marquess of Bath, (below) Punch Cartoon Library; 173 (top) *Private Eye,* (below) Sir Thomas Stockdale

Chapter VII

Page 175 Louise Cantril/Orion Books Ltd; 179 Peter Hill-Wood; 180 (below) Hulton Press; 185 (below) *Chicago Tribune;* 186 the Marquess of Linlithgow; 187 from R.Ryder, *Oliver Leese,* Hamish Hamilton 1987; 188 The National Gallery; 195 Sussex C.C.; 196 (above) Sussex C.C., (below) Julian Holloway; 200 Chrysoulla Kyprianou; 204 the Earl of Rosslyn

Chapter VIII

Page 217 Simon Sebag-Montefiore; 219 Edward Grylls; 222 The Earl of Rosslyn; 224 *The Wokingham Times*; 231 Nigel Briers; 237 Eton College; 238 Mr and Mrs Alexander van Straubenzee; 240 (centre) John Cassidy/ Replay Publishing; 241 (below) Tom Hevezi; 243 (below) Solo Agency

INDEX